Science Classroom Safety and the Law

A Handbook for Teachers

By

Kelly Ryan, Esq.

FLINN SCIENTIFIC INC.

"Your Safer Source for Science Supplies"

P.O. Box 219 • Batavia, IL 60510
(800) 452-1261 • Fax (866) 452-1436
flinn@flinnsci.com • www.flinnsci.com

ISBN 978-1–877991–65–3

Printed in the United States of America.

Table of Contents

ACKNOWLEDGMENTS

No work is ever the product of one individual and this work certainly follows form. In particular, this book is the serendipitous consequence of the synergetic interactions between and amongst a number of persons. Several individuals are most deserving of recognition for their assistance in this endeavor:

To my wife Shelley and my three children, Caitlin, Justin and Kieran, thank you for your patience, love and support for everything in our lives together, not just this book. Very special thanks to my wife Shelley, also a teacher, whose many thoughts on the subject of classroom safety have been incorporated into the final product and whose comments suggested new avenues of exploration.

To my dad, James Ryan, a safety expert, who provided encouragement and more than a few tough questions during the writing process, thanks for reading and commenting on the final draft in the van on the way to Yosemite with the family and your willingness to discuss the principles contained within a length so that the final product would contain no logical flaws I might have missed.

To my colleagues in the Science Department at San Gabriel High School, thank you for your support no matter what path I have chosen to take in the last fifteen years. Special thanks are owed to my good friends Sandy Schron (who made the introduction to Larry Flinn at the California Science Teachers convention and sparked this journey, as well as reading and commenting on the final draft) and Larry Kanow (a wise and experienced chemistry teacher and friend who read, commented, interpreted and suggested edits on several version of the manuscript and kept a sense of humor during the entire time).

To Larry Flinn III, thank you for being the true friend of science teachers across the nation. This book is his idea and without his encouragement, dedication, and support would not have ever seen the light of day. Few individuals walk the walk and talk the talk without making compromises and Larry is the real deal. His comments, edits, and tough questions clarified the analysis in the manuscript and sharpened the tools I hope that all teachers will yield wisely in changing their own laboratory practices if needed, inspiring new thinking on classroom safety in their schools, and convincing administrators and parents to work together to ensure student safety.

To the staff of Flinn Scientific and all the other individuals who worked on this manuscript, thank you for all of your hard work in shaping the final product!

To my students in the past fifteen years of teaching, this book is the reason why I always taught and enforced the safety rules.

Finally to the reader, thank you for your interest in this work. I wrote it with the intent that by giving the teachers the "rules" of the negligence game they can spark changes in the way that teachers provide science instruction—but more importantly so that the safety debate will finally end.

Kelly Ryan, Esq.

INTRODUCTION

Knowledge is power. Teachers are entrusted with the responsibility to educate our children. In carrying out this fundamental responsibility, the teacher has a number of duties. The breach of a particular duty owed to a student or others may lead to liability for both the teacher and the school district that employs that teacher. This book will discuss the tort of negligence as it applies to the high school chemistry teacher and the potential for liability as a consequence of negligent behavior in carrying out their classroom duties.[1, 2] While written with the high school chemistry teacher in mind, all teachers of science will benefit from the information provided in this book.

The law of torts provides civil remedies for the harm caused by the unreasonable actions of teachers or other actors who have a duty of care to third persons in the performance of their duties. A tort is "a civil wrong, other than a breach of contract, for which a court will provide a remedy, usually in the form of an action for damages (money)."[3]

The purpose of this book is to educate teachers and their administrators on the duties required of them in order to prevent them from becoming entangled in the war called litigation. Teachers[4] will be provided the legal tools to persuade reticent administrators to make the "right" decisions for their schools, resulting in safe, functioning, well equipped laboratories that are designed with teacher and student safety in mind. Most importantly, this book is a tool for advocacy. Teachers need to be zealous advocates for their students. Parents do not send their children to school to come home maimed.[5] An understanding of the legal principles surrounding negligence in the laboratory is a critical first step in the process of advocating for change and empowering teachers to be the advocates their profession requires for their own sake, and the sake of their students.

Most tort actions are brought in state courts. Some tort claims are brought in federal court particularly when there is the violation of a federal statute such as when civil rights are involved or when the school is under the jurisdiction of the federal government. In the context of schools, there are primarily two types of tort actions: intentional torts and negligence. Intentional torts are wrongs committed against another person that are intended by the actor. That is, if an actor has the requisite state of mind to hurt another person, the injury that results from that action will be due to that intention. The most common types of intentional torts are assault and battery, intentional infliction of emotional distress, false imprisonment, and defamation. Negligence is a species of tort that is the consequence of unintended behavior, that is, there is no intent on the part of the actor to cause another harm, however, "but for" their actions the harm would not result.

---

1. A note about footnotes. The information contained in the footnotes is to clarify some of the discussion of the cases. Most of the footnotes contain additional technical information to explain how the court reached its decision called the holding or additional information related to the point being discussed. The footnotes should be considered optional reading, but in all cases, these footnotes contain the source of the information, or provide an explanation of a term or principle, etc.
2. While the principles contained herein are applicable to all teachers, the laboratory classroom presents unique considerations inherent in classes that have more in common with an industrial work area than the ordinary classroom with desks and chairs. Rather, the science classroom is an ever-changing, fluid environment that contains potential hazards for both student and teacher.
3. W. Page Keeton (ed.), PROSSER AND KEETON ON THE LAW OF TORTS (5th ed. 1984), p. 2 (hereafter "PROSSER AND KEETON ON TORTS")
4. Parents, concerned citizens, unions, and other school safety advocates can use the cases and principles to successfully improve the safety of the science or other laboratory type classroom.
5. Ohman v. Board of Education of City of New York, 300 N.Y. 306 90 N.E.2d 474, 476 (N.Y. 1949) (Conway, J., dissenting, with whom Chief Judge Loughran concurred.)

This book discusses the liability of teachers for the negligent performance of their duties to students and others in the chemistry laboratory. While the chemistry laboratory is the setting for this book, the principles and analysis are applicable to all laboratory sciences and vocational classes taught in middle and high school. In exploring the relevant law of negligence in this limited setting, a significant number of the cases included illustrate practices that have resulted in teacher, administrator, and school district liability. In addition, there are several cases presented where the teacher's action or inaction does not result in liability. In many of the cases, subtle differences in the facts would lead to dramatically different outcomes for the teacher and his/her employer. The purpose of the case discussions serves two important functions: To change teacher behavior in the performance of their classroom duties; and as tools, convince reticent administrators and school districts to reduce the threat of liability by correcting hazardous practices or conditions that exist on their campuses.

Section I provides a technical overview of the law of negligence and the elements giving rise to the negligence cause of action.

Section II broadly outlines the circumstances surrounding teacher liability in the science and laboratory classroom. There are three areas where liability primarily may lie for the classroom teacher or the district:

- Accidents directly tied to teacher activity. These activities include supervision of students, instruction of students and maintenance of equipment;

- Accidents involving the condition of premises. This includes equipment storage and guarding (security), labeling, containment or storage of dangerous chemicals, and building design and absence of safety devices; and

- Accidents involving violations of statutes and other safety rules. This area involves situations where the failure to comply with a state law or other law regulating the school district and its activities results in a finding of negligence liability. Examples of laws regulating laboratory safety include those enacted by the Occupational Safety and Health Administration (OSHA), local building ordinances, and/or other safety regulations issued by school boards or the superintendent's office.

Section III examines a number of areas identified by teachers as being "problematic" and discusses them in terms of the teacher's duty of care to their students. Examples are drawn from existing case law, and "case links" are provided to identify relevant court cases the teacher can use to support an argument to the local administration and school board that changes should be made to the laboratory classroom on a particular issue. Section III also offers several practical suggestions for increasing classroom safety while reducing the potential for teacher and school district liability.

Section IV discusses, in detail, a number of the cases identified throughout the book. The cases selected include chemistry-related cases and several important shop cases having significant relevance to the chemistry or laboratory science teacher.

Section V outlines relevant defenses raised by teachers and school districts to prevent successful claims for negligence or reduce the amount of compensation awarded by the trier of fact,[6] even if a jury finds the teacher or district negligent.

Before we begin our discussion of the circumstances surrounding teacher liability in the science laboratory classroom, a brief explanation of the elements of negligence is in order:

---

6.   The trier of fact is most often a jury, but sometimes a judge in most tort cases.

SECTION I Negligence

A. What is Negligence?

Negligence is the breach of a duty owed to someone to protect him or her from unreasonable risks of harm. Negligence is by far the most frequently litigated tort in the educational setting. In almost every instance where the unintentional conduct of another harms someone, a negligence claim lurks. Negligence claims arise from accidental conduct that could have been prevented by the exercise of reasonable care. An accident that could not have been prevented by the exercise of reasonable care is truly an accident. That is, an accident is considered unavoidable or inevitable at law if it could not have been foreseen or prevented by the exercise of reasonable precautions.[7] The line between accident and negligence is often vague, as we shall soon see.

Example 1:[8] Kurt and Courtney are performing an acid-base titration commonly performed in high school chemistry classes. Mr. Smith ("Teacher") had given them a lab demonstration before the lesson warning them about the safe handling of acids and bases. Before the demonstration, Teacher stepped into an unlocked chemical storage room and retrieved a cart containing equipment for that day's lab. Carefully, Teacher placed bottles of stock acid and base solutions in separate fume hoods with a funnel for transferring the substances to the individual student's beakers. Teacher, after finishing the demonstration instructs the class to begin and then leaves the room to go to the bathroom, make a stock trade on e-trade in the computer lab, and get a soft drink. While Teacher is gone, Courtney has a violent seizure while performing a dilution of the base and spills 3.5 liters of undiluted base on Kurt as she drops to the floor. Kurt, who has momentarily taken off his goggles because they are uncomfortable, is seriously burned and permanently disfigured by the accident. Of note are the heroic efforts by Kurt's friend Dave who guides the blinded Kurt over to the emergency shower, only to find that there is little water pressure as the water slowly trickles from the faucet. Had Kurt been wearing the goggles the injuries would not have been as severe and would only have resulted in some minor skin charring with no loss of vision. Luckily, Kurt only loses the vision in one eye. Kurt's mother, distraught by the disfigurement of her son, files suit in State Court. Kurt's mother sues Courtney, Teacher, and the School District ("District") for negligence.[9] Assuming the doctrine of governmental immunity does not apply to Teacher and District, is anyone liable for negligence?

Certainly, Courtney's actions are not intentional, as she did not intend to cause her partner harm.[10] However, were they negligent? Teacher and District clearly have done something wrong, but exactly what actions were negligent and who is responsible? Does Kurt have some part to play in all this? How do his actions affect the outcome of this case? The answer to these questions lies, somewhat, in how the courts have interpreted the elements of the negligence cause of action:

---

7. PROSSER AND KEETON ON TORTS, p 162.
8. The issues raised by this hypothetical situation are analyzed more fully in Section III and throughout the book in order to facilitate application of the principles extracted from the cases to potentially real situations.
9. Why sue Courtney at all? As a rule, the plaintiff's attorney sues everybody remotely connected to a potential claim and then let the jury or the judge sort them out. Courtney, presumably a minor probably has no assets, but maybe her parents have homeowner's insurance or some other type of asset from which to recover.
10. However, if she threw the base at him in reaction to an inappropriate remark, her actions are intentional and she is presumed to intend the consequence of her actions. That is, she intended to hit him with the liquid, and in doing so caused him injury. If the base does not hit him because he jumps out of the way just in time, she is guilty of assault. If the base hits him, she is guilty of battery.

B. Elements of Negligence

In order to present a successful claim for negligence the following four elements must be proven:

- Duty of Care: " A duty, or obligation, recognized by law, requiring the person to conform to a certain standard of conduct, for the protection of others against unreasonable risk."[11]

- Breach of Duty: "A failure on the person's part to conform to the standard required: a breach of the duty."[12]

- Proximate Cause: " A reasonably close causal connection between the conduct and the resulting injury. This is what is commonly known as 'legal cause' or 'proximate cause' and which includes the notion of cause in fact."[13]

- Damages: "Actual loss or damage resulting to the interests of another."[14]

1. Duty of Care

The cases discussed later in Section IV generally recognize that teachers owe their students a duty of care to anticipate dangers that are reasonably foreseeable and to take precautions necessary to prevent the occurrence of those anticipated dangers. This duty of care in the classroom primarily extends to:

- Supervising students in the classroom;

- Providing adequate instructions to perform the tasks required of them;

- Maintaining in proper working order equipment to be used in the laboratory;

- Providing safe facilities and equipment for the performance of the laboratory task; and

- Warning students of the possible dangers involved in performing the activity.

The determination of the existence of a duty owed by the teacher to a student is a matter of law. That is, in determining whether the teacher or the school district owes the student a duty of care is a question for the judge to decide and is based, in part, on the analysis of a number of factors.[15]

As the likelihood of harm occurring increases, the more likely a court will find that the teacher owes a duty of care to the student. In the chemistry classroom and other specialized classes, the undertaking or burden of this duty on the teacher is somewhat greater than in the ordinary classroom setting because the risk of harm is much greater.[16] The chemistry classroom presents a greater risk of injury to the students and therefore the teacher must make a somewhat greater effort in implementing those reasonable precautions to prevent harm to the students.[17] It should be noted that the duty of care in all classroom settings remains the same: The teacher has a duty to take precautions that any ordinary and reasonable person would take.[18] That is, the chemistry teacher is not under any higher duty of care than the other types of teachers in the school. Chemistry and other

---

11. PROSSER AND KEETON ON THE LAW OF TORTS, p. 164.
12. *Id.*
13. *Id.* at 165.
14. *Id.*
15. These factors include "the social utility of the activity out of which the injury arises, compared with the risk involved, its conduct and the kind of person with whom the actor is dealing; the workability of a rule of care, especially in terms of the parties' relative ability to adopt practical means of preventing injury; and the relative ability of the parties to bear the financial burden of injury and the availability of means by which the loss may be shifted or spread." Raymond v. Paradise Unified School Dist., 218 Cal.App.2d 1, 31 Cal.Rptr. 847, 851 (1963).
16. Teachers of science and laboratory classes have a duty to take precautions that an ordinary and reasonable person in similar circumstances would exercise in the same circumstances. While the duty of care is identical, note that the *burden* on the particular teacher varies with the type of class. That is, for the teacher to meet the duty of care may take more work, because what is reasonable will vary with the circumstances.
17. Damgaard v. Oakland High School Dist., 212 Cal. 316, 298 P.2d 983 (1931) The level of care or vigilance required of a teacher or other employee is commensurate with the degree of danger inherent in a particular situation.
18. Roberts v. Robertson County Bd. of Educ., 692 S.W.2d 863, 26 Educ. L. R. 515 (Tenn. Ct. App. 1985).

laboratory teachers are not held to the expert standard of care only that of an ordinary, reasonable person standard.[19] If no duty of care is owed, then the claim is dismissed.

While often a judge determines the existence of a duty, more often than not, statute or other regulation often determines this duty of care. In some circumstances, the violation of a statute designed to protect a certain class of persons may constitute conclusive evidence of negligence or at the very least be evidence of breach of the duty of care.[20] For example, in Scott v. Independent School Dist., 256 N.W.2d 485 (Minn. 1977) a school was found negligent for failing to enforce a state statute requiring the wearing of safety goggles in industrial arts classes and such violation was found to be negligent per se.[21] In Scott, the failure to enforce the statute resulted in an electrical drill bit being embedded in the student's unprotected eye. What is important to note is that the regulation need not be legislative, but rather the violation need only be that of a local rule in order to find negligence. In Kush ex rel. Marszalek v. City of Buffalo, 59 N.Y.2d 26, 462 N.Y.S.2d, 449 N.E.2d 725, 831, 11 Educ. L. R. 582 (1983) liability was based in part on the failure to secure combustible materials in a locked fireproof cabinet as required by a rule issued from the superintendent's office.

2. Breach of Duty

Once the judge has determined the existence of a duty, ordinarily the plaintiff must show by the presentation of evidence that there has been a breach of that duty. Where there is no breach of the duty of care there can be no liability. Whether a particular teacher's conduct is a breach of the duty of care requires the plaintiff to show that the defendant's conduct (teacher and/or district) imposed an unreasonable risk of harm on the plaintiff (or a class of persons of whom the plaintiff is a member).[22]

Generally, the determination of whether a teacher has breached his/her duty of care to a student or a group of students turns on a determination of whether a reasonable person would have recognized the risk and then taken action to avoid the harm. This determination is not scientific and involves a balancing test of sorts:

> Whether the burden (B) on the teacher to prevent the occurrence of a particular foreseeable risk is greater or less (> <) than the probability of the harm (P) occurring multiplied by the gravity of the potential injury (L). [B> < P*L]

The above formula boils down to this simple statement: the more serious the potential injury to the student the less probable its occurrence will need to be before the teacher will be held liable for negligence for failing to guard against it. For example, if a student fails to wear an acid-proof apron while working with concentrated acids and is subsequently burned in an area that would have been protected by the apron, the teacher will likely be found negligent in having breached a duty of care. In contrast, if the student is working with a balance and a 250-gram weight drops on the student's foot injuring the student's toe through his running shoes, the teacher will probably not be found negligent for failing to require the wearing of a safety shoe in the laboratory. However, if the student is wearing open-toed shoes such as sandals, in violation of a safety rule, then negligence may exist.

The balancing test presented above is often very abstract for both lawyers and juries. Perhaps a better way of looking at the concept, and this is often the way that the concept is presented to a jury, is "whether a

---

19. Fallin v. Maplewood–North St. Paul Dist. No. 622, 362 N.W.2d 318, 22 Educ. L. R. 1277 (Minn. 1985) (standard of care is reasonable care and not "especially cautious" or other higher level of care); Kiser v. Snyder, 21 N. C. App. 708, 205 S.E.2d 619 (1974) (teacher subject to the standard of care that an ordinarily prudent man charged with those duties would exercise in the same circumstances).
20. PROSSER AND KEETON ON THE LAW OF TORTS, pp. 220–33.
21. This case and the other cases mentioned in this book are summarized *infra* in Section IV.
22. Restatement (Second) of Torts § 282 (1965).

reasonable person [23] of ordinary prudence in the position of the teacher, would have conducted himself or herself in the same manner as the teacher did in that situation?" If the answer is "yes," then the teacher is not negligent, if the answer is "no," then the teacher is negligent and liable for the harm caused by his/her negligence.

So what a reasonable person would do under the circumstances becomes the focus of the court's analysis, and for this book, the central focus of our discussion: What is reasonable for a chemistry or other lab science teacher to do in the performance of his/her teaching duties to safeguard students from unreasonable risks of harm? A number of general principles can be extracted from past cases involving high school students injured while performing laboratory experiments. These principles should guide the teacher in the performance of his/her duties, and put every teacher, administrator, and school district on notice that parents are willing to sue teachers and the school district for negligence. In some situations, the school district will be liable for negligence even though the teacher is not liable. This circumstance of exclusive school district liability usually follows from the school district's failure to correct a hazardous condition or defect existing within the classroom or facility of which the district has notice.[24] As will be discussed later in Section III, the best possible position of the teacher is to take affirmative steps to remedy defects or reduce the likelihood of harm to students. However, some defects cannot be remedied by teacher action. Often these are defects inherent in the construction of the facility. For example, the failure to install necessary eye washes and showers, failure to provide adequate ventilation, properly vent fume hoods, or permit the teaching of chemistry or other lab sciences in classrooms without running water, are defects that require the expenditure of money and are beyond teacher control. These types of defects would subject the school district to liability for injuries proximately caused by the defects of which the school district has "actual notice."[25]

Finally, there are certain circumstances where the plaintiff may prove negligence because negligence is inferred in the absence of direct proof of negligent conduct. These situations are rare but occur in practice often enough to merit some attention. The doctrine of "res ipsa loquitur" meaning "the thing speaks for itself" allows an inference of negligence when the injury that occurs is one that would not normally occur in the absence of negligent conduct of someone. For example, in Douglas v. Board of Educ., 127 Ill.App.3d 79, 82 Ill. Dec. 211, 468 N.E.2d 473, 20 Educ. L.R. 228 (1st Dist. 1984) a student who was sitting in her desk in a portable classroom was struck in the back when an entire window pane, still encased in its metal frame, fell from the wall. In this case, the court applied the doctrine to infer negligent conduct. Nearly all courts recognize that there

---

23. The "reasonable person" standard as applied to teachers is the essence of this discussion. For the classroom teacher the courts have made a number of pronouncements as to what a reasonable person should do under the circumstances. The failure to follow this standard of reasonableness is what determines liability.

24. See e.g., Kingsley v. Independent High School Dist. #2, Hill City, 312 Minn. 572, 251 N.W.2d 634 (1977), wherein 17 year old LaVonne Kingsley was seriously injured in attempting to retrieve her coat from the top of her locker where it had been thrown by another student. LaVonne had experienced several prior incidents where unknown students had entered her locker and thrown her coat on the floor to be stepped on. As she was jumping down from the locker, a ring that she was wearing became caught on a metal protrusion from the top of the locker. Her ring finger was torn off. She brought suit against the school district and won. The school district appealed to the Minnesota Supreme Court on the ground that no dangerous condition existed. Citing testimony from the trial, the Court stated:

> This position completely overlooks the dramatic testimony by a fellow student that after the occurrence he went to the scene and picked what remained of LaVonne's finger off the top of the locker at the point where [she] said the accident occurred. This testimony permitted the inference that the dangerous condition described by the janitor and disclosed in the pictures as in existence as of the date of trial was the same as on the date of the accident. The facts on the issue of failure to maintain [the locker] . . . adequately supported the finding of liability.

The court upheld the finding of negligence against the district. Of importance is the claim by the janitor of the existence of the defect. That is, the district was held liable for the failure of the employee to remedy the condition because the janitor had properly documented the defect and the defect had not been remedied.

25. "Actual notice" is a term of art and has a specific meaning in the law. We shall see in Section II, that the question of whether a school district has actual notice of hazardous conditions existing on their facility is a question of fact to be decided by a jury.

are situations in which "res ipsa loquitur" should be applied, and generally agree that three elements must be met before the doctrine will be available to the plaintiff:

- The plaintiff must demonstrate that the event is of the kind which ordinarily does not occur except through the negligence (or fault) of someone;

- The plaintiff must show that other responsible causes, including the conduct of the plaintiff and third persons, are sufficiently eliminated by the evidence; and

- The plaintiff must show that the indicated negligence is within the scope of the defendant's duty to the plaintiff.[26]

3. Proximate Cause (Causation)

Causation is a complex legal relationship that attempts to describe the strength of the relationship between related events. It is not necessary for the actions of the teacher to be the direct cause of the student's injury nor does the teacher's action necessarily need to be even the indirect cause of the injury. Rather the question to be asked is "but for" the teacher's actions would the student's injuries have happened. This legal causal relationship is called "proximate cause" or "legal cause" and in order to find negligence the teacher's actions must have proximately caused the student's injury. A classic example is those cases where the student claims that the proximate cause of their injuries is negligent supervision by the teacher. That is, but for the teacher's failure to supervise the student, the student would not have been injured. In every case claiming negligent supervision by the teacher, this question of proximate cause arises.

Example 2: Herbert, 13 years old, is sitting at his desk at school, suddenly turns towards a noise in the back of the classroom. As he turns, Robert, 14 years old, throws a pencil towards his friend Omar. Omar misses catching the pencil and it strikes Herbert in the eye, blinding him. Herbert's teacher, Mrs. Smith, has stepped out of the classroom for just a moment to go to the bathroom. Ohman's parents sue the board of education for negligence alleging, in part, that Mrs. Smith's absence from the classroom constituted the proximate cause of the injury.

In Ohman v. Board of Education of the City of New York, 300 N.Y. 306, 90 N.E.2d 474 (1949) the Court of Appeals of New York held that "[a] teacher may be charged only with reasonable care such as a parent of ordinary prudence would exercise under comparable circumstances. Proper supervision depends largely on the circumstances attending the event, but so far as the cases indicate there has been no departure from the usual rules of negligence."[27] In finding the teacher not negligent for failing to supervise the students, the court felt that there was no abnormal danger involved in the use of a pencil and that the failure to supervise the students was not the proximate cause of Ohman's injury. "[No one can] seriously contend that a pencil in the hands of a school pupil is a dangerous instrumentality. This is one of those events which could occur equally as well in the presence of the teacher as during her absence."[28]

The issue of whether a teacher's actions are the proximate cause of student injury usually turns on whether the student's injury was foreseeable. If the teacher or the school district could reasonably foresee that a student might be injured the failure to take reasonable precautions to prevent the occurrence of the injury will normally result in a jury finding that the teacher's actions are the proximate cause of the student's injury. This is true even if there are intervening events not under the control of the district or school personnel that take place and directly cause the injury.

---

26. Restatement (Second) of Torts §328 D (1965).
27. Ohman v. Board of Education of the City of New York, 300 N.Y. 306, 90 N.E.2d 474 (1949) reh'g denied, 301 N,Y, 662, 93 N.E. 2d 927 (1950)..
28. *Id.*

Example 3: Two unsupervised teenagers employed by a local school board in a summer program stole some chemicals from an unlocked storeroom and dropped them from a window into some bushes behind the storeroom. They intended to return later to pick them up so they could take them home. However, an eight-year-old boy who lived in the area, and frequently played at the school discovered the chemicals in the bushes. Thinking the chemicals to be sand, he began playing with the chemicals and the matches that he found earlier. The chemicals exploded, severely injuring the boy.

In Kush ex rel. Marszalek v. City of Buffalo, 59 N.Y.2d 26, 462 N.Y.S.2d 831, 449 N.E.2d 725, 11 Educ.L.R. 582 (1983), the New York Court of Appeals upheld a finding of negligence against the school district finding that school authorities had a duty to anticipate the presence of certain individuals on school grounds and keep dangerous chemicals locked away from them. The court stated that the school authorities' failure to properly supervise their employees and to safely secure the chemicals caused the chain of events leading to the boy's injury. The court stated that school district should have anticipated the theft of the chemicals. Therefore, there was no intervening act that would relieve the school district of liability.

In Kush, the key facts supporting the finding of school district negligence were the presence of unlocked dangerous chemicals and the failure to properly supervise employees. In deciding whether the school district's actions were the proximate cause of the boy's injury the court felt that the theft of chemicals from unlocked storerooms was a foreseeable intervening event and therefore would not break the chain of causation. Of course, if the intervening event was not foreseeable then this intervening event would break the chain of causation and therefore no proximate cause will exist.[29] If we change the above scenario so that the facts are that the school district properly supervised the students and had locked chemical storeroom, the result would have been very different.

4. Damages

Assuming the other three elements discussed previously are proven, the plaintiff must then prove that she has been injured by the negligence of the defendant and is entitled to collect damages. Damages are a "sum of money awarded to a person injured by the tort of another."[30] In any action based upon negligence, the existence of actual injury is a requirement.[31] In most cases, the plaintiff can only meet the actual injury requirement if they have suffered some type of physical harm, rather than purely mental or emotional harm. Once physical harm has been proven,[32] the injured plaintiff may recover a variety of damages. These generally fall into the category of compensatory damages, which may be general or special, and may be awarded for "all harm, past, present, and prospective, legally caused by the tort."[33]

General damages are "compensatory damages for a harm so frequently resulting from the tort that it is the basis of the action that the existence of the damages is normally to be anticipated and hence need not be alleged in order to be proven."[34] This include compensation for the physical harm itself (e.g., $100,000) for the loss of an eye); damages for economic loss which are those direct out of pocket expenses such as medical expenses or lost earnings that flow from the injury; physical pain suffered by the plaintiff from the injury; and the mental distress as a consequence of the injury.

---

29. *But see* Frace v. Long Beach City High School Dist., 58 Cal.App.2d 566, 137 P.2d 60 (1943) (where janitor let two other students enter into a chemical supply room from which they stole chemicals which they took home and subsequently caused plaintiff to be injured; the court held that students acts of theft broke the chain of causation) Apparently, theft from an unlocked storeroom is a foreseeable intervening event, but theft from a storeroom opened by a janitor and not a chemistry teacher is not.
30. Restatement (Second) of Torts §902 (1977).
31. *Id.* at §902 (1977) Comment a.
32. In chemistry and other science laboratory accidents, the proof is rather dramatic.
33. Restatement (Second) of Torts §910 (1977).
34. Restatement (Second) of Torts §904 (1) (1979).

Special damages are "compensatory damages for a harm other than for which general damages are given."[35] Special damages are those exceptional situations which are not readily foreseeable and would not naturally flow from the type of injury incurred by the plaintiff—for example, payments for tutors during the time the injured student was out of school recovering from his injury.

In certain circumstances, punitive or exemplary damages are awarded. Punitive damages are "awarded against a person to punish him for his outrageous conduct and to deter him and others like him from similar conduct in the future."[36] Punitive damage awards tend to be very large so the plaintiff, in his or her complaint, always requests them. Similarly, the defense counsel for the teacher or school district will work hardest to remove them from the case.

---

35. *Id.* at §904 (2) (1979).
36. Restatement (Second) of Torts §908 (1978).

SECTION II Circumstances Surrounding Teacher Liability in the Science and Laboratory Classroom

The cases in Section IV demonstrate that teacher liability flows primarily from three categories of circumstances:

- Accidents directly tied to teacher activity. These activities include supervision of students, instruction of students, and maintenance of equipment;

- Accidents involving the condition of premises. These conditions include equipment storage and guarding (security), labeling, containment or storage of dangerous chemicals, building design and absence of safety devices, overcrowding, inappropriate facility use; and

- Accidents involving violations of statutes or rules. This area involves situations where the failure to comply with a state law or other law regulating the school district and its activities results in a finding of negligence liability. Examples of laws regulating laboratory safety include those enacted by the Occupational Safety and Health Administration (OSHA), local building ordinances, and/or other safety regulations issued by school boards or the superintendent's office.

A. Teacher Activity

As mentioned previously, chemistry teachers have a duty to take those precautions that an ordinarily prudent person would take to protect students from an unreasonable risk of injury.[37] This does not mean that chemistry teachers have any higher burden than the ordinary classroom teacher. However, the definition of what is "reasonable" varies significantly between the two groups. The level of care required of a teacher is commensurate with the degree of danger inherent in the situation.[38] The laboratory situation presents unique types of dangers that teachers must guard against. That is, the chemistry teacher has a duty to anticipate foreseeable dangers and take precautions to protect students from possible harm. This duty, as we saw in Section I, extends primarily to five areas of responsibility:

- Providing adequate supervision over student activities;[39]

- Providing students adequate instructions to perform the tasks required of them;

- Warning students of possible dangers in performing the activity;

- Maintaining in proper working order equipment to be used in the laboratory, and

- Providing safe facilities and equipment for the performance of the laboratory task.

---

37. Roberts v. Robertson County Bd. of Educ., 692 S.W.2d 863, 26 Educ. L.R. 515 (Tenn. Ct. App. 1985). *See supra* notes 15–16 and accompanying text.

38. Damgaard v. Oakland High School Dist. 212 Cal. 316, 298 P.2d 983 (1931). This duty of supervision applies to the extent necessary for the adequate enforcement of a safety rule. *See* Roberts v. Robertson County Bd. of Educ., 692 S.W.2d 863, 26 Educ. L.R. 515 (Tenn. Ct. App. 1985).

39. A teacher owes the student a duty to exercise reasonable care in providing and labeling dangerous materials used in chemistry experiments, and in properly instructing and supervising the students. Mastrangelo v. West Side Union High Sch. Dist., 2 Cal 2d. 540, 42 P.2d 634 (1935).

1. Supervision

While many state statutes require educators to maintain proper supervision, there is no requirement that this supervision be constant or guard against every possible danger.[40] The levels of supervision required depend on the circumstances, including the age, maturity and experience of the students, as well as the specific activity in which the students are engaged.[41] It is important to realize that the analysis of the circumstances surrounding the accident is a question of fact that a jury will likely decide if the complaint gets to trial. Imagine a severely injured child on the witness stand telling the story of how the incident occurred and stating that the teacher was out of the room at the time the "accident." Equally disturbing would be the child describing that the teacher was unable to offer assistance after the accident because the teacher was not in the room at that time. The chemistry laboratory is not a per se dangerous place, but given the level of knowledge of the students, their maturity, and their differing capacities to find new ways to "create" in the laboratory, the expectation is that students in laboratory settings need to be closely supervised.

Not all accidents in the laboratory are caused by inadequate supervision. Under certain circumstances, courts have found the teacher not liable, even though the teacher was absent from the room for a period.[42] However, the expectation is that a teacher should be physically present to supervise wherever dangerous materials or equipment are going to be used.[43] In assessing the extent of the precautions that must be taken by the teacher to protect the students from unreasonable risk of harm, several factors must be taken into account: the age, maturity, inexperience, and physical limitations of the students; judgment as to the maturity of their conduct; and the inherently dangerous nature of the equipment and materials being used in the class.[44]

The general rule in assessing and awarding damages in lack of supervision cases is that the injury must be one that is foreseeable and preventable by the exercise of proper supervision.

Example 4: Students are seated around their teacher on a lawn outside of their classroom. The teacher, who is reviewing a safety quiz with the students, fails to notice that several of the students have been throwing a sharp metal object shaped like a knife both inside the classroom and outside on the lawn. The object strikes a student in the eye, causing permanent damage.

In Lilienthal v. San Leandro Unified School Dist., 139 Cal.App.2d 453, 293 P.2d 889 1st Dist. (1956), the court found that there was enough "evidence for the jury on the question whether the teacher knew or should have known of the knife throwing."[45] The court felt that the testimony available

> tending to prove that the knife throwing had been going on for some thirty minutes and the teacher's own testimony that the students were facing him and were all plainly visible and that he looked up frequently and viewed them to give them a chance to ask questions, would . . . warrant the jury to infer that he did observe these knife throwing activities (if the jury disbelieved his testimony that he did not

---

40. Cirillo v. City of Milwaukee, 34 Wis. 2d 705, 150 N.W.2d 460 (Wis. 1967).
41. Roberts v. Robertson County Bd. of Educ., 692 S.W.2d 863, 26 Educ. L.R. 515 (Tenn. Ct. App. 1985); Sheehan v. Saint Peter's Catholic Sch., 291 Minn. 1,188 N.W.2d 868 (Minn.1971).
42. Wentz v. Deseth, 221 N.W.2d 101,102 (N.D., 1974).
43. Fallin v. Maplewood-North St. Paul Dist. No. 622, 362 N.W.2d 318, 22 Educ. L. R. 1277 (Minn. 1985) (teacher not liable for injuries sustained by student where student had injured his finger while using a power saw after the teacher had left the room); *but see* Roberts v. Robertson County Bd. of Educ., 692 S.W.2d 863, 26 Educ. L. R. 515 (Tenn. Ct. App. 1985) (teacher found liable after admitting that the accident would not have occurred if he had been in the room and supervising the student in the use of a drill press and the drill bit struck student in the temple); Lawrence v. Grant Parish School Bd., 409 So.2d 1316, 2 Educ. L.R. 1234 (La. Ct. App.), *cert. denied*, 412 So. 2d. 1110 (La. 1982) (teacher found liable when student injured with saw while teacher out of the room).
44. Payne v. North Carolina Dept. of Human Resources, 95 N.C. App.309, 382 S.E.2d 449, 55 Educ. L. R. 753 (1989), Roberts v. Robertson County Bd. of Educ., 692 S.W.2d 863, 26 Educ. L. R. 515 (Tenn. Ct. App. 1985).
45. Lilienthal v. San Leandro Unified School Dist., 139 Cal.App.2d 453, 456, 293 P.2d 889, 891 (1st Dist. 1956).

see what was going on in front of him) or that he was inattentive and careless in failing to observe such an activity which was going on over such an extended period of time.[46]

The duty of proper supervision extends to the handling and storage of chemicals by students. Where injury results from a failure of the teacher to properly instruct or warn the students, to properly label containers of dangerous materials or to check the equipment for defects, the duty of supervision is breached and liability will follow if the injuries to the student are proximately caused by the teacher's failure to properly supervise the students. Several of the cases discussed in Section IV involve subtle variants on the duty of supervision. In one instance the duty of supervision extended to the unauthorized access of an unlocked storage room during the summer where a young child passing by a window underneath the classroom discovers dangerous chemicals dropped out of the window by two student workers and is subsequently injured.[47] Here the failure to supervise the two student workers and to lock the storage room was the proximate cause of the passing child's injuries. In another supervision case, a teacher working with a group of students in a lab across a hallway was found negligent in failing to supervise a pair of other students in an adjacent classroom. The teacher, although he periodically checked on the students, failed to detect that one student was performing an unauthorized experiment which resulted in the student being seriously injured.[48] In both cases, the teacher's liability was a direct result of the trier of fact's perception that, given the circumstances and the fact that a student was injured, the students were not properly supervised by the teacher. While courts repeatedly emphasize that teachers are not insurers of student safety, the more serious the injuries, the more likely that a court will find that the duty to supervise was breached, thereby permitting some type of recovery for the student. This "rough" justice by judges and juries is the primary reason that most cases involving serious student injury are settled long before they reach a courtroom. In most instances, the allegations will involve a claim of "intentional, willful, or malicious" failure to supervise, and expose the teacher to a potential award of punitive damages, which would permit the jury to punish the wrongdoer for his evil conduct in an amount sufficient to deter him and others from engaging in this type of behavior in the future. Large punitive damage awards promote settlement. It is precisely for this reason that insurance companies make a decision to settle particularly serious claims, when there is some indication that the teacher had not properly supervised the students during the class.

There is authority to the effect that the failure to properly store dangerous chemicals under lock and key may result in liability if a person of ordinary reasonable prudence would have done so under similar circumstances.[49] Finally, this duty of proper supervision extends to the performance of the laboratory exercise by the students. In several cases, the inconsistent requirement of a teacher relating to the use of proper safety equipment has led to liability where there was a rule requiring the use of proper safety equipment, but the teacher did not enforce the rule on a consistent basis. For example, in Scott v. Independent School Dist., 256 N.W.2d 485 (Minn. 1977) a school district was held liable for negligence *per se* for failing to consistently enforce the wearing of safety goggles in industrial arts programs that resulted in a serious and permanent eye

---

46. *Id.*
47. *See* Kush ex. rel. Marszalek v. City of Buffalo, 59 N.Y.2d 26, 462 N.Y.S.2d 831, 449 N.E.2d 725, 11 Educ. L. R. 582 (1983) (school district found liable for negligence when student workers under the supervision of custodians, stole chemicals from an unlocked laboratory storeroom placing them in containers and dropping them out of a window, and where a passing eight-year-old child who regularly played on school property discovered them, began playing with them, and was seriously burned).
48. Connett v. Fremont Cty. Sch. Dist., 581 P.2d 1097, 1102 (Wyo. 1978).
49. Reagh v. San Francisco Unified Sch. Dist., 119 Cal.App.2d 65, 259 P.2d 43 (1953). *See* Gregory v. Board of Education, 222 App. Div 284, 225 NYS 679 (1927).

injury to a student. In <u>Scott</u>, the negligence per se finding was predicated on a state statute requiring the wearing of goggles in such programs.[50]

2. Proper Instruction and Warning of Danger

Proper instruction goes a long way in insulating teachers from potential liability. Proper instruction acts as a type of shield to liability as it relates to the student's own contributory or comparative negligence. In many cases, liability has been denied for chemistry class injuries where the pupils were properly instructed and warned of the dangers of the particular activity and the students acted in disregard of the warnings or instruction. In fact, the most powerful defense in chemistry classroom accidents has been the introduction of evidence of proper instruction as to the dangers inherent in the activity.[51] It is not sufficient however, to merely give the students the directions in the form of a handout, or provide the instructions in a textbook. Rather, the duty of instruction requires personal instruction and sufficient warning.[52] In a number of cases, students have recovered where they have not received proper instruction in the use of a machine, in the use of safety equipment, or where there has been a failure to provide safety equipment, such as safety goggles. In several cases, absolute liability (negligence per se) has been imposed where the failure to provide necessary safety equipment was in violation of a state safety statute or regulation.

Given the inherent danger of liability flowing from lack of proper instruction, it is critical that chemistry instructors spend the additional time necessary to fully demonstrate the laboratory, to specifically identify and warn students of potential hazards associated with such laboratory, and properly supervise the students by monitoring the proper use of safety equipment by the students [53] While it may appear that chemistry instructors have a high burden in providing proper instruction and warnings, the benefits of this instruction cannot be understated. Warning students of the dangers and providing reasonable supervision has resulted in a denial of liability by a number of courts. This is particularly true where students have performed unauthorized experiments without the knowledge of the teacher.[54] In these cases, the adequacy of the teacher's warnings will be a factual issue. However, where the student makes a particularly dangerous device, which a teacher reasonably should know is potentially dangerous and fails to warn the student, the teacher is liable even if the injury occurs after school hours or while the student is at home.[55]

---

50. *See* <u>Ross v. San Francisco Unified School Dist.</u>, 120 Cal. App. 2d. 185, 260 P.2d 663 (1953) (where the failure of an injured pupil to wear goggles because of an inadequate supply available and the failure of the teacher to watch the pupils to see if they had found them, were using them, and the failure by the teacher to warn of the danger involved, supported a finding of negligence).
51. Documentation of instruction is discussed *infra* at Section III.
52. <u>Mastrangelo v. West Side Union High Sch. Dist.,</u> 2 Cal 2d. 540, 42 P.2d 634 (1935).
53. In practice, this duty may be met by dividing the performance of the laboratory into three distinct phases: (1) a prelab phase, where the lab is demonstrated for the students and the appropriate safety techniques and warnings are given; (2) a lab preparation/setup phase, where students set up the laboratory equipment, the instructor ensures that all students are wearing the proper safety equipment, and the apparatus is set up in the proper manner without defect; and (3) a performance phase, where the instructor monitors the students to ensure the safe performance of the lab, ensures students are complying with the safety instructions given, and warns students of potential hazards should a situation arise. In short, teachers must be vigilant in ensuring student safety, through proper supervision consistent with the degree of danger inherent in the activity; give proper instruction and warning sufficient to put the students on notice of the potential for harm; and teachers must guard against foreseeable harm by monitoring compliance with established safety procedures.
54. *See* <u>Wilhelm v. Board of Educ.</u> 16 A.D. 2d 707, 227 NYS2d 791, (2nd Dept.) *aff'd* 12 NY2d 988, 238 NYS2d 972,189 NE2d 503 (1962).
55. <u>Calandri v. Ione Unified Sch. Dist.,</u> 219 Cal.App.2d 542, 33 Cal. Rptr. 333 (3rd Dist. 1963).

In determining liability of the teacher and/or school district for "teacher activity" accidents, several patterns predominate as to whether such liability will follow:[56]

- A finding of negligence by a school district has been held to turn on the existence of three elements: first, the existence of a duty to use care; secondly, a breach of such duty by the creation of an unreasonable risk of harm; and thirdly, proximate cause.[57]

- Ignorance of the pupil in a chemistry experiment caused by a <u>failure of the teacher to properly instruct</u> as to the proper use of materials or <u>to warn of their dangerous nature</u>, notwithstanding that such instruction may be contained in a textbook given to the pupil.[58]

- The fact that a student has taken a chemical off a shelf without permission does not by itself establish that the student was negligent as a matter of law where the student did not know of its dangerous characteristics and had never received instruction as to its dangerous properties.[59]

- However, if the student knows of the dangerous characteristics of the chemicals and takes them without permission, the student may be barred from recovery as a matter of law for his/her own contributory negligence. In those states with comparative negligence statutes, the students' recovery may be significantly reduced.[60] In addition, if the chemicals are stolen by students from a chemistry lab to which they are not permitted entry, and injury results to a third person to whom the students give the chemicals, the school district may not be liable for those injuries because the chain of events was not reasonably foreseeable to school officials.[61]

- A student need not prove that the teacher had knowledge of defective equipment where it can be established that the teacher or school officials were negligent in having such piece of equipment, or in not properly inspecting it or otherwise determining its condition.[62] In the absence of a defective condition, unreasonably dangerous, no liability attaches where proper notice is posted and verbal warnings have been given and where students have been properly instructed and protected with respect to safety measures.[63] But if the injuries to the student result from the violation by a school district of a state safety regulation, then defenses such as lack of knowledge or notice are not available to the school district.[64]

- In the case where a student is injured by the failure to wear protective equipment such as goggles, factors such as the failure to have an adequate supply of goggles, or the failure of the teacher to supervise the pupils to ensure that they had found the equipment and were using them, and the failure to warn the pupils of the danger involved in not wearing them,[65] would support a finding of negligence.[66]

---

56. *See generally*, Tort Liability of Public Schools and Institutions of Higher Learning for Accidents Associated with Chemistry Experiments, Shopwork, and Manual or Vocational Training, 35 ALR3d 758 (1981) §4.
57. *See generally*, Tort Liability of Public Schools and Institutions of Higher Learning for Accidents Associated with Chemistry Experiments, Shopwork, and Manual or Vocational Training, 35 ALR3d 758 (1981) §4; Calandri v. Ione Unified Sch. Dist., 219 Cal.App.2d 542, 33 Cal. Rptr. 333 (3d Dist.1963).
58. *Id.* at 768 (*citing* Mastrangelo v. West Side Union High Sch. Dist., 2 Cal 2d. 540, 42 P.2d 634 (Cal. 1935)).
59. *Id.* at 769 (*citing* Reagh v. San Francisco Unified Sch. Dist., 119 Cal.App.2d 65, 259 P.2d 43 (1953)).
60. *Id.* (*citing* Wilhelm v. Board of Educ. 16 A.D.2d 707, 227 NYS2d 791, (2nd Dept.) aff'd 12 NY2d 988, 238 NYS2d. 972, 189 NE2d 503 (1962)).
61. *Id.* (*citing* Frace v. Long Beach City High Sch. Dist. 58 Cal.App.2d. 566, 137 P.2d 60 (1943)).
62. *Id.* (*citing* Maede v. Oakland High Sch. Dist. 212 Cal. 419, 298 P. 987 (1931)).
63. *Id.* (*citing* Peruman v. Wills, 8 Cal. 2d. 578, 67 P.2d. 96 (Cal. 1937); Klenzendorf v. Shasta Union High School Dist. 4 Cal.App.2d. 164, 40 P.2d. 878 (Cal. 1935)).
64. *Id.* at 770 (*citing* Lehman v. Los Angeles City Bd. of Educ., 154 Cal.App.2d. 256, 316 P.2d 55 (Cal.App.1957)).
65. *Id.* at 769 (citing Ross v. San Francisco Unified Sch. Dist., 120 CalApp.2d 185, 260 P.2d 663 (1953)).
66. As discussed previously, liability only flows if the injury was proximately caused by the failure to provide the required safety equipment. If the student's toe is crushed by a metal gas cylinder because he was not wearing safety-toed shoes, and he is not wearing the safety goggles required by statute, the teacher and school district will not be liable for the crushed toe just because the student was not wearing goggles. Rather in this example, liability would only follow if the statute required the safety shoes and the teacher did not enforce the rule requiring them to be worn.

- Contributory negligence by a pupil injured because of a failure to use a guard or other safety device on a machine does not bar recovery in the absence of instruction by the teacher as to the necessity of using such guard or device.[67] Whether an injured pupil has violated a safety rule is relevant to the issue of contributory negligence; a jury may be instructed that a knowing violation of a safety rule may in itself be negligence.[68] Contributory negligence is normally a fact question in the absence of compelled inferences to the contrary, particularly in the case of a minor.[69] Assumption of risk does not bar recovery in the absence of showing that the plaintiff knew or appreciated the specific danger to which he was exposed.[70]

3. Providing a Safe Working Environment for Students

Providing a safe working environment is a prerequisite to having a safe laboratory. No matter how capable the teacher, if the laboratory's physical environment is not adequate, then accidents are more likely happen. Teachers are charged with the additional duties of maintaining in proper working order equipment to be used in the laboratory, and providing safe facilities and equipment for the performance of the laboratory task. This duty of providing a safe working environment extends only to those factors that are within the teacher's control.[71] As nearly all courts have expressed, certain classroom environments are more dangerous than others are. Chemistry and other laboratory classrooms are distinguished from the regular classroom by the "inherently dangerous nature of the equipment and materials"[72] used in them.

As noted previously, any time dangerous equipment or materials are present the teacher has a duty to supervise more closely than at other times. In Lawrence v. Grant Parish School Bd., 409 So.2d 1316, 2 Educ. L.R. 1234 (La. Ct. App.), cert. denied, 412 So. 2d 1110 (La. 1982) the court found the classroom teacher liable for negligence when evidence supported that at the time of an accident wherein a child was seriously injured by a power saw, that the teacher had been out of the room.[73] The duty to provide a safe working environment is an extension of the duty of supervision. Teachers have a duty to maintain the equipment in their classroom and use that equipment safely. If the teacher does not repair the equipment or permits use of the equipment while in a state of disrepair injuries to students are foreseeable. A common example is found where the teacher fails to remove a piece of equipment that has a frayed power cord and subsequently a child is electrocuted. In one case, a basketball coach was found negligent for the electrocution death of a student in a whirlpool, because the coach, in modifying the equipment, had failed to install a GFI (Ground Fault Interrupter) as required by a national electric code.[74] In short, teachers have a duty to maintain the equipment in their classrooms and should take steps to reasonably ensure that students are not injured by a piece of defective equipment for which they have responsibility.[75]

---

67. *Id.* at 770 (*citing* Ahern v. Livermore Union High School Dist., 208 Cal. 770, 284 P. 1105 (1930); Ross v. San Francisco Unified Sch. Dist., 120 CalApp.2d 185, 260 P.2d 663 (1953)).
68. *Id.* (*citing* Swartley v. Seattle School Dist. 70 Wash. 2d 17, 421 P.2d 1009 (Wa. 1966)).
69. *Id.* (*citing* Damgaard v. Oakland High School Dist. 212 Cal. 316, 298 P.2d 983 (1931); Ross v. San Francisco Unified Sch. Dist., 120 CalApp.2d 185, 260 P.2d 663 (1953); Calandri v. Ione Unified Sch. Dist., 219 Cal.App.2d 542, 33 Cal. Rptr. 333 (3d. Dist.1963)).
70. *Id.* (*citing* Dutcher v. Santa Rosa High School Dist., 156 Cal. App. 2d 256, 319 P.2d 14 (Cal. 1957)).
71. Liability for those defective conditions existing on the premises is covered in the next section.
72. Roberts v. Robertson County Bd. of Educ., 692 S.W.2d 863, 26 Educ. L.R. 515 (Tenn.Ct.App. 1985).
73. *See* Roberts v. Robertson County Bd. of Educ., 692 S.W.2d 863, 26 Educ. L.R. 515 (Tenn.Ct.App. 1985) (liability found where teacher admitted that accident would not have occurred had he been in the room supervising the student who was injured when a drill bit broke off striking student in the temple).
74. Massie v. Persson, 729 S.W.2d 448 (Ky. Ct.App. 1987).
75. The question before the court in this type of question will be whether the teacher had knowledge of the defect. In each case, the teachers answer will be "No, of course not. If I had known the equipment was defective, I would never have given it to them to use." While this is the "A" answer to the question, the problem will be proving that there was no way that the teacher could have foreseen the injury from the defect. The teacher will need to provide evidence that:
    a.   there was a regular pattern of maintenance;
    b.   the equipment was checked for defects;
    c.   there is a written record of such inspections;
    d.   and these inspections were held on a regular basis.

B. Premises Liability[76]

While teachers will have no direct liability for the conditions of the premises, as a rule, school districts are directly liable for injuries caused by conditions of their premises, buildings, fixtures, or equipment.[77] The extent of the school district's liability often turns on the legal status of the person who is injured.[78]

At common law, there were three categories of individuals whom the law gave status. The landowner owed each of them a different duty of care. At the low end of the duty spectrum was the trespasser. A "trespasser" is simply someone who enters and remains on the land without the consent of the landowner or without a valid excuse (called a privilege) for being there. A landowner generally did not owe a trespasser any duty to make the land safe for the trespasser or not conduct activities on his land so as to place them in danger. Thus, there is no duty to inspect the land and make it safe. So if the landowner knew that there was an iron pipe sticking up out of the ground, and fails to mark it so it can be seen by someone entering the land, and a trespasser impales himself on the pipe, the landowner is not liable for the trespasser's injuries. A "licensee," on the other hand, is a person who has permission to enter the land with the consent of the owner but is only on the land for his or her own purpose (not the landowner's). A licensee is owed a limited duty of care. The landowner generally has a duty to warn of dangerous conditions of which he has knowledge, but has no duty to inspect or make safe. Finally, "invitees" are those individuals afforded special treatment under the common law. There are two types of invitees. For purposes of this discussion, only one type, the public invitee is relevant to the classroom teacher. While there are "business invitees" present on school grounds, the public invitee is the person whom teachers will encounter in their classrooms. A public invitee is a member of the public who enters land held open to the public for the purpose for which the land is held open. For example, schools are held open to the public as institutions of learning. Those individuals who enter on school grounds incident to that purpose are classified as public invitees. Generally, students are public invitees.[79]

Invitees are afforded the highest duty of care. The landowner "is subject to liability for physical harm caused to his invitees by a condition on the land if, but only if, he (a) knows or by the exercise of reasonable care would discover the condition, and should realize that it involves an unreasonable risk of harm to such invitees, and (b) should expect that they will not discover or realize the danger, or will fail to protect themselves against it, and (c) fails to exercise reasonable care to protect them against the danger."[80] Thus, a landowner has an affirmative duty to "take reasonable care to ascertain the actual condition of the premises and, having discovered it, either make it reasonably safe by repair or to give warning of the actual condition and the risk involved therein."[81]

---

76. The material in this section is in an abbreviated form because most of the issues involving premise liability do not directly involve the chemistry teacher. However, the chemistry teacher may have some negligence exposure for failing to report defective conditions. As will be discussed in Section III, the reporting of defective conditions increases the likelihood that the school district and administration will correct the defective condition(s).

77. *See generally* Annot., 34 A.L.R.3d 1166 (1970) (tort liability of public schools and institutions of higher learning for accidents due to condition of buildings or equipment); Annot., 35 A.L.R.3d 975 (1971) (tort liability of private schools and institutions of higher learning for accidents due to condition of buildings, equipment, or outside premises).

78. A minority of jurisdictions has abrogated the common law distinctions and, in general, treats everyone as an invitee. In these jurisdictions, a landowner "must exercise ordinary care in maintaining his property in a reasonably safe condition for all persons reasonably expected to be on the premises. Landau, Martin, and Thomas, Premises Liability §1.06 [1] (Mathew Bender, 2000).

79. Petersen v. San Francisco Community College Dist., 36 Cal. 3d 799, 685 P.2d 1193, 205 Cal. Rptr. 842, 19 Educ. L.R. 689 (1984); Waltz v. Wake County Bd. of Educ., 409 S.E. 2d 106, 70 Educ. L.R. 239 (N.C. Ct. App. 1991).

80. Restatement (Second) of Torts §343 (1965).

81. *Id.* at comment d (1965).

There are several general principles that have emerged from cases dealing with the issue of whether an educational institution is liable for the condition of their buildings or equipment:

- With respect to injuries resulting from an arguable defective design or plan of construction of buildings or improvements, as distinguished from negligent maintenance or operations of premises or equipment, state legislation <u>may have</u> been adopted . . . .[82] [Such legislation] gives a public entity immunity from liability for the plan or design that has been approved by a governmental agency exercising discretionary authority, unless there was no reasonable basis for such approval. While it is proper to hold public entities liable for injuries caused by arbitrary abuses of discretionary authority, to permit re-examination in tort litigation of particular discretionary decisions . . . would create too great a danger of [imprudent] interference with the freedom of decision making by those public officials. There is authority to the effect that no liability attaches under such statute notwithstanding that the defective nature of the design or plan is considered wholly unreasonable under later circumstances that the authorities have notice thereof.[83] The same conclusion has been reached, in the absence of statute, on the ground that error of judgment with respect to construction plans does not carry liability with it, since error of judgment without more is consistent with reasonable care.[84]

- Where a condition which causes injury is present on a school's premises, liability may attach only if it is established that the condition was caused by the school employees, rather than third persons, or that the

---

82. *See* Cal. Government Code § 830.6.
83. Annot., 34 A.L.R.3d 1166, 1178-9 (1970) (*citing* <u>Cabell v. State,</u> 67 Cal. 2d 150, 60 Cal. Rptr. 476, 430 P.2d 34 (1967)). The question of whether school districts have a duty to repair or remedy defective conditions in buildings that have been approved by the State architect or other governmental agency and are in essence "defective from inception" is resolved by analyzing the facts and circumstances and the particular defect(s) that caused the injury to the victim. The critical distinction that must be made is whether the victim's injury can be attributed solely to a defective building design/design flaw or does some other theory of wrongdoing explain the injury? It is very important to note that this "design flaw" language *does not* mean or imply that school districts *do not* have an obligation or responsibility to repair or modernize the facility once the conditions pose a hazard to students. Rather, a design defect *standing alone* is insufficient to bring a cause of action against a school district for injuries caused by the defective design. If the defective design is a hazardous condition, the school district has a duty to repair the condition, or prevent students and teachers from exposure to the condition. Every injury usually presents several contributing causes, one of which is the legal or proximate cause of the victim's injury. While the building may have a defective design, that defective design may create a hazardous condition for which the school district may have liability. Liability for defective conditions of the premises may be predicated on a number of alternative theories not merely the allegation that the building was defectively designed. For example, in <u>Stevens v. Central School Dist.</u>, 25 App. Div. 2d. 871, 270 N.Y.S. 2d 23, *aff'd* 21 N.Y. 2d 780, 288 N.Y.S. 2d 475, 235 N.E. 2d 448 (1966), liability was "predicated upon the type of material used in [the building's] construction where the material used was inappropriate in light of the activity to which the premises were subsequently subjected, where appropriate materials were readily available. The failure of a state school agency to comply with state building safety requirements may be a factor in rendering the state liable for injuries from such violation . . . on the theory that a state agency is required to follow the safety regulations adopted by the state". (*citing* <u>Robotham v. State</u>, 54 Misc.2d 363, 282 NYS2d 586 (1967))

   [W]hile liability may not be imposed upon a public school entity because of any errors in judgment it made with respect to the plan under which its school building and the approaches thereto were constructed, on the ground that error of judgment alone is consistent with reasonable care, failure to abate dangers which reasonable care would have revealed will charge the school entity with liability. (*citing* <u>Murphy v. Board of Educ.</u>, 20 App. Div 2d 53, 244 NYS2d 986, *app dism'd* 16 NY2d 660, 261 NYS2d 292, 209 NE2d 284 (1965) (where school district failure to provide adequate lighting for a ramp that was 6 or 7 inches lower than an adjacent walk was an inherently dangerous condition which cast upon the school district a duty to illuminate the area where the accident occurred when invitees were using the sidewalk and ramp in the nighttime).

   In analyzing the facts and circumstances surrounding a particular injury, care must be taken to frame the duty of the school in each instance with respect to the particular conditions existing at the time of the incident. For example, in a building where the fume hoods are improperly vented and arguably the product of a defective building design, the failure of the school district to take steps to prevent the use of the fume hoods until repaired, is probably negligence. Thus, a teacher reporting defective conditions, without reference to design flaws, still presents school districts with an important choice–whether to risk harm to students and teachers by doing nothing, or correct the hazardous condition which is unreasonably dangerous and of which they have actual notice.
84. *Id.* (*citing* <u>Murphy v. Board of Education,</u> 20 App. Div. 2d 53, NYS2d 986, *app. dism'd* 16 NY2d 660, 261 NYS2d 292, 209 NE2d 284 (1965)).

school had actual notice of the presence of the condition, or that the condition had been there for a sufficient length of time . . . for the school, in the exercise of reasonable care, to have discovered and remedied such condition.[85]

- Before a defendant may be held liable for an injury resulting from a dangerous condition . . . the plaintiff generally must show that the defendant had actual knowledge of the condition, or that the condition had existed for such a length of time that in the exercise of ordinary care the defendant should have known of it.[86]

- There are two exceptions to the rule requiring proof of notice of dangerous condition: (1) the dangerous condition was created or maintained by the defendant or by those for whom it was responsible; or (2) the "mode-of-operation doctrine applies. . . . The mode-of-operation rule allows a plaintiff to recover without proving the proprietor's knowledge of a dangerous condition where a patron's carelessness should be anticipated and the defendant fails to take reasonable measures to rectify the condition.[87]

The primary determinant of whether liability will attach to an educational institution for failure to properly maintain the premises or equipment is whether the educational institution had notice, actual or constructive of the dangerous or defective condition of the premises. If there is notice of a hazardous condition and the institution does not take reasonable steps to correct the hazard, then a negligence cause of action will arise. More importantly, "if a dangerous condition exists that would have been revealed by proper inspections, the liability is the same as if there were actual knowledge.[88] Thus, educational institutions have a three-fold duty to maintain the conditions of buildings and premises:

1. They have a duty to inspect the premises to detect conditions which are hazardous;

2. If they find a hazardous condition, they have a duty to take reasonable steps to repair or correct the condition and make the premises safe;

3. They have a duty to warn persons of the hazardous condition if they are not able to eliminate the condition and to prevent harm to persons from the condition.

Example 5: Every year, the local school has a Halloween haunted house in an old grain elevator to raise funds for the student body. Just before the event, as students are sweeping the elevator in order to decorate it for the spooky event, a teacher notices a large number of pigeon droppings around the elevator. The teacher had contracted histoplasmosis in the past from pigeon droppings. A student subsequently develops histoplasmosis after participating in the event.

In Drake v. Mitchell Community Sch., 628 N.E.2d 1231 (Ind. Ct. App. 1994), *aff'd in part, rev'd in part, remanded*, 649 N.E. 2d 1027 (Ind. 1995) the Indiana Supreme Court held that an Indiana school district was liable for damages for its failure to warn or to prevent a student from contracting histoplasmosis for their preparing for and participating in a Halloween activity in a grain elevator not on school premises.

---

85. *Id.* (*citing* Vreeland v. State Bd. of Regents, 9 Ariz. App. 61, 449 P.2d 78 (1969)).
86. Knowles v. Klase, 204 Kan. 156, 460 P.2d 444, 446 (1969) (Finding that evidence that it had been raining for four hours when plaintiff slipped and fell; that the defendant had not mopped the floor since it had begun to rain; and that wet leaves had accumulated at the scene of the accident as well as evidence of a skid mark leading to a leaf were sufficient for a jury to find that the moisture and leaves had caused plaintiff's fall and that the moisture and leaves had remained on the floor a sufficient time prior to the accident to charge the defendants with constructive notice of an unsafe condition).
87. Kimes v. Unified Sch. Dist. No. 480, Seward Cty. Kan., 934 F. Supp. 1275, 1280 (D. Kan. 1996).
88. Wilkinson v. Hartford Accident and Indemnity Co., 411 So.2d 22 (La. 1982) (school board was negligent in permitting a plate glass panel to remain in the foyer of a gymnasium); Gurule v. Salt Lake City Bd. of Educ., 661 P.2d 957 (Utah 1983) (failure to remove ice).

School personnel are not obligated to anticipate every possible defective condition, nor are they obligated to correct every minor defect that may exist on the school's premises as soon as the condition occurs. However, the longer the school district delays in correcting the condition, the more likely it is that the court will find the delay unreasonable.

Example 6: Earlier on that same Halloween day, Janet Kimes, a student in the welding class, was wearing a Halloween costume in anticipation of the event. At the end of the class period while students were cleaning up, Janet was eager to leave the class. As she was walking through the shop, she slipped on a puddle of water and welding beads that were on the floor. As Janet fell, she reached out to stabilize herself by grabbing a welder. A gas cylinder attached to the welder falls off and lands upon her. Janet suffers severe head and facial injuries because of the fall.

In Kimes v. Unified Sch. Dist. No. 480, Seward Cty. Kan., 934 F. Supp. 1275 (D. Kan. 1996) the district court in granting summary judgment for the school district held that:

1. The student had failed to present evidence that the school was on notice of a dangerous condition in the school welding shop work area that would support a negligence action;

2. Student failed to show that any items located on the floor of the school welding shop were concealed dangers as to which the school had a duty to warn or that the school did not use ordinary care in maintaining the work area in reasonable condition as would support negligence action;

3. School did not create or maintain allegedly dangerous condition of wet floors in school welding area such that student could prove exception to the rule requiring proof that school was on notice of the dangerous condition; and

4. Student failed to show that school did not maintain welder and its attached gas cylinder in accordance with manufacturer's recommendations and industry standards or that it was in dangerous condition as would support negligence action.[89]

In the chemistry classroom, the duty to inspect, maintain, and repair equipment is obvious. Less obvious is the responsibility of the teacher to correct student-reported hazards. Chemical spills, broken glassware, or equipment failures occur with enough frequency and regularity that chemistry teachers should be aware of the possible consequences for failure to quickly and effectively remedy the hazardous condition. Most of the time, the choice as to what to do is obvious.

Example 7: Alex , a chemistry student , spills 6M HCl on the lab bench. Teacher, asks " Alex are you alright? If you are, could you please, carefully clean up the spill, okay?" Alex, begins to clean up the spill, and splashes some acid on his face, resulting in a small, but painful burn. Alex sues teacher for negligence.

While it is usually a good idea to have a student clean up his or her own "mess," it may not always be a wise decision to permit the student to do so. Teacher directed the student in a manner consistent with the "standard practice" most individuals would use in their own homes. The difference in this example is that this is not a "standard" spill and this is not the teacher's home. This "standard" response may not meet the requisite duty of care for a chemistry teacher under these circumstances. It is important to understand that it is almost impossible to predict how a court will view the actions of the chemistry teacher in this regard. The facts and circumstances surrounding the accident control the determination of whether the teacher has acted as an ordinarily reasonable person in the particular situation. If the teacher has not properly instructed the student as to how to handle this particular hazard and subsequently is injured cleaning it up then liability attaches to the teacher's action in failing to instruct the student.

---

89.   Kimes v. Unified Sch. Dist. No. 480, Seward Cty. Kan., 934 F. Supp. 1275 (D. Kan. 1996).

Assume, in the above example, that before the lab, the student was properly instructed in the proper method of cleaning up a spill of 6 M HCl. In addition, the student receives proper instruction as to the nature of the hazard immediately following the accident. Has the teacher done enough to meet the standard of care? Perhaps not. Did the teacher warn the student as to the possible consequences if he did not perform the cleanup properly? If not, again, the teacher may be negligent in failing to provide such warning. Is the student able to clean up the chemical spill unsupervised by the teacher? Depending on the characteristics of the student and the likelihood of harm to the student, the level of supervision required by the teacher can vary. In some cases, a student may clean up a minor spill without close teacher supervision. If the spill is larger in area and the risk of harm to the student greater, then closer teacher supervision is necessary.

Now, is the student able to perform the cleanup? Of course, but before such cleanup is made by the student, the teacher must analyze the facts and circumstances surrounding the incident and make an informed decision as to how best proceed while minimizing the danger to the student. In short, the teacher must, in every instance where there is potential for harm to the student, think about what they are going to do before proceeding. Rather than responding abruptly, "Clean it up!" the teacher must not give in to the temptation or habit to make the snap or patterned decision that may not be reasonable under the circumstances.

Example 8: Teacher, instead of instructing Alex to clean up the spill, is engaged in a discussion with another teacher on the phone. Unable to get off the phone, Teacher calls over to Alex telling him to throw some paper towel on the spill on the bench. Alex does as instructed and throws some paper towel on the spill. The paper towel soaks up the acid. Alex having completed his lab begins putting away the lab equipment. His lab partner, Alice, picks up the paper towel and splashes some acid on her face. Thinking that the towel contains water, she throws the towel in the wastebasket, rubs several drops of liquid off her face with her sleeve, and heads to track practice. Expert gets off the phone and inspects the lab bench. Finding the spill is already clean; Expert calls to Alex as Alex is leaving the classroom "Thanks for cleaning up the spill." About 20 minutes into practice in the hot sun, Alice's face begins to itch, and she casually scratches at the area. Several minutes later, one of her teammates notices black spots developing on her skin. Now the area that was originally itchy begins to hurt, and bleed. Frantic, she runs to the nurse for help. The nurse, who is at the end of her workday, sends Alice home. Her parents rush her to the emergency room.

This example, loosely based on the facts contained in Duross v. Freeman, 831 S.W.2d 354 (Tex. App. San Antonio 1992),[90] illustrates how easy it is for a teacher to be negligent. Teacher knew that Alex had spilled a dangerous chemical on the laboratory bench. Rather than direct Alex to clean up the spill immediately, Teacher waited several minutes. In that time, another student unknowingly is exposed to the acid and is injured. In this case, Expert was on notice of the dangerous condition and failed in a reasonable time to correct the dangerous condition, resulting in serious injury to Alice. As should be clear by now, there are several other bases for finding teacher liable under the above facts including breach of the duty of supervision, failure to warn, failure to provide safety instruction, etc.

90. In Duross v. Freeman, 831 S.W.2d 354 (Tex. App. San Antonio 1992), the student was unable to pursue negligence claims against the teacher and the nurse for negligence because of a Texas statute giving immunity for acts "done within the scope of employment, and which involve the exercise of judgment or discretion, except in circumstances where disciplining a student, the employee uses excessive force or his negligence results in bodily injury to the student." *Id.* at 356.

C. Violations of Statute and Other Rules

The final area where teachers have exposure to liability is through violations of statutes, regulations, ordinances, or other rules enacted for the safety of employees or children. There are a large number of statutes and regulations requiring adherence to a particular safety requirement. As discussed previously, these statutes and regulations define the duty of the teacher regarding a particular practice. For example, if a regulation requires goggles in the classroom, then the failure to adhere to the standard will result in a court finding negligence per se.[91] A major source of rules is the Occupational Safety and Health Act (29 U.S.C. § 651 et seq.), or their state law equivalents.[92] Rather than detail the wide reaching effect that these specific statutes, and the large number of ordinances, regulations and other rules have on classroom operation, it will suffice to say that districts have a duty to adhere to all applicable rules of law, and it is negligence to fail to communicate those rules to employees.[93] Ultimately, the question of individual liability will rest with the teacher who fails to make a reasonable effort to know the rules applicable to his subject area.[94] The task of learning the rules is made more difficult by conflicts between different regulations or rules. A current example of this rule confusion is found in the dilemma facing California AP Chemistry teachers. Some of the approved AP Chemistry lab experiments use chemicals that are on the list of chemicals prohibited for classroom use by the Department of Education. The chemistry teacher must choose between doing the lab experiment and violating the safety regulation. The primary responsibility for the safety of the chemistry students lies with the chemistry teacher. The teacher has a duty to take reasonable steps to comply with the regulation prohibiting certain chemicals in the classroom, despite the apparent approval of the chemicals by the same regulatory body.

---

91. Scott v. Independent School Dist., 256 N.W.2d 485 (Minn. 1977). For a discussion of goggle safety and the American National Standards Institute (ANSI) standards, *see generally* Flinn Scientific Inc., Goggle Safety: What Do the ANSI Standards Really Mean?, flinnsci.com/homepage/safe/gogsafe.html (Flinn Scientific, Inc. 2000).

92. California is an example of a state that has enacted a large number of regulations affecting the chemical laboratory: California Education Code: §§ 32030, 32031, 32032, 32033 (School Eye Safety); §§ 32255.1, 32255.3, 32255.4, 32255.5 (Alternatives to Dissection); §§ 35295, 35296, 35297, 40041.5 (Earthquake Emergency Procedures); §§ 49340, 49341, 49401.5, 49411 (Hazardous Materials Education); § 51202 (Instruction in Personal and Public Health and Safety; § 51540 (Use of Animals in Public Instruction). California Code of Regulations, Title 8, General Industry Safety Orders: § 5154.1 (Ventilation Requirements for Laboratory-Type Hood Operations); § 5154.2 (Ventilation Requirements for Biological Safety Cabinets); § 5162 (Emergency Eyewash and Shower Equipment); § 5163 (Spill and Overflow Control); § 5164 (Storage of Hazardous Substances); § 5191 (Occupational Exposure to Hazardous Chemicals in Laboratories (Chemical Hygiene Plan)); § 5193 (Bloodborne Pathogens); § 5194 (Hazard Communications; Material Safety Data Sheets) California Code of Regulations, Title 22: § 66263.42 (Specific Requirements for Milkrun Operations–Hazardous Waste Disposal). Health and Safety Code: §§ 1650, 1651, 1660, 1662 (Humane Care of Animals); §§ 25153, 25205.7(o) (Repeal of Requirement for Obtaining an Extremely Hazardous Waste Disposal Permit); §§ 25163, 25163.1 (Transporting Hazardous Waste); [Summary of] § 25500 et seq. (Hazardous Materials Release Response Plans and Inventory). From "Science Safety Handbook for California Public Schools 1999 ed.," California Department of Education, Sacramento 1999.

93. For a very thorough analysis of the intersection of the various "safety statutes" as they relate to science classroom size, see Roy, Ken, "Safe Science: Be Protected! For Safety Sake, One Class Size Does Not Fit All," flinnsci.com/homepage/safe/safesci.html (Flinn Scientific, Inc. 2000).

94. A plaintiff's attorney analyzing the facts and circumstances surrounding a negligence case against a teacher will, in every instance, ask the teacher what materials, rules, etc. did they rely on in order to make their decision to act, or not act as the case may be, when a student is injured? The attorney would rather find a violation of a rule or statute affecting the teacher's classroom duty and the teacher's failure to follow the applicable rule because it raises the inference of negligence that the teacher must rebut in order to avoid liability.

SECTION III Practical Solutions to Everyday Problems: Advice for Teachers

A. Teacher Concerns

Teachers are the first targets of lawsuits because often they are in the position to best prevent the occurrence of the accident. A recent sampling of questions directed to a major scientific supply company,[95] from science teachers across the nation identified several areas of concern related to teacher activity liability:[96]

Group 1: Teacher's Duty to Provide Adequate Supervision over Student Activities

A. Class Size Supervision

Teachers need to be aware that they must provide adequate supervision over all of the classroom activities of their students. With class size increasing across the nation the importance of limiting the size of the class appropriate to the degree of risk involved in the activity becomes an important factor in determining whether a teacher should perform a particular experiment.[97] Teachers are expected to use their professional judgment to determine whether the students are properly supervised for the particular activity in which they are engaged.

Example 9: You are a first year chemistry teacher with a class size of 32 students, all freshmen with no prior chemistry experience. You are operating in a 'standard' chemistry facility. After several weeks of class, you feel comfortable to begin doing the experiments in the textbook. Laboratory No. 1 is an investigation of chemical changes that has your students using an open flame. You decide that they should work in teams of two students in order to reduce the number of open flames to 18 in the classroom. Is this lab safe for this group of students?

---

95. Flinn Scientific Inc. "Your Safer Source for Science Supplies."
96. Rather than list each question separately, each question was analyzed in terms of the duty of care applicable to the question and grouped accordingly. Following the discussion of each frequently asked question, a "case link" is included to identify those cases found in Section IV that are on point and address the issue(s) being discussed.
97. The issue of class size and safety is hotly debated. For current thinking on the topic, the National Science Teachers Association (NSTA) recently published a special issue of *The Science Teacher*, Vol. 66 No. 6 (September 1999) devoted to issues of Science Safety and specifically addressed the issue of class size. In the view of the NSTA laboratory class size should be no more than 24-1. National Science Teachers Association 1999. NSTA Handbook, (Arlington Va.: National Science Teachers Association). While not disputing the need for smaller class sizes, this author's belief is that the imposition of a fixed number of students does not properly address the duty of care. A discussion of the varying "standards" in effect in some states is obviously fraught with difficulty because the minimum amount of space required by a student, is going to vary with the type of experiment, the type of teacher, the age and maturity of the students and a whole host of other factors. For a discussion of the various "standards," *see generally,* Flinn Scientific Inc., Overcrowding in the Science Laboratory, flinnsci.com/homepage/safe/ovrcrowd.html (Flinn Scientific, Inc. 1998).

If in your judgment, you reasonably believe it is safe, and you proceed with the experiment and an accident occurs from that flame, you can also be assured that some attorney will say that you were not being reasonable, and a jury will likely find that to be so. Why? There is no set number of students that makes a classroom safe or unsafe. Rather the question is whether you can safely monitor and supervise all students in the room. Smaller class size reduces the likelihood of an accident occurring, and increases the adequacy of the teacher supervision. The determination of how many students can safely participate in a particular activity depends not only on the number of students in the classroom but also on several other closely related factors, such as the knowledge, training, and experience of the teacher; the risk of harm inherent in the activity; the ability level of the students; the number of lab stations; design of the classroom; etc.

Unfortunately, few teacher contracts or collective bargaining agreements provide guidance as to having large numbers of students in chemistry and other science classrooms.[98] Increasingly, chemistry and other science teachers are asked to accept larger numbers of students in their classrooms on a basis equal to other classes. Apparently, there is a widespread belief that science classrooms do not present a special situation justifying fewer students than other non-laboratory classrooms. That is, science teachers should have 32 students just as history teachers have 32 students. Acceptance of these "additional" numbers of students increases the risk that serious accidents will occur and increases the risk of liability for all involved.

For example in Bush v. Oscoda Area Schools, 405 Mich. 716, 275 N.W.2d 268 (1979), *sub appeal*, 109 Mich.App.373, 311 N.W.2d 788 (Mich.Ct.App.1981) a chemistry class that was originally meeting in the chemistry lab had been rescheduled in order to accommodate increased enrollment and was meeting in a math room in the interim. The chemistry laboratory was equipped with a safety shower, ventilation or exhaust hoods, sinks, enclosed storage areas, stationary laboratory desks and water and gas outlets. The substitute room was not so equipped. The classroom teacher had previously complained to the principal about the overcrowded conditions existing in the classroom and the increased potential for accidents. She said "[y]ou cannot keep sending us this many students and expect us to do lab work in rooms this size where the tables move too easily. It's just too crowded." "When you throw more students in that classroom . . . [y]ou have more hands to get into things, more bodies in the small amount of space, more confusion at times. People sometimes bump into each other. You tend to have more clumsiness occurring and it's just too hard to manage too many students." Bush v. Oscoda Area Schools, 405 Mich. 716, 275 N.W.2d 268, 270 (1979). The principal using, initially, good judgment in deciding that the chemistry laboratory was not adequate for the students' safety, then makes an extremely poor decision in deciding to use a math classroom, not properly equipped, as a substitute laboratory.

While it would be easy to come up with a number as the maximum size for a chemistry class, that number would be arbitrary at best. While current thinking places this optimal class size at approximately 24 students for every science teacher, there are circumstances where even this many students may be unreasonable in the context of the teacher's duty to provide adequate supervision. Each school must evaluate their facility, the safety codes and other state and local regulations, the nature of their student population, the capabilities and

---

98. Approaching your union representative, if you have one, with your concerns about your students and your own safety due to large class numbers is the first step in beginning the process of changing the thinking of teacher unions that "one size fits all." In almost every district in the nation, class sizes vary from class to class depending on whether or not special funding is available. For example in California, many ninth grade English classes are 20 students to 1 teacher because the legislature has determined that many students are unable to read. It should make sense that these same non-reading students are also the same ones in your chemistry class except that now there are 32 of them and they are going to use fire, hazardous chemicals and other potentially dangerous objects. Teacher unions need to be sensitive to the fact that for some of their unit members, which they have a duty to represent, uniform class size numbers (e.g., 32 in a classroom) may not adequately protect the teacher or the students. Given the latest thinking on the subject, the implication for those unionized teachers who now have 24 or more students in a chemistry classroom, negotiating larger class sizes for chemistry teachers to accommodate English teachers who have classes of 20 might be a violation of their union's duty of fair representation. See *infra* note 111 and accompanying text.

experience of their staff and students in reaching a decision as to the optimal class size for their facility. While efforts to come up with an objective measure of the amount of space necessary are appropriate, they are only as useful as the ability to quantify the other significant factors which affect the ability of the teacher to meet his/her duties of care to their students. In some of the cases discussed in Section IV, accidents occurred with a few students in the lab room,[99] or in one case while there were only 12 students in the room.[100] Perhaps it may be more productive to meet with school district decision-makers and describe what steps must be taken by the teacher in order to meet their duty of care. The reduction in class size in laboratory environments is an effective way to reduce the risk of liability for negligence for both teachers and school districts.

Case Links:

1. Bush v. Oscoda Area Schools, 405 Mich. 716, 275 N.W.2d 268 (1979), *sub appeal,* 109 Mich.App.373, 311 N.W.2d 788 (Mich.Ct.App.1981)

2. Connett v. Fremont Cty. Sch. Dist., 581 P.2d 1097(Wyo.1978)

3. Rixmann v. Somerset Public Schools, St. Croix County, 83 Wis. 2d 571, 266 N.W.2d 326 (Wis.1978)

B. Supervision of Student Aides

Student aides are to be treated the same as every other student in the chemistry classroom. They are students first, and aides last. The chemistry teacher owes student aides the same duty of care as every other student for which they are responsible. Often teachers use these aides to assist them in supervising the laboratory, preparing chemicals, and other chores related to the chemistry laboratory. While this is an appropriate use of these individuals, the teacher must remember that they are still students with limited skills. Therefore, the teacher must always supervise their activities (not leave them alone in the back room or another room to mix chemicals for a laboratory exercise); ensure that they are following proper safety procedures (goggles, aprons, and other appropriate safety equipment), and that there are no other hazards in the environment where they are working.[101]

Example 10: Teacher allows several sophomore boys enrolled in a first year chemistry course to assist him in the setup and preparation of a laboratory for the next class day. Two boys are working alone in another lab room. Although the teacher is in the room next door, with the door open, he is not able to see the boys and only checks on them every couple of minutes. Inevitably, one of the boys decides to help his friend with an experiment. Using a can of alcohol left by the teacher to fill alcohol burners, one of the boys decides to see if adding alcohol to different salt solutions changes the boiling point. The can catches fire and explodes. The teacher hearing the explosion rushes to the student and puts out the flames with a blanket. Testimony at the hearing indicated that the teacher did not instruct the boys on the danger of alcohol and open flames.

In Connett v. Fremont Cty. Sch. Dist., 581 P.2d 1097(Wyo.1978), the court concluded that the question of whether the teacher was negligent in failing to supervise the students was one of fact for the jury to decide. In short, teachers are not relieved of their duty to supervise just because they are not instructing a class. Rather, they are going to be charged with the supervision of the lab, even if there is no class instruction going on. Consequently, if teachers are not able to supervise the students directly, students, including student aides, should not be permitted to work unattended.

---

99. *See* Connett v. Fremont Cty. Sch. Dist., 581 P.2d 1097 (Wyo.1978).

100. *See* Rixmann v. Somerset Public Schools, St. Croix County, 83 Wis. 2d 571, 266 N.W.2d 326 (Wis.1978).

101. In addition, student aides increase the number of students in the classroom for which the teacher is responsible, triggering the duty to provide adequate supervision discussed above.

In one instance, a teacher was not liable for serious injuries sustained by a student aide who performed an unauthorized experiment without the teacher's knowledge or presence. In Shifton v. North Clackamas School Dist. No. 12, 18 Ore. App. 90, 523 P.2d 1296 (Ore. App. 1974) a teacher who permitted a student aide to work alone in a room with access to phosphorus, successfully defended a negligence suit at trial on a showing that the student was conducting unauthorized experiments with the chemical, and violated safety rules given by the teacher at the beginning of the year.

Case Link:

1. Connett v. Fremont Cty. Sch. Dist., 581 P.2d 1097 (Wyo.1978)

2. Kush ex rel. Marszalek v. City. of Buffalo, 59 N.Y.2d 26, 462 N.Y.S.2d 831, 449 N.E 2d 725, (Ct.App. 1983)

3. Moore v. Order Minor Conventuals, 164 F. Supp. 711 (W.D.N.C. 1958), *aff'd,* 267 F.2d 296 (4th Cir. 1959)

4. Shifton v. North Clackamas School Dist. No. 12, 18 Ore. App. 90, 523 P.2d 1296 (2d Dept.) (Ore. App. 1974)

5. Wilhelm v. Bd. of Educ. of New York, 16 A. D.2d 707, 227 N.Y.S.2d 791, *aff'd without opinion* 12 N.Y.2d 988, 238 N.Y.S.2d 972, 189 N.E.2d 503 (N.Y.1962)

C. Security of Chemicals/Theft of Chemicals

Theft of chemicals is a recurrent theme in many of the cases discussed in Section IV. The answer to the question as to whether a teacher will be found liable for negligence is determined by whether it was foreseeable that the chemicals are going to be stolen or taken from the lab without permission. If it is foreseeable, then the teacher will be found to have breached the duty of care. Once a jury determines that there has been a breach in the duty of care, then the jury must determine if the type of harm (injury) to the student is consistent with the danger inherent in the misuse of the particular chemical stolen. If it is, then liability will attach.

Example 11: Student, unbeknownst to teacher, steals a bottle of 12 M HCl and subsequently receives severe burns when he accidentally spills the acid on his pants. If it was foreseeable that student would steal the acid, the teacher will be liable for negligence because burns are consistent with the misuse of HCl.

Another example of a chemical theft case is found in Kush by Marszalek v. City. of Buffalo, 59 N.Y. 2d 26, 449 N.E 2d 725, 462 N.Y.S.2d 831 (Ct.App. 1983) where an eight year old who lived near a school was severely injured when he discovered chemicals that had been dropped from a chemistry lab window along a pathway where he lived. Two student janitors had stolen the chemicals. They had taken them while the regular janitorial staff was on a coffee break. In finding the school district liable for the eight-year-old boy's injuries, the court stated that

> [w]here the school purposely maintained a store of chemicals, some of which were inherently dangerous, and recognized that, in the environs of the school, a serious hazard would arise if deliberate safeguards were not in place, reasonable care required the securing of the chemicals in such a way that their unsupervised access could not be readily obtained by children, and school which failed to adequately supervise its student employees and failed to adequately secure the dangerous chemicals breached that duty.[102]

---

102. Kush ex rel. Marszalek v. City. of Buffalo, 462 N.Y.S.2d 831, 834 (Ct.App. 1983).

The chemistry teacher must be on guard for the loss of chemicals from the classroom. An excellent way to minimize costs is to use smaller quantities. More importantly, the use of smaller quantities during the laboratory activity means smaller amounts being stolen by students. Logically, the danger from a small amount of chemicals should be smaller than if large quantities are stolen. It is highly likely that a modern jury would find that chemicals, particularly those whose properties are particularly attractive to teens, because they cause severe burns, are "dangerous," cause explosions, etc., would find that these types of chemicals are likely to be the ones stolen.[103] In that case, the teacher, and the school district would have a duty to secure the chemicals properly. In particular, the use of locked storage areas and cabinets is mandatory.

The good news for teachers is that in some fact situations, courts are split on whether the teacher was negligent in detecting whether students removed chemicals from the classroom. Several of the cases discussed in Section IV point to the level of knowledge and maturity of the student, and whether the student should have known of the danger of harm as critical factors in determining whether the student was contributorily negligent for injuries sustained in the laboratory.

In Rixmann v. Somerset Public Schools, St. Croix County, 83 Wis. 2d 571, 266 N.W.2d 326 (Wis.1978) Ron Rixmann was performing a starch extraction from a leaf that required the students to transfer the leaf into alcohol that was being warmed by an electric plate. The teacher, whom had demonstrated the experiment the previous day, had warned the students to have no open flames near the experiment because alcohol is flammable. Ron and two of his friends were working in a group and had become bored with the lab. Apparently, one of the pupils decided to ignite some of the alcohol in a plastic spoon with a match provided by Rixmann. Eventually, the spoon itself caught fire. The student waved the spoon in the air to put out the flames, and then proceeded to place the spoon in a beaker of water, but in doing so ignited the fumes from the beaker of heated alcohol. The teacher seeing the beaker was on fire tried to put it out by placing a notebook over the mouth of the beaker. The beaker tipped over and spilled the flaming liquid onto Ron severely burning him. In determining whether the teacher was negligent, the court looked at not only the teacher's actions but also the student's actions:

> It may be true, as the trial court stated, that these students "weren't the brightest." But all three of the students were bright enough to know that alcohol was flammable and that they were not supposed to have open flames near it. On the basis of these admitted and undisputed facts, we conclude that the students, by collaborating to set fire to the puddle of alcohol on the table, did not conform their conduct to that which would be expected of a similarly situated child of the same age and with the same capacity, discretion, knowledge, and experience in creating the initial fire.[104]

In a similar vein, a student's act of stealing a large amount of sodium chlorate was considered to be a "superceding force" breaking the chain of causation between the teacher's negligence and the student's injuries. In Brazell v. Bd. of Educ. of Niskayuna Schools 161 A.D. 1086, 557 N.Y.S.2d 645 (3d Dept. 1990) a teacher was not liable for negligence where a student, after making a measurement of 5.0 grams of sodium chlorate, decides to put an extra amount in his pocket so he can set fire to it at home. That night the chemical ignites and burns his leg. The teacher specifically had told the class to never remove chemicals from the classroom and had gone over safety procedures in the classroom with him. The court in addressing whether the teacher was negligent stated: "[I]t is our opinion that even if the science teacher was negligent in any way by reason of being unable to watch some 28 students every minute of the time they were there, Colin's intervening

---

103. While no court has done so, an argument can be made that dangerous chemicals are "attractive nuisances" that must be guarded against, much as swimming pools are attractive to young children. Defining something as an "attractive nuisance" has some very important legal consequences, and raises the liability bar to almost a form of strict liability.

104. Rixmann v. Somerset Public Schools, St. Croix County, 83 Wis. 2d 571, 266 N.W.2d 326,333 (Wis.1978).

culpable act of intentionally stealing the chemical constituted a superceding force absolving defendant from any liability."[105]

It is important to note that the issue of whether a teacher is liable for injuries sustained by students who have stolen chemicals from the classroom is not clear. Several factors seem to influence the court's determination of liability. These include the age of the student and his/her experience with the chemicals, the degree of supervision exercised by the chemistry teacher, the adequacy of the safety instruction related to the particular chemical, and the efforts made by the teacher and the school to safeguard and secure potentially dangerous chemicals. Several of the cases discussed in Section IV return differing judgments on substantially similar facts. Thus, it becomes very challenging to predict whether the chemistry teacher will escape some liability. This is particularly true in modern jurisdictions where comparative negligence principles apportion fault between all negligent actors. In almost all of the "stolen" chemical cases, a strong argument can be made that the student's injuries were caused by their own negligence and would result in a reduction in any damage award.

Case Links:

1. Kush ex rel. Marszalek v. City. of Buffalo, 59 N.Y.2d 26, 462 N.Y.S.2d 831, 449 N.E 2d 725, (Ct.App. 1983)

2. Rixmann v. Somerset Public Schools, St. Croix County, 83 Wis. 2d 831, 266 N.W.2d 326,333 (Wis.1978)

3. Brazell v. Bd. of Educ. of Niskayuna Schools, 161 A.D. 2d 557, N.Y.S. 2d 645 (3d Dept. 1990)

4. Hutchison v. Toews, 4 Or. App.19, 476 P.2d 811, (Or. App. 1970)

5. Moore v. Order Minor Conventuals, 164 F. Supp. 711 (W.D.N.C. 1958), aff'd, 267 F.2d 296 (4th Cir. 1959)

6. Frace v. Long Beach City High School Dist., 58 Cal.App.2d 566, 137 P.2d 60 (1943)

7. Mastrangelo v. West Side Union High School Dist., 2 Cal.2d 540,42 P.2d 634 (1935)

8. Reagh v. San Francisco Unified School Dist., 119 Cal.App.2d 65, 259 P.2d 43 (1953)

9. Shifton v. North Clackamas School Dist. No. 12, 18 Ore. App. 90, 523 P.2d 1296 (Ore. App. 1974)

10. Brown v. Tesack, 556 So.2d 84, 58 Ed. Law Rep.846, review granted 556 So.2d 1288,58 Ed. Law Rep.1378, aff'd in part, revised in part, 566 So.2d. 955, 62 Ed. Law Rep.1287, rehearing denied (La. App. 4 Cir. 1990).

D. Student Horseplay, Misuse of Equipment and Chemicals/Unauthorized Experiments/Failure of Students to Follow Instructions

Student horseplay or misuse of chemicals and equipment, like the theft of chemical situation discussed above poses significant problems for the chemistry teacher. Again, the determination of liability in these cases is fact dependent and often liability turns on whether it was foreseeable that an injury would occur because of student misbehavior in using a piece of equipment, handling a dangerous chemical or by engaging in horseplay. If the teacher sees the horseplay and fails to intervene to protect the student, and the resultant injury is of the type that would not have occurred but for the horseplay, the teacher will be liable. Horseplay and equipment/chemical mishandling or misuses are really supervision questions. If the chemistry teacher is properly supervising a class, then the probability of these types of occurrences should be significantly reduced. Many courts are quite lenient in assessing the number of students that a teacher is able to supervise properly in a classroom. For example, in Rixmann v. Somerset Public Schools, St. Croix County, 83 Wis. 2d 571, 266

---

105. Brazell v. Bd. of Educ. of Niskayuna Schools, 557 N.Y.S.2d 645, 646 (A.D. 3d Dept. 1990).

N.W.2d 326,333 (Wis.1978), the student misbehavior occurred in a class of 12 students. The courts have mentioned class size as a factor influencing the ability of teachers to properly supervise their students. However, in the majority of cases analyzing the adequacy of teacher supervision related to student misbehavior, the factor that appears to determine liability is the physical proximity of the teacher to the student at the time of the accident. If the teacher is far from the student who is injured, or out of the room, then it is more likely the teacher is liable if a reasonable chemistry teacher should have been in the room or closer to the student. If the teacher is within close physical proximity to the student who is injured, the analysis changes. In these cases, the court asks whether a reasonable chemistry teacher should have detected the student misbehavior. The longer the student was misbehaving, the more likely the teacher is negligent.

Teachers have a duty to prevent injuries from occurring in the laboratory. Students who engage in horseplay, perform unauthorized experiments, or alter the intended performance of a piece of equipment, are a danger to themselves and others. To avoid liability, chemistry teachers must take affirmative action to deal swiftly with the misbehaving student. The teacher should *immediately*[106] remove the student from the lab. Chemistry teachers have a duty to prevent foreseeable harm to students. Removal of a misbehaving student removes the risk of harm to all. More importantly, as several of the cases demonstrate, allowing the horseplay to continue opens the door for a jury to find liability. Remember, while teachers are not the insurer of children safety, parents do expect teachers to protect their children from harm, both to themselves and to others.

Teachers are expected to control their students' classroom behavior. If the student is a continuing discipline problem, or willfully disregards the laboratory's safety rules, it is negligent to permit the student to remain in the room. Teachers must balance the need to maintain a safe learning environment with the need of the student to be in the classroom. A student's failure to follow the rules jeopardizes everyone's safety. Permitting the misbehaving individual to remain in the classroom sends a negative message to the other students: It is okay to play in the laboratory.

Case Links:

1. Lilienthal v. San Leandro Unified School Dist., 139 Cal.App.2d 453, 293 P.2d 889 (1st Dist. 1956)

2. Connett v. Fremont Cty. Sch. Dist., 581 P.2d 1097 (Wyo.1978)

3. Rixmann v. Somerset Public Schools, St Croix County, 83 Wis. 571, 266 N.W.2d 326 (Wis.1978)

4. Wentz v. Deseth, 221 N.W.2d 101 (N. D., 1974)

5. Hutchison v. Toews, , 4 Or. App.19, 476 P. 2d 811 (1970)

6. Wilhelm v. Bd. of Educ. of New York, 16 A.D.2d 707, 227 N.Y.S.2d 791, (2d Dept.) *aff'd without opinion* 12 N.Y.2d 988, 238 N.Y.S.2d 972, 189 N.E.2d 503 (1962)

7. Moore v. Order Minor Conventuals, 164 F. Supp. 711 (W.D.N.C. 1958), *aff'd*, 267 F.2d 296 (4th Cir. 1959)

---

106. Immediate removal sends an important message to other students that safety is important to the teacher, and reinforces the concept that the chemistry teacher should have a "zero tolerance" policy for students engaged in activities that endanger themselves and their classmates. Following the student's removal from the classroom, the teacher must make every effort to document the safety violation or behavior(s) that triggered the chemistry teacher's decision in that situation. Documentation serves several important functions in improving classroom safety. *See infra* Section 3, part 2. The student and his parents should receive a notice of their student's removal from the chemistry laboratory and the reason for the removal. This report does not have to be very detailed but providing enough information to put the parent(s) on notice of their child's misbehavior. This notice is important because it "transfers" responsibility, to some extent to the parents, to instruct the student on the consequences of his inappropriate and unsafe acts in the laboratory. If a safety contract is being used (and it should), then the notice to parents should refer to this safety contract. The purpose of the notice is to allow the student to correct his behavior or face permanent removal from the laboratory. If the teacher permits the student to continue his misbehavior and the student is injured, the teacher will be negligent in permitting the student to remain in the laboratory.

8.   Mastrangelo v. West Side Union High School Dist., 2 Cal.2d 540,42 P.2d 634 (1935)

9.   Gregory v. Bd. of Educ. of City of Rochester, 222 A.D. 284, 225 N.Y.S. 679 (1927)

10.   Lawrence v. Grant Parish School Bd. 409 So. 2d 1316, 2 Educ. L. R. 1234 (La. Ct. App.) *cert. denied,* 412 So. 2d 1110 (La. 1982)

11.   Shifton v. North Clackamas School Dist. No. 12, 18 Ore. App. 90, 523 P.2d 1296 (Ore. App. 1974)

E. Substitute Teacher/Primary Teacher Responsibility

If the school district places an unqualified substitute in a chemistry or other science laboratory, then the school district will be liable for negligence arising from the negligence of the substitute teacher. The primary teacher is not responsible for the hiring of personnel to work in the classroom. Consequently, he/she will have no liability for the misguided actions of a substitute that is temporarily instructing a class because the regular teacher is absent. The employer has a duty to hire qualified individuals. If they are unable to find a qualified individual to replace the teacher, they should insist that the teacher who is supervising is engaged in activities consistent with his/her level of ability. If the district is negligent in supervising its teachers, it is rather difficult to blame the regular classroom teacher who has no authority, right, or duty to determine the capabilities of another teacher. While it is true that districts often have few qualified chemistry or science substitutes, it is not the employee's job function to determine whether someone is qualified, it is the administration's responsibility to staff the classroom. Prudence suggests, however, that if you are in a situation where you suspect that your substitute may not be qualified to run the activity you had planned for your absence that you select an alternate activity because you care about your students' safety. However, the classroom teacher will not be liable for the substitute's negligence even if they do not change the lesson plan.

Case Links:

1.   District of Columbia v. Howell, 607 A.2d 501 (D.C. App. 1992)

F. Violations of Safety Rules, Their Enforcement, and Consequences/The Importance of Safety Rules

The general and unspoken rule is that the teacher must enforce all safety rules, consistently, every time. As noted previously, there are a large number of rules enacted by various authorities at the federal, state, and local levels that impact the chemistry teacher and the chemistry classroom. Teachers have a duty to know those safety rules applicable to the classes they are teaching because the failure to follow a rule may result in teacher liability. In particular, if the safety rule has its basis in a state statute, the teacher will be found negligent per se.[107]

Example 12: Teacher tells students to put their safety goggles on at the beginning of each lab. State law requires that all students in chemistry labs shall wear goggles. Teacher fails to enforce the rule and the student receives an eye injury. Teacher is negligent per se.

Example 13: Same as Example 12, but now there is no state law requiring goggles. Teacher notices student without goggles and tells student to put them on. Ten minutes later teacher notices that the goggles are off again. Teacher tells student again to put goggles on. Student does so again, but takes them off three minutes later. Teacher is about to say, "put the darned goggles on," when some acid splashes into the student's eye. Teacher is also going to be found negligent. The lesson from Scott v. Independent School Dist. #709, 256

---

107. Yet again, this principle comes from Scott v. Independent School Dist. #709, 256 N.W.2d 485 (Minn. 1977).

N.W.2d 485 (Minn. 1977) is that even though each pupil had been assigned a pair of safety goggles to wear, and each student had been instructed to wear them, the teacher was found negligent for not consistently enforcing the rule.

Safety rules are important because, if enforced, they make the laboratory environment a better place to be in and around, for everyone. As the slogan says, "Safety is job one." If the emphasis is on safety, and students are taught the importance of safety, then serious accidents are averted. The teacher has not only a duty to teach safety rules, as discussed below, but in most courts' views, has also a duty to ensure that those rules that are taught are also enforced. Enforcement is a function of supervision. If the students are properly supervised and their activities monitored so that the chemistry teacher can intervene early while the danger is low, then the chemistry teacher can re-teach the rule without having to discipline for more serious violations. As a general observation, if the safety rule being broken is the subject of a state statute or other legislative rule, the failure to consistently enforce the rule will result in a finding of teacher liability.

Case Links:

1. Scott v. Independent School Dist. #709, 256 N.W.2d 485 (Minn. 1977)

2. Maxwell v. Santa Fe Public Schools, 87 N.M. 383, 534 P2d 307 (N.M.App.1975)

3. Brazell v. Bd. of Educ. of Niskayuna Schools 161 A.D. 2d 1086, 557 N.Y.S.2d 645 (3d Dept. 1990)

4. Station v. Travelers Ins. Co., 236 So.2d 610, *writ refused* 256 La. 857, 239 So.2d 359 (La.App.1974)

G. Taking Home Chemicals for Experimentation with Teacher Approval

Do not permit students to take chemicals home for home experiments. This is insanity and you are asking for a lawsuit.[108]

Case Links:

1. Hutchison v. Toews, 4 Or. App.19, 476 P.2d 811 (Ore. App. 1970)

2. Reagh v. San Francisco Unified School Dist., 119 Cal.App.2d 65, 259 P.2d 43 (1953)

Group 2: Teacher's Duty To Give Proper Instruction and To Warn Students of Possible Dangers

A. Failure to Provide Safety Instruction or Provision of Poorly Written or Oral Instructions

Chemistry teachers must teach chemical and laboratory safety. It is not enough for the chemistry teacher to merely provide written instructions or warnings on the classroom board on how to perform the laboratory activity or even to ask the students to read the instructions in their textbooks, which presumably also includes the safety instructions for that laboratory activity. Chemistry teachers must actually teach the safety rules related to the activity the students are to perform. In some cases, verbal warnings or instructions are also

---

108. While an explanation of this fundamental chemistry principle probably needs little explanation, one is provided here to clarify why permitting students to take home chemicals is insanity. Chemistry is performed in specially designed laboratories, with qualified supervision, and proper safety equipment to prevent harm to students. Permitting students to take any chemical home for "experimentation" is inconsistent with all of the duties mentioned in this book. The risk of harm to the student is greatly enhanced because the chemistry teacher is not supervising, the environment where the experiments are taking place probably does not have any approved safety devices, equipment, or any of the features of a properly equipped chemistry laboratory. Even if the chemistry teacher, in his/her best reasoned judgment, determines that there is no risk of injury to the student, the fact remains that the student is not following established classroom procedures that are consistently enforced and is operating without adequate and appropriate supervision.

insufficient to meet the requisite duty of care. Chemistry teachers must *routinely* give appropriate safety information to their students. Teachers must write down safety information and must review this information with their students.[109] This review of information should be in a series of well-planned stages. Initially, teachers should provide a comprehensive review of general safety rules at the beginning of each semester.

Following the safety "unit," all students must be tested on their general safety knowledge. Teachers must provide written feedback[110] on the test to the student and take time to review the test material with them. Teachers should maintain on file a copy of the student's safety contract signed by their parents, and all safety tests or quizzes, in the event an accident occurs injuring a student.[111] Before each laboratory exercise, the teacher should review the specific safety rules applicable to the laboratory. If a pre-laboratory quiz is given, always test safety information. Teachers should remind students of specific safety procedures that may be required in the event of an accident. Taking the time to review specific safety information and procedures in the event of an accident or injury is important. In many of the cases described in the following section, the teacher is not liable for negligence where they can demonstrate proper safety instruction before the student injury.[112]

Case Links:

1. Station v. Travelers Ins. Co., 236 So.2d 610, *writ refused* 256 La. 857, 239 So.2d 359 (La.App.1974)

2. Brazell v. Bd. of Educ. of Niskayuna Schools 161 A.D. 2d 1086, 557 N.Y.S. 2d 645 (3d Dept. 1990)

3. Cazsador by Cazsador v. Greene Cent. Sch., 220 A.D. 2d 862, 632 N.Y.S. 2d 267 (3d Dept. 1995) *amended on reh'g.* 1996 N.Y. App. Div. Lexis 128, *appeal denied, without op.* 87 N.Y. 2d 812, 664 N.Y.S. 2d 145, 666 N.E. 2d 1059 (1996)

B. Notice to Parents of Chemical Safety Rules/Safety Contracts

Teachers should send home, at a minimum, a notice to parents informing them of the potential for serious harm in a chemistry classroom if the instructions of the teacher or the safety rules applicable to the laboratory are not followed. This notice is important because the parent cannot later claim that they were unaware of the hazards that could befall their child, and if they had known they would have never let him take a subject as dangerous as chemistry. Attached to the notice should be:

* a copy of the general laboratory rules; and

* a student safety contract.

The signed safety contract is evidence of two things of importance to the teacher. First, it is evidence of the instruction given by the teacher to that student regarding his/her physical safety in the laboratory. Second, a safety contract provides the parent's signature, acknowledging that they are aware of the dangers, the

---

109. After several years or less of teaching chemistry, most chemistry teachers stop writing down lesson plans for each class. For many years, teachers have written lesson plans that their administrators never ask for, have no interest in reading, and probably do not require. So, what is the purpose of the lesson plan in chemistry? It is perhaps the single most important tool a chemistry teacher has to insulate himself from liability for negligence, to place responsibility for classroom conditions on reticent administrators who cry "no money for books, no money for equipment, no money for you!," and most importantly, as a document that can be admitted in a court proceeding as a contemporaneous record and admissible to prove the truth of the matter asserted. Lesson plans are not for detailing the topic covered in class. They are important daily calendars that document the efforts made by the teacher to warn students of hazards, to record activities related to the maintenance of a safe learning environment, and to recount conversations related to the conditions in the classroom. Without a lesson plan, there is no proof that the teacher did what she is testifying to in court. Lesson plans are persuasive evidence and win lawsuits.

110. This may be a copy of the answer key to the test.

111. *See* Group 2b, *infra*, regarding the use of safety contracts in chemistry laboratory classrooms.

112. This assumes proper supervision by the teacher during the laboratory and in a safely maintained laboratory environment.

importance of following the attached safety rules, and most importantly their *consent* to their child's participation in the laboratory classroom activities with the knowledge that their child may be injured if they do not follow the safety rules. Consent is a very powerful defense to liability, and this may lead to a finding of comparative negligence of both student and parent if a failure to abide by the safety rules harms the child. Properly constructed safety contracts include language that provides for parental consent for certain types of activities that may occur in the laboratory; indicates the types of dangers that the students may be exposed to in the chemistry classroom; and the potential harm that may occur if proper safety precautions are not adhered to by the student or the teacher. Parents are not giving their consent to teachers to cause harm to their student. Rather, they are consenting to their student's participation in activities that have some degree of risk of harm.

The safety contract is also a powerful tool when it becomes necessary to remove a child for violating safety rules. The contract is not legally binding on the child in a court of law, but schools are not courts of law. If the child is so dangerous in the classroom that the chemistry teacher is considering permanent removal, the safety contract is evidence of the potential harm that can result to the student if he does not follow classroom safety rules. The safety contract also is evidence that the parent knew the consequences that may follow for their child's misbehavior or other failure to abide by the rules.

Case Links:
1. Brazell v. Bd. of Educ. of Niskayuna Schools, 161 A.D. 2d 1086, 557 N.Y.S. 2d 645 (3d Dept. 1990)

C. Choosing Experiments of an Appropriate Nature and Age Level

Teachers must choose experiments that are appropriate for the level of students they are teaching. While the goal for many chemistry teachers is to provide experiments that are interesting and challenging, the decision of what laboratory exercises to perform must be based on the characteristics and abilities of the students as well as the ability of the teacher to properly supervise the students while they are performing the experiment. If the experiment is beyond the abilities of the students or the risk of harm to the students is not outweighed by the educational benefits to the students, then teachers risk serious injuries and negligence liability.

Example 14: A summer school teacher in an elementary school enrichment program decides that he is going to liven up his class by having his students make homemade sparklers. While the children were grinding the homemade gunpowder, Dedrick, who was specifically told not to dip the hanger in the material until instructed to do so, dipped his metal hanger into the gunpowder. Moments later the chemicals exploded in front of Dedrick. The chemicals burned at 5000 ºF, and Dedrick was burned over 25 percent of his body including his hands, arms, chest, and face. He was rushed to Children's Hospital. His burn treatment in the following months included several stays in the hospital and rehabilitation centers, multiple skin grafts, surgery to reopen the scars that constricted his movement and circulation, painful physical therapy that was continued at home, both in-patient and out-patient psychotherapy.

In District of Columbia v. Howell, 607 A.2d 501 (D.C. App. 1992), the teacher, a Ph.D. candidate in chemistry, was found negligent while performing what the court described as "inherently dangerous" work for the school district.

The chemistry teacher is responsible for the safety of the students in whose care parents place significant trust.[113] As part of that responsibility, the teacher must choose appropriate activities for the level of

---

113. This trust may very well be misplaced. As noted in Group 3a. *infra*, teachers are expected to be safety experts by administrators and parents. That is, if you are a chemistry teacher you should know something about chemical and laboratory safety. The practical reality is that most chemistry safety is learned on the job, through trial and error, or with the assistance of master teachers. This is woefully inadequate. Chemistry teachers need comprehensive initial

students and the characteristics of that particular class. If an accident occurs because the teacher selected an experiment that was not appropriate for the level of the class, a smart attorney will certainly notice, and will pay an "expert" chemistry teacher to say that the activity was inappropriate for the level of student. Howell is an easy case because the jury could reasonably conclude that nine-year-old children should not be playing with or working with gunpowder.

As the California Supreme Court in Mastrangelo v. West Side Union High School Dist., 2 Cal. 2d 540, 42 P2d 634, (1935) noted:

> It may well be doubted whether it is proper in an introductory school course in chemistry to require pupils to make and ignite an explosive. It would appear that the dangers of such an experiment, incorrectly performed by young children, might be anticipated; and the benefits to be derived from its actual performance by each pupil are not so great as to justify the risk of serious injury to the child. But the very least, if it is to be performed, it necessarily requires the strictest personal attention and supervision of the instructor. We have no sympathy with the defense that the book called for certain ingredients, and that the 'idea of putting in some other ingredient was out of his (the plaintiff's) own mind.'[114]

In choosing experiments to perform in the classroom, teachers must deliberately choose those experiments that their students can safely perform. This choice as to the appropriateness of any experiment necessarily involves an analysis of the performance abilities and maturity of the students in the chemistry class. Chemistry classes vary from section to section in high schools depending on the teacher and the composition of a particular class. The teacher must recognize that not all students can safely perform all experiments in every class. Far too many teachers place misguided reliance on the fact that an experiment is in a textbook approved by the school district for use in the classroom. This may be evidence of school district liability. However, if a student, while performing an inappropriate or inherently dangerous activity contained in the text, is injured, the teacher is negligent for failing to select an appropriate activity for that particular class. A chemistry textbook or laboratory manual is not to be relied on in making the decision on whether to include the activity.[115]

Case Links:

1. District of Columbia v. Howell, 607 A.2d 501 (D.C. App. 1992)

2. Mastrangelo v. West Side Union High School Dist., 2 Cal 2d 540, 42 P2d 634 (1935)

3. Simmons v. Beauregard Parish School Board, 293 So.2d 226, 315 So.2d. 883 (La. App. 1975) cert. denied 320 So. 2d 207 (La. 1975)

4. Station v. Travelers Ins. Co., 236 So.2d 610, writ refused 256 La. 857, 239 So.2d 359 (La.App.1974)

5. Wentz v. Deseth, 221 N.W.2d 101 (N.D. 1974)

6. Calandri v. Ione United School Dist., 219 Cal.App.2d 542, 33 Cal. Rptr. 333 (3d Dist. 1963)

---

safety training and a yearly review session in order to stay current with the standard of care. As the chemistry teaching industry changes, develops, and grows, so does the standard of care. Recall that the general standard of care is what an ordinary reasonable person would do under the circumstances. As chemistry safety devices and practices have improved, a device that was "reasonable" at one point in history may no longer meet the standard of care. For example, the failure to install GFI (Ground Fault Interrupter) outlets in chemistry laboratories would be a negligent act if a student was electrocuted and only a standard outlet was installed. Standard outlets were reasonable for the past 50 years but may not be reasonable now.

114. Mastrangelo v. West Side Union High School Dist., 2 Cal 2d 540, 549-50, 42 P2d 634, 638 (1935).
115. See Shifton v. North Clackamas School Dist. No. 12, 18 Ore. App. 90, 523 P.2d 1296 (Ore. App. 1974).

7. Shifton v. North Clackamas School Dist. No. 12, 18 Ore. App. 90, 523 P.2d 1296 (Ore. App. 1974)

Group 3: Teacher's Duty To Provide a Safe Learning Environment

A. Lack of Teacher Safety Training/New Teacher Training

All teachers need safety training on a regular basis.[116] New teachers need more safety training. New teachers need more than just more training. They also need knowledgeable mentors who have the experience to deal with the safety issues that arise in the chemistry classroom. Experience allows chemistry teachers to intervene and prevent accidents before they become "problems." The lack of safety training for chemistry and other science teachers will become more noticeable as more experienced teachers begin retiring from the classroom in the next several years. As a consequence of this "brain drain," the number of chemistry-related injuries will increase as "rookie" teachers enter the classroom. Many teaching positions are filled with excellent chemistry academicians, but with little practical experience or knowledge in running a safe chemistry laboratory. The equipment has become more complex, and as the technology improves, more tools will enter the chemistry classroom to improve the capability of students. The crisis that is developing is that there will be a shortage of knowledgeable, safety-aware teachers with the technical skill and training to deal with the potential injuries from these new tools. The tools are getting safer, but the students are still exposed to dangers that the teacher needs to identify and minimize.

As the emphasis in the education community has turned again to a more "hands-on-science" approach, teachers need current training and information on not only the "general" applicability of safety rules to their performance, but specific training on meeting their duty of care. Teachers need training in a number of areas specific to their work environment:

- Managing the laboratory environment to meet the standards of care of the applicable safety statutes.[117]

- Maintaining accurate logbooks of student safety training and testing, laboratory maintenance and repair, and techniques to report hazardous conditions to administrators and state agencies.

- Practical solutions and suggestions for conducting potential hazard assessments in the laboratory. Chemistry teachers must be able to identify potential chemical, operational, and environmental hazards in the chemistry lab to determine whether the applicable safety standard is being met.

- Demonstrations on how to properly label, and store, laboratory chemicals and maintain chemical storerooms and equipment. Chemical storage, ventilation, laboratory design and maintenance are also very important components of a safety-training program.

- First aid training related to the possible types of injuries expected in the laboratory.

- Demonstrations and information on the cleanup and disposal of chemicals and other hazards in the laboratory.

Administrators also need information related to their specific duties and responsibilities in supervising an "industrial" work area. The school district may have some responsibility to provide safety training to their employees that is specific to the area in which they work. Evidence of a routine safety training program, may also relieve districts of liability for failure to supervise their employees in the performance of their classroom

---

116. All teachers means *all* teachers. Every teacher should have some type of safety training related to the hazards that exist in their work environment. While not every classroom presents the same type of hazards as the science classroom, each teacher needs regular, specific, safety training related to the types of hazards they are likely to experience in their classrooms.

117. *See infra*, Group 3, part d.

duties. Effective safety training programs prevent accidents and are less expensive than the resultant injury to students, staff, and the enhanced risk of civil lawsuits.

Case Links:

1. District of Columbia v. Howell, 607 A.2d 501 (D.C. App. 1992)

2. Brown v. Tesack, 556 So.2d 84, 58 Ed. Law Rep.846, *review granted* 556 So.2d 1288,58 Ed. Law Rep.1378, *aff'd in part, revised in part,* 566 So.2d. 955, 62 Ed. Law Rep.1287, *rehearing denied* (La. App. 4 Cir. 1990)

B. Teaching in a Non-Science Laboratory

Teachers should never perform laboratory experiments in a "non-science" classroom. Performing chemistry experiments in a classroom not properly equipped with appropriate safety features and equipment is per se negligence. Teachers must refuse to perform laboratories under those conditions. In fact, pressuring a teacher to work in an unsafe environment is a form of hostile work environment, and possibly an unfair labor practice.[118] Teachers should immediately report the practice to their administrator, and if available to their local union representative to ensure that the district is on notice of the defective conditions. There is no problem with chemistry teachers lecturing or performing other non-laboratory functions in a "regular" classroom, but they should *never* attempt to perform any laboratory exercises in that "regular" classroom, even if they reasonably believe the exercise can be performed safely. It is also good practice to immediately notify, in writing, the administrator in charge of the facility of the conditions that exist in the classroom including remedies for the conditions.[119]

Case Links:
1. Damgaard v. Oakland High School Dist., 212 Cal. 316, 298 P. 983 (1931)
2. Station v. Travelers Ins. Co., 236 So. 2d 610, *writ refused* 256 La. 857, 239 So.2d 359 (La.App.1974)

C. Failure to Maintain and Repair Laboratory Equipment

Knowingly permitting students to use defective equipment is negligence per se. If the teacher has knowledge of a condition impairing the performance of a particular piece of equipment to be used by students, the teacher has a duty to prevent the students from using the defective equipment. It does not matter if the equipment is not part of the chemistry classroom or being stored in the classroom at the time of the accident. Chemistry teachers owe the children a duty to take reasonable precautions to keep them from harm caused by unsafe equipment.

Example 15: Teacher is helping students to set up their experiment in the school's gymnasium for a school science fair. The teacher provides the students with an alcohol burner that he knows the students have had difficulty lighting and has, on several occasions, unexpectedly "gone out." The teacher also provides them with a one-gallon plastic jug containing alcohol to refill the burner. The teacher then leaves the students and returns to his classroom. The students, unable to get the burner lit, decide that they will try again. While pouring

---

118. In most collective agreements, teaching in an inappropriate or unsafe classroom would be a grievance under the appropriate "working conditions" section of the agreement.

119. The more difficult question to answer in this situation is whether the chemistry teacher can refuse to work in the regular classroom environment. The answer to this question is quite complex and beyond the scope of this book. While, in principle, the chemistry teacher may be correct for refusing to work in an improper environment, the teacher may also be jeopardizing her job.

alcohol from the jug into the burner, another student lit the stream of alcohol. This caused the jug to explode burning a girl standing nearby who later died.

In <u>Station v. Travelers Ins. Co.</u>, 236 So.2d 610, *writ refused* 256 La. 857, 239 So.2d 359 (1974) the court held the teacher negligent for several reasons but specifically identified the teacher's failure to properly supervise and warn the students about the defective burner:

> Here, a dangerous instrument was placed in the hands of children without any special degree of care, supervision, or direction. Alcohol, a highly flammable substance, was left in their control to be used in connection with a faulty alcohol burner that had continually given trouble. That the situation was fraught with danger is proven by the results. The duty incumbent upon Wilson under these dangerous circumstances was to either positively warn these girls not to attempt to light the burner if it went out or to personally supervise their use of the equipment or provide adequate adult supervision in his absence. He did none of these things. [120]

Chemistry teachers have a duty to warn of known dangers to students, inspect the premises for hazards, and make the premises safe for student use. In making the premises safe for students, teachers should not expose students to conditions they know are dangerous. In the <u>Station</u> example above, something as common as a defective burner was sufficient to impose negligence liability when combined with a lack of supervision and an injury that resulted in the death of a student.

Case Links:

1. <u>Station v. Travelers Ins. Co.</u>, 236 So.2d 610, *writ refused* 256 La. 857, 239 So.2d 359 (1974) *and appeal after remand,* 292 So. 2d 289 (La. App. 1st Cir. 1974) (broken alcohol burner)

2. <u>Ross v. San Francisco Unified School Dist.</u>, 120 Cal.App.2d 185, 260 P.2d. 663 (1953) (safety goggles broken)

3. <u>Matteucci v. High School District No. 208, Co. of Cook</u>, 4 Ill.App.3d 710, 281 N.E.2d 383 (Ill. App. 1972) (Guard on a power saw)

4. <u>Lawrence v. Grant Parish School Bd.</u> 409 So.2d 1316, 2 Educ. L. R. 1234 (La. Ct. App.), *cert. denied,* 412 So. 2d 1110 (La. 1982)

D. Storage, Maintenance, and Disposal of Chemicals/Acids/Flammables/Poisons

Teachers must properly and safely store and dispose of all chemicals in their laboratories. This duty of care is governed in significant part by a large number of state statutory enactments. For example in California, there are several legislative enactments which apply to every science classroom:[121]

*   California Education Code: §§ 32030, 32031, 32032, 32033 (School Eye Safety); §§ 49340, 49341, 49401.5, 49411 (Hazardous Materials Education).

*   California Code of Regulations, Title 8, General Industry Safety Orders: § 5154.1 (Ventilation Requirements for Laboratory-Type Hood Operations); § 5162 (Emergency Eyewash and Shower Equipment); § 5163 (Spill and Overflow Control); § 5164 (Storage of Hazardous Substances); § 5191 (Occupational Exposure to Hazardous Chemicals in Laboratories (Chemical Hygiene Plan)); § 5193 (Blood Borne Pathogens); § 5194 (Hazard Communications; Material Safety Data Sheets).

*   Health and Safety Code: § 25500 et seq. (Hazardous Materials Release Response Plans and Inventory).

---

120. <u>Station v. Travelers Ins. Co.</u>, 236 So.2d 610, *writ refused* 256 La. 857, 239 So.2d 359 (1974).
121. From "Science Safety Handbook for California Public Schools 1999 ed.," California Department of Education, Sacramento 1999.

A California teacher's failure to meet these standards of care in the science classroom as defined by the above California regulations is negligence per se. Other states may have legislative enactments controlling the safe handling, storage, and disposal of hazardous materials.[122] Chemistry and other science teachers need specific training directed towards meeting the prescribed duty as defined by their state's statute. In addition, teachers require additional funds specifically targeted to have facilities meeting these requirements. School districts must not operate in the belief that science classrooms are similar to every other classroom and should receive exactly the same amount of funds to operate their classrooms. Chemistry and other classrooms handling potentially "dangerous" materials are industrial areas which require sufficient funding to provide appropriate facilities to safely store, handle, and dispose of "dangerous" chemicals.[123]

Case Links:

1. Frace v. Long Beach City High School Dist., 58 Cal.App.2d 566, 137 P.2d 60 (1943)

2. Brazell v. Bd. of Educ. of Niskayuna Schools, 161 A.D. 2d 1086, 557 N.Y.S.2d 645 (3d Dept. 1990)

3. Bush v. Oscoda Area Schools, 405 Mich. 716, 275 N.W.2d 268 (1979), *sub appeal,* 109 Mich. App. 373, 311 N.W.2d 788 (Mich.Ct.App.1981)

4. Shifton v. North Clackamas School Dist. No. 12, 18 Ore. App. 90, 523 P.2d 1296 (Ore. App. 1974)

5. Brown v. Tesack, 556 So.2d 84, 58 Ed. Law Rep.846, *review granted* 556 So.2d 1288,58 Ed. Law Rep.1378, *aff'd in part, revised in part*, 566 So.2d. 955, 62 Ed. Law Rep.1287, *rehearing denied* (La. App. 4 Cir. 1990)

E. Prohibited Chemicals

Some states and school districts have developed lists of prohibitive chemicals.[124] If a student is injured in an accident involving a prohibited chemical that can be traced back to the chemistry teacher, the chemical storeroom, or some other area on the school campus, then this is negligence and someone is going to be liable. The teacher has a duty to know what chemicals are on the list, to inspect the facility to identify and remove any chemicals on the list, and if the teacher cannot safely remove them, to ensure that these chemicals undergo proper disposal by someone qualified. A number of the cases in the next section involve several chemicals that now appear on prohibited chemical lists nationwide. For example, Phosphorus (White/Yellow), Sodium Azide, Picric Acid, and Perchloric Acid, In addition, teachers must develop and follow a chemical hygiene plan. This plan is mandated by OSHA's Laboratory Standard–Occupational Exposure to Hazardous Chemicals in Laboratories, which amended the Occupational Safety and Health Act ("Act") to include Part 191.1450 *et. seq.* and provides specific guidance on how implement the new safety standard for chemistry laboratories.[125]

Case Links:

1. Mastrangelo v. West Side Union High School Dist., 2 Cal.2d 540,42 P.2d 634 (1935)

---

122. *See generally Flinn Chemical & Biological Catalog Reference Manual 2000* (Flinn Scientific, Inc. 2000) pp. 870–894, for a thorough discussion of national "Right to Know Laws."

123. For guidance and suggestions on an appropriate "Chemical Hygiene Plan" *see generally the Flinn Chemical & Biological Catalog Reference Manual 2000* (Flinn Scientific, Inc. 2000), which contains a significant amount of quality current information related to chemistry classroom safety. More importantly, this information is provided free. A similar resource is found at Flinn Scientific Inc.'s company Website at www.flinsci.com providing detailed analysis of "Right to Know" legislation and "ANSI Standards" as well as other valuable safety information.

124. *See supra* discussion part 3d.

125. 29 CFR Part 1910 § 191.1450 (1990). A copy is located at OSHA's Website: www.osha-slc.gov/OshStd_data/1910_1450.html.

2.   Brazell v. Bd. of Educ. of Niskayuna Schools, 161 A.D. 2d 1086, 557 N.Y.S.2d 645 (3d Dept. 1990)

3.   Brown v. Tesack, 556 So.2d 84, 58 Ed. Law Rep.846, *review granted* 556 So.2d 1288,58 Ed. Law Rep.1378, *aff'd in part, revised in part,* 566 So.2d. 955, 62 Ed. Law Rep.1287, *rehearing denied* (La. App. 4 Cir. 1990)

F. Facilities Issues Part I: Personal Safety Equipment: Goggles, Aprons, Fire Blankets, First Aid Kits, etc. [126]

Chemistry teachers and schools must provide the necessary and appropriate safety equipment to the students. Most items, such as goggles, aprons, fire blankets, etc. are mandated by state law or other regulation and therefore the failure to provide the equipment falls squarely in the lap of the school district. All of the equipment provided to students should also be in good working condition. If the equipment is damaged or broken and cannot be repaired it should be disposed of in a proper manner. Providing defective safety equipment is treated in a similar manner as if no safety equipment was provided. In short, if the teacher has students perform an experiment without the teacher providing the appropriate safety equipment in good working condition, they are negligent per se, if the missing safety equipment would have prevented the injury. Of note in this area, school districts may have some exposure to penalties and fines even if there are no injuries to students if the proper safety equipment is not present during a safety inspection by a state agency such as OSHA.

Case Links:

1.   Goodman v. Pasadena City High School Unified Dist., 4 Cal.App.2d 65, 40 P.2d 854 (1935)

2.   Ross v. San Francisco Unified School Dist., 120 Cal.App.2d 185, 260 P.2d. 663 (1953)

3.   Bush v. Oscoda Area Schools, 405 Mich. 716, 275 N.W.2d 268 (1979), *sub appeal,* 109 Mich. App. 373, 311 N.W.2d 788 (Mich.Ct.App.1981)

G. Facilities Issues Part II: Laboratory Design/Storage Areas/Proper Ventilation, Shelving, Storage Cabinets, Fume Hoods, etc.

Later in this book there is a brief discussion regarding immunity of school districts for design defects.[127] That discussion of the importance of immunity in the law is relevant in addressing this particular facilities concern. Schools are aging. Chemistry teachers go years without improvement in their facilities. Laws continually change requiring new safety equipment, storage units, ventilation, etc. Few changes are made to existing facilities. Laboratory designs that were state of the art when schools were built in the 1950s and 1960s may not conform to modern safety and design standards. School districts have no duty to provide modern laboratory facilities. However, they do have a duty to provide safe facilities. Thus, the impetus to renovate must come from a need to bring aging facilities up to modern safety standards and not from some design defect because school districts, generally, are not liable for designs that fail to meet some building standard. In those cases where the state's architect has approved a proposed laboratory design, the failure of the builder to follow the approved plans and the failure of the school district to object to defects in the design, are insufficient to hold the school district liable for the flawed design. School districts are liable for non-compliance with safety statutes. For example, a building built in the 1950s may not have adequate, or proper, ventilation under modern

---

126. The following two sections entitled "Facilities Issues" address questions directed at existing facilities defects in the chemistry classroom. They are separated primarily by the type of defect: Part 1 discusses the failure to provide personal safety equipment, and Part 2 discusses the installation of specific safety features in the classroom and the consequences of failing to provide these items and issues related to defective design laboratory in existing buildings.

127. *See infra* Section V, Part C.1 Immunity.

building and safety codes because at the time those buildings were designed there was no such ventilation requirement or the design met the code requirements at the time of construction. The school district is not liable for the design defect that existed from the time of construction, but it may have a duty to modernize or provide ventilation for the building under modern education, building and safety codes.

In short, teachers must assess their facility to identify specific defects or safety hazards existing in laboratory equipment or environmental conditions that are not solely attributable to design defects. For example, "this room is required to have eyewashes in at least one location because of the danger from chemical splashes to the eyes." Rather than point out the obvious design flaw in a room that does not have eyewashes, teachers must present the environmental problem as a specific hazard that can be remedied. In certain circumstances, the room may be so lacking in appropriate safety equipment and features, that the room is not appropriate for the planned activity and therefore should not be used at all.[128] All communications with administrators, board members, parents, should be in writing to give the district actual notice of the defect(s). Subsequently, if an accident does occur, some school principal, board member or other administrator, will have their names along with the school district added to the complaint filed by the student's attorney.

Case Links:

1. Nielsen v. Community Unit School Dist. No. 3, 90 Ill.App.3d 243, 45 Ill.Dec.595, 412 N.E.2d 1177 (Ill. App. 1980)

2. Bush v. Oscoda Area Schools, 405 Mich. 716, 275 N.W.2d 268 (1979), *sub appeal,* 109 Mich. App. 373, 311 N.W.2d 788 (Mich.Ct.App.1981)

3. Kush ex. rel. Marszalek v. City. of Buffalo, 59 N.Y.2d 26, 462 N.Y.S. 2d 831, 449 N.E 2d 725 (Ct. App. 1983)

Practical Solutions

There are several important ways that science teachers can limit their potential for liability by decreasing the risk of harm to their students. This list is different from the standard list that many chemistry teachers are familiar with on classroom safety. The following list, in no particular order, identifies several areas where teachers have the most exposure for liability and where small improvements can greatly reduce the probability of student injury and lawsuits:

• Know the safety statutes that affect your classroom and carefully abide by them. The lesson of Scott v. Independent School Dist. #709 is that the violation of a statute is tantamount to a finding of negligence, and is the first area a plaintiff's attorney will look to see if the teacher did not meet their duty of care. There are always numerous rules that affect the classroom, some enacted by the federal government, some by the state, and the ones most often overlooked, those enacted by the school board or the school site administration. It is important to generate a list of a summary of the safety statutes you must comply with for your school. The science department should meet regularly to ensure that such list is communicated and that teachers are following these rules. Recall that while most of the cases turn on facts, if a violation of a safety statute or rule is found, no one will care what facts are out there, and a jury will find your actions negligent per se. These are the rules that must be followed in order to avoid liability. Some of the more common ones that are found regulate the use of safety goggles, aprons, and required footwear in the laboratory. Some, such as those requiring ventilation in laboratory classrooms are less well known.[129]

---

128. *See generally* Bush v. Oscoda Area Schools, 405 Mich. 716, 275 N.W.2d 268 (1979), *sub appeal*, 109 Mich. App. 373, 311 N.W.2d 788 (Mich.Ct.App.1981).

129. If your administrator insists that you teach chemistry or another laboratory science in a room not properly ventilated or equipped, notify them, in writing, of the specific features you feel are lacking and are necessary in order to make the room safe for the proposed activity or instruction, as well as their individual potential for liability, if you are forced to

- Document all efforts to resolve safety issues in your classroom. Document all safety violations or problems affecting your safety or your students, and that you are unable to resolve yourself. Put your observations, concerns, and possible solutions, in writing to the administrator in charge, with copies to everyone.[130] This puts everyone on notice that there is a safety hazard that cannot be ignored. If you fail to document your efforts to resolve a problem, any problem, your oral testimony may not be believed when someone is badly hurt. If you have properly documented your efforts, then your school district may be negligent, but not you.

- Do not leave your classroom during any lab period. Most of the cases discussed in Section IV turn on whether the classroom teacher properly supervised the students. Ask yourself whether any of the students can possibly be hurt in the laboratory while you are gone. Students may suffer injury through their own negligence, or by the negligence of fellow students. If it is foreseeable that one or more students may be injured while the teacher is gone, then the teacher is liable. Recall that the duty of supervision is not necessarily constant, but depends on a number of factors based on the characteristics of the students in your classroom and the environmental factors affecting their safety. Rather than guess at whether you are meeting the duty of care, staying in the classroom and being attentive will reduce the chance of injury. Supervision also reduces the amount of chemicals and equipment that students steal during the laboratory exercise. Recall that theft of dangerous substances is foreseeable and therefore teachers have a duty to monitor the laboratory to ensure that students do not steal dangerous chemicals.

- All students should wear all of the appropriate personal safety equipment while working in the laboratory. Students at a minimum should always wear safety goggles, aprons, and proper footwear in the laboratory for all experiments. What is the harm in having too much safety equipment, compared with the harm that comes from having too little equipment?

- Teach safety all year and review safety procedures often. Properly drafted, safety contracts place students (and parents) on notice of the potential dangers of the laboratory environment and the consequences of failing to follow the classroom rules.

- Make safety a priority in the classroom. Establish and model safe chemical handling practices. These practices when documented establish that the teacher made efforts to meet the standard of care. When a student is injured because they consciously disregarded those practices, the teacher is in a much better position to argue that the student was comparatively negligent and knowingly disregarded established safety procedures. More importantly, modeling the expected practices of the chemistry laboratory, teaches students to respect the hazards involved in this science and the methods of safely handling hazardous materials.

- Use smaller volumes and amounts of chemicals. There is no need to keep large quantities of chemicals on hand, nor is there any necessity to use large volumes when performing laboratories. Using smaller quantities is cheaper and significantly reduces the potential severity of injuries due to some accidental mishandling of a chemical.

- Demand appropriate safety training related to your duty of care in the chemistry classroom. Learn the regulations that affect your workplace and your students and take steps to ensure that students and the administration follow these regulations for their safety and your physical, emotional, and financial safety.

- Do not permit students to use damaged or defective equipment.

- Do not permit students to take chemicals or any other school equipment home to perform "experiments." This is an invitation to disaster.

---

teach in a classroom. Have them read Bush v. Oscoda Area Schools, 405 Mich. 716, 275 N.W.2d 268 (1979), *sub appeal,* 109 Mich. App. 373, 311 N.W.2d 788 (Mich.Ct.App.1981). This notice of defective conditions will be important evidence at the trial when there is a question of whether the school knew or should have known that the class was not suited for the particular activity.

130. At a minimum, copies should go to school board members, particularly if the problems are serious, such as inadequate ventilation, building defects, or lack of safety equipment. This puts the school board on notice, and increases the likelihood that problems will be fixed.

- Be proactive rather than reactive. Take steps to avoid accidents by planning the laboratory exercise to include the relevant safety procedures applicable to the laboratory. Check all equipment to see that it is in good working condition in advance of each laboratory. Replace or repair defective equipment as soon as possible. Establish a regular maintenance schedule for the laboratory and stick to the schedule. Finally, document all of your lab and safety activities.

SECTION IV   Relevant Cases

Introduction

The cases included in this section comprise those involving the chemistry classroom or involve the use of chemicals. In addition to the chemistry cases are several important vocational (shop) cases that have relevance to the chemistry classroom. It is critical to note that the principles applicable to the chemistry classroom are relevant in other laboratory classrooms. The importance of the included cases for the chemistry teacher is not the technical discussions of tort law. Rather chemistry, or other science teachers should approach these cases with an eye to understanding their duty to students and to improving the conditions in their laboratories and on their campuses. Administrators should evaluate their exposure to civil liability for their direct actions and indirectly under the doctrine of respondent superior. In some states, teachers and school districts are immune from suit, can be ordinarily negligent[131] to their hearts' content, and cannot be sued for their casual acts of neglect. Rather, these cases are presented with the singular goal of improving the safety conditions in the laboratories that we work in as teachers and that our children experience as students in these classes.

Teachers should present these cases to administrators to educate them about their duty to provide safe buildings, equipment, and other tools necessary to ensure the safety of all. In every district, money is always an issue. Money also plays a role in the litigation process. Perhaps the money spent on improving conditions and practices in our chemistry labs is a better investment than hiring attorneys to defend lawsuits. The included chemistry cases represent those that have survived a trial court determination and have subsequently been appealed on some issue of law. A maxim of tort law is that 90 percent of all cases are decided before trial, that is, they are settled. Insurance companies, which often have to pay the costs of such litigation, often determine that settlement is in the best interest of all involved. Of the 10 percent of the cases that actually go to trial, 90 percent of those cases are not appealed.

In editing the cases, issues that are not relevant to teacher, school district, or school board liability have largely, but not always, been omitted. In reading the cases, keep in mind that a number of them involve the concepts of contributory negligence and assumption of risk.[132] These two concepts predate most state's legislative enactments of the 1980s and 1990s adopting comparative negligence statutes to replace these ancient doctrines and mitigate their harsh effects. This legislative trend is significant because in most of the early cases contributory negligence and assumption of risk were complete bars to recovery by the plaintiff against the teacher, school district, and school board. In a contributory negligence state, a plaintiff's own negligence barred recovery against a clearly negligent teacher or school district. The harshness of the contributory negligence rule has been mitigated in almost all states today by the enactment of a comparative negligence statute. Under these statutes, a plaintiff's own negligence is not a bar to recovery but rather, reduces the plaintiff's amount of recovery in proportion to their own fault. For example, if the jury finds the defendant 70 percent negligent in causing plaintiff's injuries, and also finds the plaintiff 30 percent negligent, and the jury awards the plaintiff $100,000 the plaintiff's award will be reduced by $30,000, the amount of his or her own negligence and will only receive $70,000 from the defendant. In some states, the comparative negligence statute will act as a bar to recovery when the plaintiff's negligence is greater than the defendant's, that is, when the plaintiff's negligence is greater than 50 percent, there is no recovery. With this in mind, here are the cases:

---

131 In those states with immunity statutes, teachers and administrators are immune from suit for their ordinary negligent acts, but not those that are reckless or "grossly" negligent.

132. *See infra* section V for a discussion of the predominant defenses to negligence liability.

A. Chemistry Cases [133]

<u>Gregory v. Bd. of Educ. of City of Rochester,</u>

222 App. Div. 284, 225 N.Y.S. 679 (1927)

Concepts:

- Chemical Storage
- Duty of Care

Facts:

Howard Gregory, 14 years old, was injured in an explosion occurring in the chemistry department of the Rochester Shop School. The student had been performing an unauthorized experiment when the explosion occurred. No details of the actual chemicals used by the plaintiff were described. At trial, the plaintiff was awarded $433.75 damages and costs. The Board of Education of Rochester appealed the award of damages and the denial of its motion for a new trial.

Issues:

1. Whether the school board could be held liable for injuries to a chemistry student in a public school resulting from the nonperformance of the board's duty of exercising reasonable care in the keeping and distribution of chemicals which are potentially dangerous when used in combination?

2. Whether board could be held liable for injuries sustained by a pupil while conducting an unauthorized experiment, on the ground that the board failed to prescribe a suitable course of study in chemistry, where the experiment was unauthorized and was not a part of the course of study, and where a syllabus prepared by the board of regents was in actual use in the laboratory but had not been formally adopted by the board?

---

133. The following cases are arranged chronologically from oldest to most recent and all involve the use of chemicals or have occurred in chemistry labs or biology labs. The selected shop cases, following this section are also arranged chronologically. In both instances, the decision to arrange the cases in a chronological order is to illustrate the changes in the law of negligence and to demonstrate that certain fundamental principles have not changed in the past century. Finally, there is one case dealing with pigeon droppings included in the shop case group because it is an issue for those teachers who utilize live materials in the biology classroom (it is also really interesting!).

Holding:[134]

1. Yes. "It was the duty of the defendant to use reasonable care in the keeping and distribution of chemicals potentially dangerous in combination."[135]

2. No. "We think the trial court erred . . . in charging the jury in substance that defendant might be held liable if it had omitted to prescribe a suitable course of study in chemistry . . . . Whether it was formally prescribed is immaterial. The experiment which plaintiff was conducting was unauthorized and was no part of the course of study in actual use."[136]

Comment:

Gregory, a case decided December 30, 1927, is one of the earliest chemistry cases and the principles announced in the case are still valid today. Teachers have a duty of care to the students they teach and that duty is one of reasonableness under the circumstances. In the handling and distribution of dangerous chemicals, this duty extends to their storage. As we will see in Mastrangelo, *infra,* this duty of care is met through the maintenance of proper facilities. The following cases say as much about teacher behavior as they do about the duty of the district to assist teachers in meeting the duty of care. This includes the maintenance of a safe learning and working environment for teachers and students. Note in particular that the court found the school board liable in this case even though the student was obviously performing an unauthorized experiment. We shall see that under certain conditions the performance of an unauthorized experiment and the disregard of safety warnings given by a teacher is a bar to plaintiff's recovery.[137]

---

134. The holding of a case is the court's decision on the issue(s) before it.
135. Gregory v. Bd. of Educ. of City of Rochester, 222 App Div 284, 225 N.Y.S. 679 (1927).
136. *Id.* at 284–85.
137. *See* Hutchison v. Toews, 4 Or. App.19, 476 P. 2d 811 (Or. App. 1970); Rixmann v. Somerset Public Schools, St. Croix County, 82 Wis. 2d 571, 266 N.W. 2d 326 (Wis. 1978).

Damgaard v. Oakland High School Dist.,

212 Cal.316, 298 P. 983 (1931)

Concepts:

- Class Size
- Duty to Instruct

Facts:

Rudolf Damgaard, a 17-year-old high school student, was seriously injured when "an experiment conducted by the teacher . . . requiring the use of certain substances and apparatus involving the production and use of explosive gases"[138] exploded resulting in the loss of Rudolph's right eye. At trial before a jury, Rudolph was awarded $15,000.00 for his injuries and his parents were awarded $387.00 for medical and surgical expenses incurred by the accident. The School District appealed the sufficiency of the evidence to support the jury finding the district negligent and the application of the doctrine of *res ipsa loquitur*[139] to the facts of the case. The court of appeals reversed the trial court finding in favor of the district and ordered a new trial. An appeal followed.

Issues:

1.   Whether there was sufficient evidence to support the award of damages to the plaintiff based upon negligence by the defendants?

2.   Whether the doctrine of *res ipsa loquitur* was applicable to find the teacher and the school district liable for negligence?

Holding:

1.   Yes.

2.   Yes.

The California Supreme Court, in a rather lengthy and technical discussion, held that the plaintiff's general complaint of "negligent omission" without alleging any details amounted to no more than an "averment that the defendant school district through their agents and employees negligently failed to take proper precautions for the safeguarding of their pupils during the performance of a dangerous experiment in chemistry . . . . ."[140] As such, the plaintiff was entitled to the application of the *res ipsa loquitur* doctrine to aid his case.

Analysis:

In sustaining a judgment against the school district, the California Supreme Court indicated that the doctrine of *res ipsa loquitur*[141] was applicable to the facts of this case. Questions as to whether the

---

138. Damgaard v. Oakland High School Dist., 212 Cal.316, 318, 298 P. 983, 984 (1931).

139. *Res ipsa loquitur*, means the "thing speaks for itself," and allows the inference of negligence in the absence of direct proof. It is a substitute for proof of causation, either because the evidence of causation is destroyed, or is entirely in the hands of the defendant. In real life terms, bad things happen for a reason, and the reason is that you did not do something you were supposed to do. So if you cannot prove that you did everything correctly, we are going to infer that you did not. In short, the accident would not happen if someone were not negligent. *Res ipsa loquitur.*

140. Damgaard v. Oakland High School Dist., 212 Cal.316, 319, 298 P. 983, 985(1931).

141. *See supra* note 139. "The thing speaks for itself." In discussing the doctrine the Court stated that the "doctrine of *res ipsa loquitur* ought to be given precise application, since the pupils in a public school receiving instruction in the rudiments of chemistry could not in reason be expected to know in advance the very matters with respect to which they were undergoing instruction; while on the other hand, their teachers undertaking to instruct them by the method of experimentation through the employment of substances, materials, and gases liable to explode,

teacher was negligent and the student's own contributory negligence was for the jury, and that the evidence sustained the jury's findings in this regard. The Court cut through the heart of the plaintiff's complaint stating that it essentially boiled down to no more than a statement that the district and its employees were negligent and that "[t]he essence of negligence is the failure to exercise due care and take proper precaution in the particular case."[142] The court stated "[i]f the experiment which the defendants' employees undertook to conduct in their classroom was one in which dangerous explosions were likely to occur from no known cause, it would clearly be negligence to conduct the same without properly safeguarding the pupils from the likelihood of such explosions."[143] The court noted that "the evidence, however, disclosed that the particular experiment was one wherein explosions did not occur without such ascertainable causes as defective appliances, or the presence of combustible matter in the test tubes or carbonaceous matter in the materials or chemicals made use of in the experiment or the improper application of heat in the course of the experiment."[144] Finally, the Court indicated that "[t]he evidence offered in the course of the trial presented several probable causes of the explosion involving the foregoing elements, but which particular cause or combination of causes actually produced the explosion remained a matter of doubt . . . which was a question for the jury to unravel.[145]

Comment:

Damgaard is an excellent case illustrating that in the absence of direct proof of negligence the court will often struggle to apply the doctrine of *res ipsa loquitur* to the facts, reasoning that if a student is injured in chemistry or other laboratory experiment, then someone must be negligent. The more serious the injury, the more likely the court will apply the doctrine.

The Damgaard facts are not very clear because the California Supreme Court was concerned with the technical requirements of pleading the doctrine. In the underlying case, the appellate court indicated that it was Damgaard, and not the teacher, who was conducting the experiment when a glass tube used in the experiment exploded.[146] However, the court stated that teachers have a duty of care to take reasonable precautions to safeguard the students.[147] In the underlying case, the court indicated that

> [t]he evidence showed that proper instruction and warnings were given, but that some means of protection against injuries might have been used—such as gloves to protect the hands and glasses to protect the eyes. The evidence also disclosed that the explosion probably was caused by the entrance of some carbonaceous matter into some of the chemicals used in the experiment, but there was no evidence of any character which showed carelessness or negligence on the part of the teacher or of any other employee of the defendant except the evidence above noted relating to their failure to give "instruction, warning or protection."[148]

Damgaard is a useful case for science teachers currently facing overcrowded classrooms. If an accident occurs in an overcrowded laboratory classroom, in the absence of any direct proof of negligence, the court will likely find the doctrine applicable. In placing too many students in a classroom equipped to

---

unless handled and brought into combination with scientific delicacy and care, should know and should be able to explain in the event of an explosion, why or how it occurred, and that no negligence on their part constituted or contributed to its causation. Damgaard v. Oakland High School Dist., 212 Cal.316, 324, 298 P. 983, 987 (1931).

142. *Id.* at 212 Cal.316, 319, 298 P. 983, 985 (1931).

143. *Id.* at 212 Cal.316, 324, 298 P. 983, 987 (1931).

144. *Id.*

145. *Id.* at 212 Cal.316, 325, 298 P. 983, 987 (1931).

146. Damgaard v. Oakland High School Dist., 290 P. 1047 (Cal. Ct. App. 1st Dist. 1930).

147. Throughout the cases, an unmistakable pattern emerges. Teachers have a duty to take reasonable cautions to safeguard against those behaviors that the majority of children of average intelligence would not engage in. Later cases, while concluding that the child is partially responsible for his own injuries, will still hold the teacher and the school district liable for failing to take reasonable precautions to prevent these aberrant students from harming themselves. A classic example of this principle is found in Kush ex. rel. Marszalek v. City of Buffalo, 59 N.Y.2d 26, 462 N.Y.S. 2d 831, 449 N.E 2d 725 (Ct. App. 1983) discussed *infra*.

148. Damgaard v. Oakland High School Dist., 290 P. 1047 (Cal. Ct. App. 1st Dist. 1930).

safely hold a smaller number, the probability of accidents increase, and the ability of the teacher to supervise the class properly decreases. Under these circumstances, a plaintiff's attorney would argue that "but for" the overcrowded conditions the accident would not have occurred. That is, the overcrowding of the classroom is the proximate cause of the accident, and a breach of the duty of care that requires the teacher to take reasonable safety precautions to safeguard the students. Proof of overcrowded classroom conditions would be a factual determination for the jury. That is, the plaintiff would be able to discover relevant information related to the safety procedures in the classroom, and take depositions related to the conditions existing in the classroom at the time of the accident. The teacher should put in writing his observations and concerns related to overcrowding and the impact such overcrowding has on the safety of all in the classroom. This document should then be sent to the administrator responsible for the safety of the facility for action.[149] If the administrator refuses or fails to act, the school district is now on actual notice of a hazardous condition that must be remedied.

---

149. The decision to send notice of defect is an important step in transferring responsibility for unsafe decisions away from the teacher. This does not however mean that the chemistry teacher is relieved of her duty to act reasonably under the circumstances. In addition, sending the notice to the building administrator represents the minimal notice to the district. Depending on the facts and circumstances, notices of defective or hazardous conditions should go to the union representative, district personnel including the superintendent and individual school board members.

Mastrangelo v. West Side Union High School Dist.,

2 Cal.2d 540, 42 P. 2d 634 (1935)

Concepts:

- Chemical Labeling
- Chemical Storage
- Custom in the Industry
- Duty To Instruct and Warn
- Duty To Supervise
- Educational Value of the Experiment
- Educational Value of the Experiment
- Experiment Selection
- Eye Safety
- Maintenance of Facility
- Safety Equipment
- Science Facilities

Facts:

Elge Mastrangelo, a junior in high school, was in a chemistry lab conducting an experiment designated Number 40 in his chemistry laboratory book when he deviated from the directions given by the lab. The result of this detour was a massive explosion that blew off his left hand, severely injured his right hand, destroyed his right eye and seriously injured the left. The lab called for the pupils to make a type of crude gunpowder in very small quantities and then ignite it to observe the properties that make solids explosive. Mastrangelo, in the company of two other students, had previously and successfully performed the experiment twice.

> In the laboratory, under the supervision of the chemistry teacher . . . Elge was attempting to repeat the same experiment for the third time. Instead of pulverizing the ingredients upon separate sheets of paper as directed by the textbook, they were mixed together and ground in an iron mortar by means of a pestle. Instead of using potassium nitrate as directed by the textbook, either by mistake or otherwise, potassium chlorate was substituted or both substances were used. Both of these ingredients were kept in similar separate boxes on the shelf directly in front of the bench where the students were performing the experiment.[150]

In addition, it appears from the testimony at the time of the explosion, the chemistry teacher was standing behind the student as he performed the experiment, that he "saw or may have seen not only the selection of ingredients, but the fact that they were being mixed together in the iron mortar instead of pulverizing them separately on sheets of paper as directed by the textbook; and that he failed to warn the students of the danger of that method." [151]

It was during this third attempt that the explosion occurred. The court summarized his injuries as "serious and permanent." Mastrangelo brought suit against the chemistry teacher for negligence; however, the trial court dismissed the suit without allowing the jury to decide the issues (nonsuit). The pupil appealed the case to the California Supreme Court.

---

150. Mastrangelo v. West Side Union High School Dist., 2 Cal 2d 540, 543–4, 42 P2d 634, 635 (1935).
151. *Id.* at 2 Cal 2d 540, 546, 42 P2d 634, 637(1935).

Issues:

1. Whether there was substantial evidence to reasonably infer that the chemistry teacher was guilty of negligence?

2. Whether there was evidence that Elge was contributorily negligent in causing his own injuries?

Holding:

1. Yes. The California Supreme Court, in a *per curiam* opinion[152] reversing a lower court's judgment of nonsuit,[153] held that it may be reasonably inferred that there "is substantial evidence to indicate that the [chemistry teacher] was guilty of negligence in failing to exercise reasonable care in providing and labeling dangerous materials to be used in chemical experiments, and in failing to properly instruct and supervise the selection, compounding, and handling of dangerous ingredients in manufacturing explosives.[154]

2. The court passed on this issue, instead remanding to the trial court for a determination of the issue of whether Elge was contributorily negligent.

Analysis:

In so holding and reversing the lower court's granting of a nonsuit to the defendants, the Court felt that the two primary issues in the case, negligence by the teacher and contributory negligence of the students, were best decided by a jury. The court also questioned the appropriateness of the particular experiment:

> It is not unreasonable to assume that it is the duty of a teacher of chemistry, in the selection, mingling, and the use of ingredients with which dangerous experiments are accomplished, rather than to merely hand them the textbook with general instructions to follow the text. This would seem to be particularly true when young and inexperienced students are expected to select from similar containers a proper, harmless substance rather than another dangerous one which is very similar in appearance.[155]

The Court also seemed concerned with the level of knowledge of Elge, indicating that it found evidence that Elge was ignorant of the dangerous character of the experiment and that this would seem to be particularly true when young and inexperienced students are expected to select from similar containers substances that are very similar in appearance.[156] The court felt that these factors were relevant in a jury determination of the student's contributory negligence.

Comment:

Mastrangelo appears to hold that the teacher has a number of duties to the student:

---

152. A *per curiam* opinion is one issued by the court as a whole but is not attributed to any particular justice or justices.
153. A dismissal of the lawsuit at trial by a judge without allowing a jury to decide the issues.
154. Mastrangelo v. West Side Union High School Dist., 2 Cal 2d 540, 545, 42 P2d 634, 636(1935).
155. *Id.*
156. "It may well be doubted whether it is proper in an introductory school course in chemistry to require pupils to make and ignite an explosive. It would appear that the dangers of such an experiment, incorrectly performed by young children, might be anticipated; and the benefits to be derived from its actual performance by each pupil are not so great as to justify the risk of serious injury to the child. But the very least, if it is to be performed, it necessarily requires the strictest personal attention and supervision of the instructor. We have no sympathy with the defense that the book called for certain ingredients, and that the 'idea of putting in some other ingredient was out of his (the plaintiff's) own mind.' " Mastrangelo v. West Side Union High School Dist., 2 Cal 2d 540, 549-50, 42 P2d 634, 638 (1935).

1. To ensure the proper labeling and storage of all chemicals used in the laboratory. This is critical today. As more states enact legislation making their schools accountable to OSHA regulations for the handling and storage of chemicals on their campuses, more school districts will face penalties, fines, and enhanced liability for their improper chemical handling practices.

2. To supervise students commensurate with the level of potential harm. More supervision is required when there is a greater potential for harm.

3. To select experiments appropriate for the level of student. The court appears to criticize the teacher for failing to select appropriate laboratory exercises for the students. That is, just because the laboratory is in the textbook, does not make it appropriate for all students. Thus, the teacher's duty to instruct students appropriately also includes the duty to select appropriate material.

4. To warn students of danger and protect students from harm. This is significant because numerous courts have held that teachers are not insurers of student safety, but rather they have a duty to act as a reasonably prudent person would under the circumstances. Here a chemistry teacher would have superior knowledge of the great potential for harm from this experiment and should have taken appropriate measures to warn students and protect the student from injury.

5. There is no testimony that safety glasses were used by anyone in conducting the experiment. This case, from 1935, predates the widespread use of safety glasses and face shields that would have certainly reduced the damage to the student's eyes. In determining negligence today, a court would have placed emphasis on the student's failure to wear proper safety equipment and this would be a factor in determining the student's comparative negligence. Recall that in analyzing the applicable standard of care, often custom in the industry is determinative. If the standard in schools is to use a safety shield when performing experiments with potential for explosion, then the failure to use such safety device by the student or to provide such safety devices by the school or district would be considered negligence per se.

Frace v. Long Beach City High School Dist.,

58 Cal.App.2d 566, 137 P.2d 60 (1943)

Concepts:

- Chemical Theft
- Duty to Supervise
- Unauthorized Experiments

Facts:

A high school janitor, on several occasions, permitted two high school students to enter a locked chemical storeroom and remain unattended and leave without observation while the janitor went about his other duties. This was contrary to school rules. These two students took potassium chlorate and phosphorus from the storeroom without authorization. They kept these chemicals in the garage at the home of one of the boys, where the plaintiff, Frace, 17 years old, watched the other two boys experiment with them without injury.[157] One day, Frace asked one of the boys if he could use some of the chemicals for an experiment. He gave Frace a small quantity of the chemicals he had stolen. Frace mixed them in a container and shook them causing an explosion and the injuries for which he sued.[158] Frace alleged that "by reason of their immature age, inexperience and lack of knowledge of chemicals neither the [other boy] nor the plaintiff knew that use of said chemicals by them was dangerous and hazardous or would cause an explosion or that the use of said chemicals by plaintiff was likely to injure person or property."[159] In addition, Frace alleged that the school district was negligent because

> . . . at all times the [school district and the janitor] knew: that the use of said chemicals by students, except under the personal supervision and direction of one skilled in the science of chemistry, was apt to cause injury to person and property; that said supply room and the chemicals therein was an attraction and allurement to the students of the high school; and that if given an opportunity some of said students would steal chemicals therefrom for the performance of their own and unsupervised tests and experiments thereby exposing themselves and others to serious personal injury.[160]

Issues:

1. Whether the facts as alleged in the complaint were sufficient to find the defendants (the janitor and school district) liable for negligence and survive a motion to dismiss the complaint for failure to state a cause of action?[161]

---

157. <u>Frace v. Long Beach City High School Dist.</u>, 58 Cal.App.2d 566,569, 137 P.2d 60, 61 (1943).
158. *Id.*
159. *Id.*
160. *Id.* at 58 Cal.App.2d 566,570, 137 P.2d 60,62 (1943). The court, referring to plaintiff's complaint noted that the primary thrust of Frace's allegations against the school district were through the janitor's alleged misconduct; that [the janitor] "negligently and in violation of his duties as such custodian, permitted two students of said high school . . . to take certain chemicals from said supply room, in that with knowledge that said students were not authorized by any teacher or other agent or employee of his codefendants, to enter said chemical supply room or to take chemicals therefrom; he unlocked said supply room for said students and permitted them to remain therein and leave therefrom unobserved by himself or any other agent or employee of his codefendants; all of which was in violation of the rules and regulations of said high school and of his duties as such custodian." *Id.* at 58 Cal.App.2d 566,571, 137 P.2d 60,62 (1943).
161. The technical term for this type of motion is a "demurrer." There are several types of demurrers that all ask the court to do the same thing: strike offensive material from the complaint filed by the plaintiff or the answer of the defendant, or strike the entire complaint. In this case, the defendants had filed such a motion before the trial court, which was granted with the plaintiff given a period of time in which to amend the complaint. The plaintiff failed to amend and the trial court dismissed the case. The plaintiff now appeals the dismissal.

2. Whether the theft of chemicals was foreseeable and therefore not an "intervening independent cause"[162] which would break the chain of causation?

Holding:

1. No. The facts as plead were not sufficient to state a claim for negligence on the part of the district.

2. No. The theft of the chemicals from the storeroom was not foreseeable and therefore this "intervening independent cause" broke the chain of causation.

Analysis:

The court offered this insight as to why the janitor and the school district were not liable for negligence:

> It is obvious that the facts thus far set forth are not sufficient to impose any liability on the defendants. They show merely that unauthorized persons took, in legal effect stole, some chemicals from defendant's storeroom, and that plaintiff, obtaining possession of some of these chemicals, was injured by reason of his unwitting mishandling of them.[163]

In the opinion of the court, it was not foreseeable that the two boys would steal the chemicals from the storeroom, even though they were left unattended by the janitor, and were in the room in violation of school rules. As such, the theft of the chemicals was an "independent intervening cause" which broke the chain of causation, and therefore the school district owed no duty to the plaintiff, Frace.

The court determined that although the school district was liable for its own negligence or that of its officers or employees by virtue of statute, it was not liable for Frace's injuries, because the mere act of permitting the two students to enter and remain in the storeroom did not constitute actionable negligence, and that even if it did constitute negligence, it was not the proximate cause of the injuries, inasmuch as the independent, intervening acts of the two students in stealing the chemicals and in giving them to the plaintiff, as well as the latter's act in experimenting with them, were not reasonably foreseeable by the school authorities.[164]

Comment:

The court finds that the act of the two students in stealing the chemicals from the storeroom is not foreseeable. The court then goes on to say that had the plaintiff alleged that if the room was accessible to all, an allegation that *some* students left alone would steal the chemicals would be sufficient to show negligence on the part of the school district. As we shall see in Kush ex. rel. Marszalek v. City. of Buffalo, 462 N.Y.S.2d 831 (Ct.App. 1983) in some circumstances the theft of chemicals from an unlocked or unsupervised chemical storeroom is foreseeable and will not act to relieve the school district from liability.

---

162. The rule regarding an independent intervening cause on which plaintiff relies is thus stated . . . where the original negligence of a defendant is followed by an independent act of a third person, which results in a direct injury to a plaintiff, the negligence of such defendant may nevertheless constitute the proximate cause thereof if, in the ordinary and natural course of events, the defendant should have known the intervening act was likely to happen; but if the intervening act constituting the immediate cause of the injury was one which it was not incumbent upon the defendant to have anticipated as reasonably likely to happen, then, since the chain of causation is broken, he owes no duty to the plaintiff to anticipate such further acts, and the original negligence cannot be said to be the proximate cause of the final injury." Frace v. Long Beach City High School Dist., 58 Cal. App. 2d 566,570 137 P.2d 60,62 (1943) (citations omitted).

163. *Id.* at 58 Cal. App. 2d 566,569 137 P.2d 60,61 (1943).

164. *Id.* at 58 Cal. App. 2d 566,572 137 P.2d 60,63 (1943). "The complaint fails to show either that defendants were negligent in admitting the two students to the storeroom or that they should have anticipated that their acts in doing so would or might result in such an accident as that which occurred to plaintiff." *Id.*

Reagh v. San Francisco Unified School Dist.,

119 Cal.App.2d 65, 259 P.2d 43 (1953)

Concepts:

- Chemical Storage
- Custom in the Industry
- Duty To Supervise
- Standard of Care
- Teacher Judgment

Facts:

Reagh, a 16-year-old chemistry student and member of the school's ROTC program, sought out his chemistry teacher for some red phosphorous. Reagh wanted to use the phosphorus to create a smoke screen on a particular maneuver that he was going to participate in on the weekend with the ROTC. The teacher, the day before the explosion, gave him a small slice of white phosphorus, which the student told her he could use as a trigger to ignite the red phosphorus, since white phosphorus ignites spontaneously upon exposure to the air. The teacher at the same time told him that the red phosphorus, which is more inert than the white and will not spontaneously ignite, was in short supply and for that reason she doubted how much of it she could let him have. The student testified, although the teacher contradicted this part of his testimony that he then asked her if it would be all right to add potassium chlorate and sugar to the red phosphorus to increase the smoke and that the teacher told him that it would.

The day of the explosion the student brought a clean glass container to school with him and the teacher permitted him to take from a locked cabinet a small quantity of red phosphorus, about 100 cc which he placed in the container. Following the class the minor remained in the classroom after the other students had left. The teacher stood with her back to him in an office adjoining the classroom talking to another chemistry teacher. The student then went to an open shelf upon which there were bottles of various chemicals including potassium chlorate and sugar and took a small quantity of sugar, about 35 cc and a smaller quantity of potassium chlorate, about 15 cc, and placed them in the container with the red phosphorus. He then said good-bye to the teacher and left. On his way downstairs the mixture in the container exploded spontaneously causing him to be seriously injured.[165]

The trial court entered judgment for the school district, and the plaintiff appealed. The district court held that the giving of a certain [jury] instruction referable to the issue of what was the proper standard of care with respect to the storing of potassium chlorate under lock and key or on open shelf, and refusal of requested instruction on same issue, constituted reversible error. This appeal followed.

Issues:

1. Whether a jury instruction which in effect said that if the student was not familiar with the use and characteristics of the chemicals, which were inherently dangerous, it was the duty of the school district and the chemistry teacher to exercise that degree of supervision in connection with the use of such chemicals as was ordinarily furnished students of the same age, intelligence, and experience "by other similar schools" which carried on the same type of work in the locality was error?[166]

---

165. Reagh v. San Francisco Unified School Dist., 119 Cal. App. 2d 65, 68, 259 P 2d 43,45 (1953).

166. The instruction in full was: "If you find that the defendant, through its teacher, Frances Dealtry, undertook to instruct the plaintiff Theodore Reagh in a course of study in elementary chemistry, which course involved the use of chemicals which were inherently dangerous and hazardous to a person who was not familiar with their use and their characteristics, and if you further find that the plaintiff was not familiar with their use and characteristics and

2. Whether the evidence at trial supported the finding that the student was contributorily negligent as a matter of law because he wrongfully took the potassium chlorate?

Holding:

1. Yes. The trial court giving of the above instruction was reversible error.

2. No. The student could not be found to be contributorily negligent on the weight of the evidence and the issue of his negligence was for the jury to decide.

Analysis:

The court added that the error in the above instruction was aggravated by the trial court's refusal to give a correct instruction proposed by the plaintiff: that if a person of ordinary prudence, in the position of the school district and its teachers, would have kept a supply of potassium chlorate under lock and key, or would otherwise have controlled it so as to prevent its being used by a student except under a teacher's supervision, then it was the duty of defendant school board to observe such precaution.[167]

On the issue of whether the student was contributorily negligent as a matter of law as found by the trial court, the court further held that it could not be said that the boy's action in taking the chemicals from an open shelf of the classroom and placing them in a container with red phosphorus established that he was contributorily negligent as a matter of law, where he testified that he did not know that the mixture would result in a spontaneous combustion, and where his teacher had never instructed him as to the danger of combining the substances, although she knew that such combination might explode and another chemistry teacher did not know before this explosion that the mixture might result in an explosion.[168]

Comment:

This case illustrates that the standard of care is not based on what other schools in the area are doing or not doing in the area of safety.[169] Rather, the standard of care for storage of potentially hazardous chemicals is:

> If you find that a person of ordinary prudence, in the position of the defendant, and its officers, teachers and employees, would have kept the supply of potassium chlorate under lock and key, or would otherwise have controlled the same so as to prevent its being used by a student except under the supervision of a teacher, then you are instructed that it was the duty of the defendant to have observed such precautions.[170]

In Reagh, the court was concerned with the proper application of the standard of care. The school district attempted to define the standard based on local practice. That is, if every chemistry teacher in the

---

the dangers incidental thereto, it was the duty of the defendant and of the plaintiff's teacher, Frances Dealtry, to exercise that degree of supervision in connection with the use of said chemicals which you find was ordinarily furnished to students of the same age, intelligence and experience, by other similar schools which carried on the same type of work in the locality." Reagh v. San Francisco Unified School Dist., 119 Cal. App. 2d 65, 71,259 P2d 43,46(1953).

167. Id.

168. The court seemed to overlook the fact that the student "had been making gunpowder and similar explosives for a number of years, and that he had used potassium chlorate with other chemicals for the purpose." Reagh v. San Francisco Unified School Dist., 119 Cal. App. 2d 65,70, 259 P 2d 43,46 (1953).

169. As the court noted in defining the appropriate standard that evidence was introduced by appellant [student] that in certain private schools in the vicinity potassium chlorate was not kept on open shelves in the laboratory classroom but was always kept in locked cabinets, and by respondent school district that in other high schools under its jurisdiction, potassium chlorate was kept on open shelves. Evidence of custom in the same trade or occupation is admissible for the consideration of the jury but it is not conclusive on the question of what constitutes ordinary care. Conformity to "the general practice of custom would not excuse the defendant's failure unless it was consistent with due care." Reagh v. San Francisco Unified School Dist., 119 Cal. App. 2d 65,71, 259 P 2d 43,46 (1953).

170. Id.

school district is doing the same thing, then it must be evidence of what a reasonable person would do under the circumstances. This is not the rule. Rather, custom in the industry is only one measure of what a jury may consider in determining what a reasonable person would do under the circumstances. This case, decided in the fifties, shows the rather lax attitude towards safety. Teachers should always have potentially hazardous chemicals under lock and key. At no time should a student work unsupervised in the laboratory, and at no time should students be permitted to take chemicals from the lab. Since this case was decided, the standard of care has remained the same, but what was reasonable then, is no longer reasonable today. As Ohman instructs, parents do not expect their children to go to school and come home maimed because of the negligence of the teachers in giving very hazardous materials to students to take home. This case serves as landmark example of poor teacher judgment and, more importantly, an example of district negligence in the supervision of their employee.

Moore v. Order Minor Conventuals,

164 F. Supp. 711 (W.D.N.C. 1958), *aff'd*, 267 F.2d 296 (4th Cir. 1959)

Concepts:

- Chemical Storage/Security
- Duty of Care
- Duty To Instruct and Warn
- Duty To Supervise
- Responsibilty for One's Own Actions

Facts:

Terrell Moore was a student at St. Francis High School, a private school run by a Franciscan order. A few weeks after the beginning of the school year, Terrell, a tenth grader enrolled in a first year chemistry class, was given permission with several other classmates to set up the equipment for a lab that was to be run later in the day. Friar Faneuff, who was in charge of the lab, had given the boys a key to the lab but did not accompany them to the lab while they were setting up the equipment. The chemicals in the lab were in an unlocked cabinet. There were no written warnings posted with respect to the use of the lab, and Terrell testified "he had no other experience in chemical laboratories, and no instruction had been given him with respect to safety in the laboratory, and no warnings as to the dangers involved in mixing chemicals."[171] Apparently, Terrell had learned from some source other than the school how to make gunpowder.

While the others went about setting up the lab, Terrell assembled the ingredients for making gunpowder. Unable to find an ingredient he needed, he made a substitution, using manganese dioxide instead of charcoal. This mixture didn't produce the desired results producing only a "fizzle" upon ignition. Not satisfied, Terrell obtained some red phosphorous in order to produce a more volatile explosive, despite the warnings and protests of the other boys. "His efforts were successful beyond his expectation, for the unstable mixture exploded in the beaker as he stirred it, resulting in grave and tragic injuries to him, including the loss of one eye and a hand."[172] Terrell sued alleging that Friar Faneuff was negligent for failing to properly supervise and instruct Terrell. The trial court did not reach the issue of whether Friar Faneuff was negligent, holding as a matter of law that Terrell was contributorily negligent as a matter of law and directing a verdict in favor of the school district.

Issues:

1. Whether the trial court committed error in finding Terrell contributorily negligent as a matter of law?

2. Whether Terrell could not have anticipated the explosion of the chemical combination and therefore would not be contributorily negligent?[173]

Holding:

1. No. The trial court committed no error. "Whether there was such a want of care on the part of school officials as would warrant recovery by a plaintiff who might reasonably be said to be free of negligence, we need not consider, for we think the district Judge was correct in concluding that

---

171. Moore v. Order Minor Conventuals, 267 F.2d 296, 297 (4th Cir. 1959).
172. *Id.*
173. If Terrell could not have anticipated the explosion, then under the view of contributory negligence existing at this time, he would not be negligent as a matter of law and not barred from recovery for his own negligence.

Moore's injuries were the result of his own acts which were so imprudent as to require . . . the direction of a verdict for the defendant." [174]

2.   No. "It is perfectly clear that Moore's companions were voicing their objections and warnings. There was testimony that almost every one of the other boys voiced such warnings, one of them testifying that he told Moore that if he wasn't careful he would "kill us all." Moore persisted in the face of these warnings, as a venturesome boy sometimes persists even in the face of obvious danger." [175]

Analysis:

The Court was concerned, not with the school or teacher's breach of the duty of care but, with whether Moore could be said to recognize that "explosives are dangerous" and that he "should have recognized that his course of conduct exposed himself, or others, to risk of harm, even though it would be perfectly clear that he did not anticipate the particular way in which the injury occurred."[176]

In reaching its conclusion that Moore recognized the potential for harm, the court perhaps said it best:

> Judges may understand his conduct and sympathize with him in the loss of his eye and hand, but they cannot permit him, in order to place responsibility for his loss upon others, to be heard to say that he was acting with that degree of care and prudence expected of the average boy his age. Even boys of extraordinary intelligence sometimes act imprudently. Sir Winston Churchill is said to have blown himself high into the air with a self-made bomb when he was a student in Harrow. (Citation omitted) Fortunately for the history of our age his wounds were only minor, and it is good fortune of most of us that we are not made to suffer from the consequences of our youthful imprudence. Moore was not so fortunate, but it cannot be said on this record that his imprudence was not the cause of his injuries.[177]

Comment:

Moore demonstrates the harshness of the rule of contributory negligence, and it is precisely this harshness why the doctrine has all but disappeared in the United States. In its place, almost all states (46) have adopted some type of comparative fault rule, where the amount of fault of each party is apportioned. Under a more modern analysis, Friar Faneuff clearly breached his duty of care for negligently failing to properly instruct the students as to the hazardous nature of the chemicals present in the lab, for failing to provide appropriate signage and warnings, failing to secure the chemicals in a secure manner, and for failing to adequately supervise his students in the lab. Under a comparative negligence standard, a jury would have found Moore comparatively negligent, but he would have still won a substantial amount of money for his injuries.

---

174. Moore v. Order Minor Conventuals, 267 F.2d 296, 297 (4th Cir. 1959).
175. *Id.* at 298.
176. *Id.* at 297.
177. *Id.* at 298.

Wilhelm v. Bd. of Educ. of New York,

16 App. Div.2d 707, 227 N.Y.S.2d 791, (2d Dept.) *aff'd without opinion*

12 N.Y.2d 988, 238 N.Y.S.2d 972, 189 N.E.2d 503 (N.Y.1962)

Concepts:

- Chemical Storage/Security
- Duty To Supervise

Facts:

A 13-year-old, Harold Wilhelm, together with a classmate, both ninth grade students enrolled in a program for superior students at a junior high school, were assigned a project of building a record player. They were working alone in a laboratory with the approval of the teacher. "After spending about 10 minutes in their respective projects and without permission to do so, the two boys began to "fool around" with chemicals and glass bottles which were on the shelf in the laboratory."[178] Wilhelm was intent on mixing the chemicals for a rocket fuel, which exploded, burning him. The trial court awarded damages to the boy. Defendant Board of Education appealed.

Issue:

1. Whether Wilhelm was contributorily negligent as a matter of law thus barring his recovery of damages?

Holding:

Yes. "In our opinion, under all the circumstances, the plaintiff was guilty of contributory negligence as a matter of law"[179], the judgment was to be reversed and the complaint against the board of education dismissed.

Analysis:

Apparently the court focused on the following facts in reaching the conclusion that Wilhelm was contributorily negligent as a matter of law and therefore barred from recovering against the school board: Wilhelm was in a gifted program; he was not doing the project that he was assigned; and that he knew that the chemicals he was mixing were dangerous as they were to be used for rocket fuel.

Comment:

Wilhelm like Moore v. Order Minor Conventuals, 267 F.2d 296, 298 (4th Cir. 1959) is an example of the harshness of contributory negligence. Again, it appears that the students had unfettered access to dangerous chemicals, without appropriate supervision by the teacher. However, as we will see shortly, this trend will start to change and the teacher and school district's duty of care change correspondingly.

---

178. Wilhelm v. Bd. of Educ. of New York, 16 App. Div. 2d 707, 227 N.Y.S. 2d 791 (N.Y. 1962).
179. *Id.*

Hutchison v. Toews,

4 Or. App.19, 476 P 2d 811 (Or. App.1970)

Concepts:

- Duty of Care
- Inappropriate Experiment Selection
- Student Risk
- Unauthorized Experiments

Facts:

Fred Hutchison and his friend Phillip Brown, both 15 years old, attempted to fire a homemade pipe cannon using a mixture of potassium chlorate and sugar which exploded, severely injuring Fred's hands. The students had badgered the chemistry teacher Mr. Toews for several weeks to give them some powdered potassium chlorate. Finally, he reluctantly gave them a small amount of powdered potassium chlorate that they put in a baby food jar. Several days later, after Toews had stepped momentarily out of the school's chemistry storeroom, Brown stole some crystalline potassium chlorate. This crystalline form caused the explosion. The chemical storeroom was locked except when in use.

In addition, the students sent for and received a pamphlet that gave 100 formulas for explosives. They admitted that they had read the pamphlet and all of the warnings it contained. They also showed the pamphlet to Mr. Toews, who cautioned them against doing any of the experiments described in the pamphlet. Several of the formulas in the pamphlet called for the use of potassium chlorate and without exception these formulas contained the strongest warnings to be found among all of the formulas. Brown mixed the chemicals and then they attempted to light it. Previously they had experimented with homemade gunpowder in the cannon, using up all their fuses. Instead they attempted to light the cannon by sticking a match into the fuse hole. They had some difficulty lighting the cannon because the match they were using kept blowing out. So the pupils decided to keep the wind from blowing the match out by covering the fuse hole with their hands. When the match finally lit, the cannon exploded, "peeling back like a banana," and severely injuring the hands of both boys. They later admitted that they knew what they were doing was dangerous, yet continued the experiment. In their complaint the students alleged that Mr. Toews had negligently given them the potassium chlorate that caused the explosion. However, approximately two years after filing, Brown revealed that he had stolen the crystalline potassium chlorate. At trial, the court held that the students had known what they were doing was dangerous and that they had assumed the risk that someone was going to get hurt if extreme caution was not taken. The trial court dismissed the suit, from which Hutchison appeals.

Issue:

1. Whether Fred Hutchison was contributorily negligent thereby barring his recovery against the teacher and the school district?

Holding:

1. Yes. The court found this to be a clear case of contributory negligence. The court explained that the general rule in these types of cases was that ". . . the kind of contributory negligence which consists of voluntary exposure to a known danger, and so amounts to assumption of risk, is ordinarily a defense . . . . " Prosser, Torts 539 § 78 (3rd ed. 1964) We think the only reasonable conclusion from the evidence was that plaintiff had knowledge of the risk involved, and that he was contributorily negligent as a matter of law.

Analysis:

The court in determining whether Hutchison was contributorily negligent focused on what Hutchison knew. Did he have knowledge that the chemicals were dangerous? Yes. Brown and Hutchison both testified that they had read the pamphlet warnings, had experimented with the cannon and other explosive mixtures prior to the accident, and that they knew that they might get burned if they held onto the cannon, or if they stood too close when it did fire that it might fly up and hit them in the face.

Comment:

The court does not discuss the teacher's actions in giving the students a quantity of the powdered potassium chlorate that he knew the boys were using with the cannon. In a comparative negligence jurisdiction, this fact alone may have lead to liability for the teacher and the school district. The students, obviously, were familiar with Mr. Toews. They had at least a dozen discussions related to explosives according to Brown who testified that they had bothered Toews a dozen times before he reluctantly gave in. In giving the students a dangerous chemical that, used improperly, could lead to serious injury, as it did in this case, Toews breached the duty of care because it was foreseeable that the boys could be injured in the performance of an unauthorized experiment.

Station v. Travelers Ins. Co.,

236 So.2d 610, *writ refused* 256 La. 857, 239 So.2d 359 (La.App.1974)

Concepts:

- Defective Equipment
- Duty To Instruct and Warn
- Duty To Supervise
- Equipment Safety
- Inappropriate Experiment Selection
- Student Access to Chemicals

Facts:

Geraldine Station, an eighth-grade pupil, was severely burned when an alcohol burner, known to be defective, exploded when Station attempted to re-light it. The science teacher had helped Station and a friend set up a science project in the school gym. The teacher lit the burner and returned to class. Apparently, the burner went out. A boy poured alcohol from a jug and a girl lit a match near the mouth of the jug, which exploded, severely burning a 14-year-old girl who was standing nearby, and who later died. The trial court awarded $7,889.95 in damages to Station finding the science teacher Wilson, guilty of negligence. The science teacher appealed that finding.

Issue:

1.   Whether the science teacher was guilty of negligence in failing to supervise and properly instruct the pupils as to the safe handling of the burner?

Holding:

Yes. The appeals court upheld the finding of the trial, stating: "The district judge . . . found that Wilson [the science teacher] was negligent in that he failed to fully instruct the girls, or anyone else who might assist them, of the dangerous nature of the alcohol and further [in] that he did not positively warn that the burner was not to be re-lighted by them should it go out."[180] The court further found that "Wilson should have anticipated that the burner would go out, due to his prior experience with it, and that his failure to warn or provide adult supervision amounted to negligence under the circumstances that negligence being the proximate cause of the minor's' injuries."

Analysis:

In reaching the conclusion that Wilson was negligent, the court of appeals found Wilson's behavior blatantly negligent, given the extreme danger of the situation. The court of appeals harshly criticizes Wilson and clarifies the duty of care Wilson owed to the girls:

The jurisprudence of this state is firmly established that where one creates, deals in, handles or distributes an inherently dangerous object or substance, that an extraordinary degree of care is required of those responsible. This duty is particularly heavy where children are exposed to a dangerous condition, which they may not appreciate. Here, a dangerous instrument was placed in the hands of children without any special degree of care, supervision, or direction. Alcohol, a highly flammable substance, was left in their control to be used in connection with a faulty alcohol burner that had continually given trouble. That the situation was fraught with danger is proven by the results. The duty incumbent upon Wilson under these dangerous circumstances was to either

---

180. Station v. Travelers Insurance Co., 292 So. 2d 289, 291–2 (La. App. 1974).

positively warn these girls not to attempt to light the burner if it went out or to personally supervise their use of the equipment or provide adequate adult supervision in his absence. He did none of these things. He testified that he did not teach the children how to light the burner because they were not mature enough to do so, but that he had instructed them as to the flammable properties of alcohol. Nowhere in the record, however, is it established that Wilson directed these children not to attempt to light the burner should it go out. Neither was adequate adult supervision provided which was commensurate with the danger involved. We agree with the trial judge that this was negligence on the part of Wilson and that this negligence was the proximate cause of Geraldine Station's injuries.[181]

Comment:

The court in Station freely heaped abuse on the science teacher in this case for his negligence in failing to supervise, warn, or instruct the students in handling a flammable chemical, in this case alcohol. On the surface, this appears to be a negligent supervision case. It is in reality, a failure on the part of the teacher to exercise due care in selecting an activity appropriate for the level of students in his care. The court does not directly admonish the teacher for this failure, possibly because they could not find a polite way to indicate that the teacher was incredibly ignorant. To be fair to the teacher in this case is difficult. The teacher had knowledge of the defective burner and failed to remove it from use or have it repaired. The teacher left the students unsupervised, without appropriate safety instructions, in a gymnasium. This is classic negligence.

---

181. Station v. Travelers Insurance Co., 292 So. 2d 289, 291–2 (La. App. 1974) [citations omitted].

Shifton v. North Clackamas School Dist. No. 12,

18 Ore. App. 90, 523 P.2d 1296 (Ore. App. 1974)

Concepts:

- Chemical Storage/Security
- Duty To Supervise
- Lab Assistants
- Lab Manuals
- Safety Rules
- Unauthorized Experiments

Facts:

Shifton was a 17-year-old senior and a student laboratory assistant to the chemistry instructor at Rex Putnam High School. Lab assistants were an aid to instructors while enriching their own education. A starting chemistry class was in the first month of its instruction and in class at that time, when Shifton requested permission of McGoldrick, the class instructor, to go into the laboratory and prepare an experiment.[182] "Permission was granted and McGoldrick continued lecturing. The experiments done were generally prepared and executed as demonstrations for the benefit of class instruction as it progressed. The class was studying Chapter 1 in its chemistry book at that time. There was no instruction concerning explosions or the means of making them in this chapter of the book. The laboratory was open only to McGoldrick and laboratory assistants."[183]

> When [Shifton] went into the laboratory, he leafed through a manual entitled 'Tested Demonstrations in Chemistry' until in Chapter 18 he came upon those involving the use of phosphorus. One such experiment described the mixing of .10 gram each of red phosphorus and potassium chlorate which together would approximate the size of a match head and which, when combined and struck, would produce a 'deafening report.' Shifton mixed in a glass test tube somewhere between 65 and 100 times the volume prescribed in the manual and proceeded to stir the ingredients with a metal spatula. On about the third stir of the material it exploded causing plaintiff serious injury.[184]

Shifton sued the chemistry teacher and the School District for negligence alleging that:

1. Inadequate supervision was provided,

2. Quantities and types of chemicals were provided capable of resulting in a violent explosion, and

3. The chemistry laboratory was equipped with books containing suggested experiments that could result in violent explosions without providing sufficient warnings thereof.

A jury reached a decision in favor of the defendant school district and Shifton moved for a new trial based upon an affidavit of his attorney. The judge on the motion for a new trial heard oral arguments and granted the new trial. The teacher and the school district appeal from the resulting order setting aside the verdict and allowing the new trial.

---

182. Shifton v. North Clackamas School Dist. No. 12, 18 Ore. App. 90, 95, 523 P.2d 1296, 1297 (Ore. App. 1974).
183. *Id.*
184. *Id.*

Issue:

1. Whether the trial judge erred in granting a new trial and setting aside the jury verdict in favor of the defendants because there was no ground for setting aside the verdict under the Oregon Statute and there was no other ground stated in an affidavit supporting Shifton's motion for a new trial.?

Holding:

1. Yes. "Given the uncertainty shown by the record for the reason for granting the motion, lack of indication that the outcome would be changed by a changed shading in McGoldrick's testimony, and lack of opportunity afforded defendant School District to demonstrate how little or great that shading might really be, we are persuaded by the language used in Schmitz v. Yant, 242 Or 308, 314, 409 P2d 346 (1965):

    > It should be made clear that as between the conflicting principles of allowing the trial judge wide discretion in granting new trials and of protecting the jury system as an effective method of deciding disputes this court believes the latter to be of the greater consequence." Reversed and remanded for reinstatement of the verdict.[185]

Analysis:

This case concerns the discretion of a judge in granting a new trial against the weight of a jury verdict. Here, a jury had already found the teacher and the school district not liable for the student's "unauthorized" experiment, only to have the trial judge indicate that a new trial was necessary because of information contained in an affidavit filed by Shifton's attorney. The court indicates that the only relevant paragraph in the affidavit was found in Paragraph 1 of the motion:

1. Defendant McGoldrick [the instructor], having testified at trial that he gave plaintiff a mimeographed set of safety rules which included directions not to stir compounds with metal spatulas and not to mix compounds in vials, now reportedly feels that testimony was erroneous.

    McGoldrick testified [at trial] that he had handed out to the class at the beginning of the year safety instructions containing a list of do's and don'ts. These included instruction against using a glass vial or test tube or a metal spatula in any experiment such as that which plaintiff undertook.[186]

Shifton's attorney in his motion that a new trial should be granted because the teacher's attorney had called up Shifton's attorney to tell him, that his client, "on further reflection, felt that his testimony was incorrect as he was not sure that the safety rules had been given to plaintiff's class . . . ."[187] and that "Mr. McGoldrick made quite a point in his testimony concerning the rules of safety passed out to all students which provided specific and correct instructions on the two points Dr. Wesley [an expert witness] felt to be important."[188]

The remainder of the court's analysis concerns the Oregon Statute that gives the grounds available for new trials in Oregon. After enumerating the grounds on which a new trial may be granted the court concludes that none of the grounds are applicable but in any event the grounds are not inclusive, rather "[t]he enumeration in the statute does not restrict the inherent power of courts to relieve a party where justice has not been done, nor to grant new trials for any other sufficient causes not enumerated."[189]

In analyzing the facts before the court, and giving weight to the fact that the teacher had recanted that portion of his testimony as it relates to the provision of safety rules and instruction to Shifton, the fact

---

185. *Id.* at 97.
186. *Id.* at 92.
187. *Id.*
188. *Id.*
189. *Id.* at 93.

remained that it was doubtful to the court that the outcome of the case would have changed even if the teacher's testimony was changed.

Comment:

Shifton is an unauthorized experiment case where the student loses, a rarity. However, this case might have been decided differently if a jury had believed the student and not the teacher. The appellate court makes a mistake in this case, by minimizing the effect on the credibility of a witness who changes his testimony, particularly when an expert witness has testified that the teacher's testimony as to the provision of safety instruction was important. The appellate court, unlike the trial judge, ignores the fact that the chemistry teacher was not providing supervision over his aide, that the chemicals involved were those known to be "inherently dangerous" and were not placed out of reach of an unsupervised student working in the room. The question of liability turns on foreseeability. In this case, whether it was foreseeable, that a student aide, left alone unsupervised in a room where phosphorus, a very hazardous chemical if handled improperly, was accessible to the student in some manner. The opinion leaves unanswered a number of factual areas that were probably available to the trial judge.

Wentz v. Deseth,

221 N.W. 2d 101 (N.D. 1974)

Concepts:

- Duty To Supervise

Facts:

Arlan Wentz sues his eighth grade teacher, Deseth, for burns he suffered causing him permanent injury during a candle-making project supervised by Deseth. The class had seven or eight students, all boys, who were instructed to extinguish their candles before Mr. Deseth left the room. The boys put out their candles. Mr. Deseth left the room for approximately 15 minutes. During his absence, however, someone relit the candle sitting on Wentz's desk, and while Wentz was seated at his desk and engaged in conversation with [other students] . . . to his left, someone poured after-shave lotion on the flame of his candle.[190] The after-shave lotion, supplied by Wentz, had been used to scent the candles. The lotion was highly flammable and caught fire. The flames spread from the container to Wentz's clothing, severely burning him, and causing him permanent injury.[191] Testimony by other students indicated that the only students in the room who had matches were Wentz and another boy and that the other students in the room borrowed matches from them to light their candles. Wentz sues Deseth for negligence. At trial the court found that the evidence did not support a finding of teacher negligence, and that Wentz had assumed the risk. Plaintiff files an appeal alleging that the evidence offered at trial was sufficient for a finding of negligence against the teacher and therefore he was entitled to a judgment in his favor notwithstanding the verdict of the jury, and secondly that the court erred in instructing the jury on the defense of assumption of risk.

Issues:

1. Whether the court erred in instructing the jury on the defense of assumption of risk?

2. Whether the evidence was sufficient to have found the teacher, Deseth, liable for negligence.

Holding:

1. Yes. "Since there is no basis for an instruction on assumption of risk, no instruction on the subject should have been given."[192]

2. No. "If the [jury] instruction had been clearly correct, we might have assumed that the jury found for the defendant on the ground of intervening cause, in which case we would have affirmed the judgment. But where [jury] instructions are confusing to us, and presumably the jury . . . [a] general verdict of the jury returned under a proper and an erroneous instruction cannot be upheld . . . . The general verdict of the jury makes it impossible for us to determine upon which theory the jury's verdict is based."[193]

---

190. Wentz v. Deseth, 221 N.W. 2d 101, 102 (N.D. 1974).
191. The dissent filed in this case points to a significantly different set of facts: "The evidence reveals that Wentz was seated at his desk, talking with other students gathered around; that his candle had been relighted, and one of the students poured shaving lotion onto the flame of the candle; that it flared up and the top of the bottle containing the shaving lotion was aflame when he removed it from the candle; that he put the flame out and set the bottle of shaving lotion down. Thereafter, another student picked up the bottle and he also poured shaving lotion onto the flame of the candle. It was during this second episode that Wentz was burned." Wentz v. Deseth, 221 N.W.2d 101,105 (N.D. 1974).
192. *Id.* at 103.
193. *Id.* at 104.

Analysis:

The court's focus in this case was on a rather confusing jury instruction that had been given to the jury.[194] The court found that the instruction was a combination of three doctrines that had been lumped into a single jury instruction: assumption of risk, contributory negligence, and the degree of care required of infant plaintiffs. In the majority of the court's view there was no evidence of assumption of risk and the instruction relating to that defense should not have been presented to the jury. The majority outlined the elements necessary for the defense of assumption of risk: knowledge of an abnormal danger, voluntary exposure to it, freedom of choice to avoid it, and injury proximately caused by the abnormal danger. The majority stated that the burning candle was not the proximate cause of Wentz's injuries. There was an intervening cause which broke the chain of causation, and that was "put in motion by another student's pouring or squirting of the aftershave lotion, which resulted in flames spewing from the container. It was these flames, which caused the injury, not the flame of candle.[195] Since there was in the court's view an intervening cause, there could be no assumption of the risk by Wentz. As such, the jury instruction was confusing and the majority felt that this was prejudicial and required reversal of the trial court's decision to deny a request for a new trial made by the plaintiff. The court at the end of its opinion noted that the law of negligence had recently been changed by statute, with the legislature determining that the defenses of contributory negligence and assumption of risk no longer being the law of North Dakota, being replaced by a comparative negligence statute. The new laws however did not apply to this case because the case was tried prior to the enactment of the changes.

The dissenting justices in this case disagreed on whether the assumption of risk instruction should have been given in this case, with one justice indicating that based upon the facts as he perceived them from the testimony, Wentz was a participant in the events, which he knew were dangerous, and therefore assumed the risk of the "dangerousness of his voluntary exposure to the known danger by continuing to sit at his desk under these circumstances."[196]

---

194. "Another defense affirmatively interposed by the Defendant is that of assumption of risk. You are instructed that a student assumes the ordinary hazards of his everyday life which he either knows, or should know and appreciate through his degree of intelligence. He assumes those dangers that are so open and obvious to his senses that one of his mental capacity and experience would in the ordinary exercise of care and prudence common to persons of like mental capacity and experience, would know and appreciate, and would be expected to be sufficiently attentive and understanding to avoid. In other words, the student's assumption of the hazards and dangers incident to his studies is determined by his capacity to know, understand, and appreciate them, and his caution, alertness, and aptitude to avoid them. In that regard you have a right to consider the Plaintiff, Arlin Wentz, as he appeared before you and his apparent ability as to experience, alertness and understanding." Wentz v. Deseth, 221 N.W.2d 101,103 (N.D. 1974).
195. *Id.* at 103.
196. *Id.* at 105.

Maxwell v. Santa Fe Public Schools,

87 N.M. 383, 534 P2d 307 (N.M.App.1975)

Concepts:

- Eye Safety
- Safety Equipment

Facts:

Charles Maxwell was a student in Mr. Smith's general science class at the junior high school. Following a lecture on cloud formation, Mr. Smith performed a cloud formation experiment himself, and then let the students perform it. "The students would drop a lighted match into a quantity of water contained in the base of a Pyrex® flask. The match would extinguish, creating visible smoke in the flask. At this point a two-hole stopper containing two hoses would be placed in the neck of the flask. One student would pump air into one hose by means of a bicycle pump. A second student would pinch the second hose, i.e., the release valve, thereby blocking the exit of air from the flask and permitting the pressure to build up within the flask. Once the smoke from the match disappeared, the pumping would cease, the release valve would be opened and small vapor clouds would form in the flask. The students were not wearing eye protection at the time of the explosion and no such eye protection devices were available in the Santa Fe Public schools. Charles, apparently holding the release valve, loses an eye when the flask explodes due to the pressure in the flask. Charles sues the school district, the school board, the sauperintendent, and the teacher for negligence for failing to provide eye protection during the experiment. The superintendent was let off the hook, and the jury found Smith, the teacher not liable for negligence. However, the jury found against both the school district and the school board finding them negligent. The school board and district appeal this finding of negligence.

Issues:

1. Whether the introduction of a State Board of Education regulation requiring that eye devices be worn when participating in or observing activities that may be hazardous to the eyes was error requiring reversal?

2. Whether the jury's determination that Smith was not liable for negligence but the school board and school district were negligent was fatally inconsistent and therefore error requiring reversal?

Holding:

1. No. "Even if the regulation's admission was error, it was harmless error."

2. No. "The theory of liability against the [district and the board] was broader than against the [teacher]."

Analysis:

On the admission of the regulation, the board and district contended that the regulation only applied to activities that took place in chemistry or combined chemistry–physical science classrooms and not a general science classroom as the one in which the accident took place. The court found this hair splitting to be trivial and indicated that even if the admission of the regulation was error it was harmless error because if the jury had believed the regulation to be relevant then it would have required them to find all of the defendants guilty. In finding Smith not guilty of negligence, the court concluded that the jury must have concluded the regulation did not apply.

As for the inconsistent verdicts brought by the jury, the court examined the theories of liability against the teacher and against the school board and district. Finding that the theory against the board and district was broader than against the teacher, the court concluded that such inconsistency was possible. That is, the school board and district could be liable for negligence, even though the teacher was not. The court stated how this was possible:

> The jury could only find Smith liable for using improper equipment for the experiment if they found the glass container was improper. The jury could find the [board and district] liable if they found any of the equipment was improper. The [board and district] candidly admit that there is evidence to support a finding of negligence in failing to use a pressure gauge in this type of experiment . . . [and] no pressure gauge was in use on the day Charles was injured aside from the visible disappearance of the smoke in the flask.[197]

Comment:

The interesting portion of this case lies in the instruction given to the jury supporting the finding of negligence on the part of the school board and district when compared with Smith, the teacher:

1. The teacher, Mr. Douglas Smith, was negligent in using a *glass container* not designed for use in an experiment such as was carried on here and that the use of this glass container created a hazard for Charles Maxwell and the other students in the class. [Emphasis added.] . . .

2. Defendants Santa Fe Public Schools, Board of Education, and the members of the Board of Education of the Santa Fe Schools were negligent in failing to properly govern, supervise and regulate the activities of officers, agents and employees of the School District so as to avoid injury to Charles Maxwell's eye, in that:

    a) They failed to establish regulations and procedures to assure that proper *equipment* was available for science experiments of this type. [Emphasis added.][198]

These different theories of liability explain how the jury could achieve different and apparently inconsistent results in finding Smith not liable and the board and district liable but nothing contained in the above instructions explains the failure of the court to address the real issue in this case: Whether it was negligence to perform the experiment without some type of eye protection? The court mentions a pressure gauge in its holding that the failure to provide a pressure gauge was the proximate cause of Charles' injuries, but in reality there was no way of preventing Charles' injuries even if they had several gauges. The flask might have had some defect that would have caused it to explode with only slight pressure. Clearly, proper eye protection would have saved Charles' eye in this instance, and eye protection devices such as goggles or shields clearly fall into the definition of equipment the court uses to find that a gauge was necessary.

---

197. Maxwell v. Santa Fe Public Schools, 87 N.M. 383, 534 P2d 307, 309 (N.M.App.1975).
198. *Id.*

Simmons v. Beauregard Parish School Board,

293 So. 2d 226, 315 So. 2d. 883 (La. App. 1975), *cert. denied*, 320 So. 2d 207 (La. 1975)

Concepts:

- Duty To Supervise
- Inappropriate Experiment Selection
- Non-Science Classroom
- Self Designed Experiments
- Unauthorized Experiments

Facts:

Lesley Simmons, a 13-year-old student originally in Mr. Wellborn's science class, but following a switch of teachers during the year ended up in Mr. Bryant's class, had built a simulated volcano model with the help of his father and older brother (who had presented a similar project in the past) for School Display Day. During "display day" students were to prepare and present projects relevant to what they were studying and bring them to school. Mr. Bryant's class was studying "Earth surfaces" and a working model volcano seemed perfect. The volcano was constructed of mud and clay molded around a large bottle. A small metal can attached to a wire at the top of the volcano was lowered into the mouth of the jar and served as a container to receive "powder" which was to be ignited and create the effect of erupting. The "powder" used in the volcano was the inside of firecrackers that had been purchased by the father. The student transported the powder in a small medicine bottle with a plastic cap. The Display Day arrived and Lesley brought his volcano to school and demonstrated it in class. The following day, Lesley was instructed to bring the volcano home including the medicine bottle. While waiting for the school bus, Lesley decided, with the encouragement of some other students, to demonstrate the volcano one last time.[199] Lesley gave one or two demonstrations and while pouring in the powder for either the second or third demonstration, an explosion occurred resulting in serious injuries to Lesley. A spark had apparently entered into the small medicine bottle and had ignited the rest of the powder causing the explosion. At the time of the impromptu demonstrations the children waiting for the bus were under the supervision of a teacher assigned to "bus duty," Mr. Evans. The main injuries to Lesley's hand were to his right hand and they were extensive, requiring amputation of most of his hand. The student sued everyone for his injuries: the school board, the school district, the principal, assistant principal, both science teachers, the bus duty teacher and the insurance company which had policy limits of $100,000. The jury found the science teacher (Jefferson Bryant) liable for exercising no control over the pupils' science projects and the school bus teacher liable for not providing adequate supervision at the school bus stop:

> Under the foregoing facts there was ample evidence for the jury to conclude that Mr. Bryant was negligent in allowing Lesley, a 13-year-old student, to build and demonstrate exactly what substances were used or whether the project was dangerous to the student himself or others. The lack of supervision on the part of this school board employee was negligence, resulting in serious injury to the child.

---

199. Apparently, there is some dispute between a dissenting justice and the majority of the importance of Lesley purportedly going across the street to obtain the matches to use in his final demonstration. In his dissent, Justice Miller believing the testimony of the only one of Lesley's friends to testify, that Lesley went across the street to a store to obtain the matches and that Lesley knew that possession of matches on school property was a violation of school rules, concluded that Lesley's actions amounted to contributory negligence and therefore should be a bar to recovery. The majority, assuming arguendo that this fact was true, promptly dismissed this fact indicating, "the harm suffered by Lesley was simply not the kind which the school rule was intended to prevent. Therefore violation of the rule was not contributory negligence." Simmons v. Beauregard Parish School Board, 315 So.2d. 883, 889 (La. App. 1975).

The school district used contributory negligence as a defense, but the court held neither the 13-year-old pupil nor his father (who helped him build the project) liable for such negligence. The school Board was held liable under the doctrine of respondeat superior by reason of lack of supervision over the science teacher, Bryant, who allowed a 13-year-old student to build and demonstrate a volcano exhibit employing firecracker powder. Several appeals ensued, with the final appeal presented by the school board on several issues.

Issues:

1.   Whether the trial judge erred in refusing to grant the school board a new trial on the ground that a statute prohibited a jury trial against a public body?

2.   Whether the jury erred in finding actionable negligence on the part of the school district for actionable negligence under the doctrine of respondeat superior?

3.   Whether Lesley and his father were guilty of contributory negligence in addition to assumption of the risk?

4.   Whether the jury award was excessive given that the policy limits of the school district's insurance policy were only $100,000 and the jury awarded $104,000 as general damages for injuries suffered by Lesley and $1,104.85 as special damages to the father for medical bills incurred?

Holding:

1.   No error. In failing to object until after the jury had rendered its decision, the school board waived its right to assert the prohibition.

2.   No error. The record reveals that the jury had ample evidence upon which to base its verdict finding the district liable under the doctrine:

> There was ample evidence for the jury to conclude that Mr. Bryant was negligent in allowing Lesley, a 13-year-old student, to build and demonstrate a project without even determining exactly what substances were used or whether the project was dangerous to the student himself or others. The lack of supervision on the part of this school board employee was negligence, resulting in serious injury to the child.

3.   No. "We conclude the jury had sufficient evidence to find that Mr. Simmons was not negligent in the manner in which he instructed his child in the use of the project."[200] Additionally, "[t]he jury apparently concluded Lesley did not fully realize and appreciate the risk involved. In addition . . . the jury also evidently concluded he did not intentionally and voluntarily expose himself to obvious danger, within his capacity to understand."[201]

4.   No. "Medical evidence indicates that the type of injury which was sustained by this youth was severe and very painful. Additionally, the child will be physically deformed for the rest of his life. The award of the jury cannot be termed excessive under these circumstances."[202]

Analysis:

Simmons is a great fact case. The court harshly criticizes the science teacher, Bryant for his negligence and sarcastically summarizes his testimony:

> Mr. Bryant testified essentially that he made no suggestions for the projects, laid out no guidelines, made no approval of projects, required no explanations of the projects by students to

---

200. <u>Simmons v. Beauregard Parish School Board,</u> 315 So. 2d. 883, 888 (La. App. 1975).
201. *Id.* at 889.
202. *Id.* at 890.

him, and never discussed or supervised any of the projects. He indicated that it was his belief that a 13 year old had a concept of what was dangerous and what was not, and that a child of that age would not do anything dangerous to himself. He stated further, that in demonstrating the project that he had used firecracker stems, did not know that Lesley had firecracker powder, saw no potential danger in the project, and did not warn Lesley in any way on the day he was allowed to remove the project from the classroom. Finally, Mr. Bryant concluded that his responsibility ended at the classroom.

In finding the school district liable under a theory of respondeat superior, the court found it significant that the principal had abdicated his authority and responsibility by failing to impose any regulations or standards upon the teachers and that no one individual was responsible for supervision of the event. The court found it particularly significant that the principal "did not require any reports on the type of projects to be made by the students nor did he set any guidelines, but stated in effect that he relied on teachers' overall mature judgment and responsibility."[203]

The dissent makes clear that the majority worked hard to present little factual argument supporting a finding that Lesley and his father were contributorily negligent. This may be due to the severity of Lesley's injuries, which the court, in discussing whether $104,000 was sufficient, lists in graphic detail.[204] As Justice Miller makes clear, "[t]here was no reasonable basis for concluding that Lesley did not knowingly violate school rules, and this violation was a direct cause of plaintiff's injuries."[205] "It is respectfully submitted that the record is subject to only one finding: that Lesley grossly disregarded his own safety in the face of known, understood, and perceived danger, and exposed himself to obvious danger within his capacity to understand."[206] In addition, Justice Miller felt that Lesley's father's contributory negligence was established as a matter of law. "He knew that firecracker powder was an explosive. Explosives are inherently dangerous. Lesley's father had a duty not to place inherently dangerous substances in the hands of his 13-year-old son without providing adequate supervision or at least ascertaining whether his son appreciated the dangers involved [citations omitted]."

---

203. *Id.* at 887.
204. According to the court:
    The main injury which Lesley received was to his right hand. . . . This injury was described as an extensive laceration of the palm of the hand, the third and fourth fingers hanging by a skin, the fifth finger almost completely destroyed, and the distal phalanx of the index finger destroyed. Corrective surgery has amputated the third, fourth, and fifth fingers of his right hand, and the distal phalanx of the index finger. The third and fourth metacarpal bones of the hand were removed. The metacarpal bones are those which give strength to the grip of the hand. The hand has undergone considerable reconstructive plastic surgery, including skin grafts to cover the denuded part of the thumb and finger which remain. In addition, numerous lacerations about the chest, abdomen, thighs, and head involving the skin, and fatty area under the skin, which resulted from fragmentation of he glass bottle which Lesley held in his hand, have left him scarred for life. . . Medical evidence indicates that the type of injury which was sustained by this youth was severe and painful. Additionally, the child will be physically deformed for the rest of his life. *Id.* at 889–90.
205. *Id.* at 890.
206. *Id.* at 892.

Comment:

Simmons is an interesting case because it illustrates the difficulty in predicting the outcome of a case when liability is predicated on the failure to do an act that causes an injury that is foreseeable. Could Mr. Bryant have foreseen that Lesley would have demonstrated the volcano in front of the school while waiting for the bus? More importantly, were Mr. Bryant's actions the proximate cause of Lesley's injuries? That is, but for Mr. Bryant's actions the injury to Lesley would not have occurred, or in the substantial factor jurisdictions, was the teacher's negligence in supervision a substantial factor in causing the harm? The court does not address these questions and massages the facts to produce, what the majority believes, is a just result. Similarly, in the chemistry classroom, the decision to let students perform certain activities in an inappropriate environment may lead to serious injuries, i.e., *non-science classrooms*. In almost all instances of serious harm to a child a lawsuit will follow. In order to minimize injury, teachers must be proactive rather than reactive.

Rixmann v. Somerset Public Schools, St. Croix County,

82 Wis. 2d 571, 266 N.W. 2d 326 (Wis. 1978)

Concepts:

- Duty To Supervise
- Student Conduct
- Student Negligence

Facts:

Ron Rixmann was a sophomore in Mr. Ammerman's sophomore general science class. The class was performing a starch extraction from a leaf. The lab required the students to transfer the leaf into alcohol that was being warmed by an electric plate. Mr. Ammerman, who had demonstrated the experiment the previous day, had warned the students to have no open flames near the experiment because alcohol is flammable. Mr. Ammerman had divided the class into two groups of six students. Ron and two of his friends (also named defendants) were working in one of the groups and had become bored with the lab. Apparently, one of the pupils decided to ignite some of the alcohol. He took a small amount of it out of the beaker with a plastic spoon, poured it onto the tabletop, and lit the substance with a match provided by Rixmann. Eventually, the spoon itself caught fire. The student waved the spoon in the air to put out the flames, and then proceeded to place the spoon in the beaker of water, but in doing so ignited the fumes from the beaker of heated alcohol. Mr. Ammerman, who had been working with the other group of students, saw that the beaker was on fire and tried to put it out by placing a notebook over the mouth of the beaker. The beaker tipped over and spilled the flaming liquid onto Ron, who was severely burned.

Ronald's father sued Ammerman, Ron's two friends, and the school district for negligence arising out Ammerman's attempt to put the beaker out with a notebook. The trial judge held the science teacher negligent as a matter of law but allowed the jury to consider whether the school district and the two students should also be held responsible. The jury found the science teacher 60 percent negligent and the school district 40 percent negligent, and awarded damages of $656.33 for past medical expenses, $8,400 for future medical expenses, $25,000 for past pain, and $30,000 for future pain for a total of $64,056.33. The trial judge limited that amount to $25,000, because of a Wisconsin statute limiting damage awards, and Rixmann's father appealed that decision.

Issues:

1. Did the trial court err in refusing to find the defendant students negligent and liable as a matter of law?

Holding:

Yes. It may be true, as the trial court stated, that these students "weren't the brightest." But all three of the students were bright enough to know that alcohol was flammable and that they were not supposed to have open flames near it. On the basis of these admitted and undisputed facts, we conclude that the students, by collaborating to set fire to the puddle of alcohol on the table, did not conform their conduct to that which would be expected of a similarly situated child of the same age and with the same capacity, discretion, knowledge, and experience in creating the initial fire. The evidence does not reasonably admit an alternate conclusion. Thus, the trial court erred in not holding these students, Ronald included, negligent as a matter of law.[207]

---

207. Rixmann v. Somerset Public Schools, St. Croix County, 266 N.W. 2d 326,333 (Wis. 1978).

Analysis:

The Wisconsin Supreme Court spent several pages discussing an argument advanced by one of the students related to the "collateral source rule." The collateral source rule is a doctrine that limits double recovery by victims for expenses paid by third parties (usually insurance companies). After ruling on the various legal technicalities related to this issue, the court dealt squarely with the issue of the student's negligence, including Ron, that contributed to Ron's injuries. In reversing the trial court on the issue of contributory negligence, the Wisconsin Supreme Court found the evidence of contributory negligence undisputed and insurmountable when it stated that, [i]t does not shock the conscience of this court to hold the defendant students liable for their negligence; indeed, it would be shocking if the court were to relieve them of liability."[208]

The student defendants next contended that even if they were negligent that the actions of their science teacher were a superceding cause of Ron's injuries. The court noted that in order for an act to be a superceding cause, it must first be an intervening force. An intervening force is "one which actively operates in producing the harm to another after the actor's negligent act or omission."[209] The court then went on to find that the science teacher's actions, although negligent did not act as a superceding cause of the harm to Rixmann, stating that "the boys knew at the time they set fire to the puddle of alcohol that Ammerman would make an effort to extinguish the flames. The manner in which he attempted to do so, though not most effective or prudent, was not extraordinarily negligent. This court has stated that "in order for the intervening act of negligence to constitute a superceding cause it must be such that the conscience of the court would be shocked if the first actor would not be relieved from liability. It does not shock this court to hold the defendant students liable for their negligence . . . . [W]e hold that the negligence of the students . . . as well as Ronald himself—was a substantial factor in bringing about Ronald's injuries."[210] The court goes on to say that

> [t]hese three, to various degrees, joined forces to create an open flame in the proximity of a heated beaker of alcohol. Once this condition was created, none of the boys alerted Ammerman to the danger, nor did Ronald take even the most elementary steps to remove himself from the scene. Rather, [one student] increased the danger by setting fire to the spoon and then to the beaker of alcohol. Though Ammerman's negligence intervened at this juncture, it did not supercede the boys' negligence in bringing about Ronald's injuries.[211]

---

208. *Id.* at 334.
209. *Id.*
210. *Id.*
211. *Id.*

Connett v. Fremont Cty. Sch. Dist.,

581 P.2d 1097 (Wyo. 1978)

Concepts:

- Duty of Care
- Duty To Supervise
- Study Hall in Science Classroom

Facts:

John Connett, a 14-year-old student was working with another student in a chemistry lab during study hall. His teacher and three other students were cleaning up an adjoining lab while Connett was working with geo-blocks, and Mike Degner, the other student in the lab, was performing a boiling point determination of solutions. One solution contained sugar and water, the other contained salt and water. An alcohol burner was heating both solutions. After working with blocks for a short period of time, Connett decided to join Degner. After discussing Degner's experiment with him, Connett decided to see if the boiling point would change if he added alcohol to each of the solutions. Degner told Connett not to do it because he did not want his experiment disturbed. Ignoring Degner, Connett located a can containing alcohol that his teacher had used to fill the alcohol burners Degner was using. The can was located in the sink approximately four feet away from where Degner was working. The science teacher had left the can out intending to use it again for the next class period. Connett then poured alcohol into one of the beakers without mishap, but when he poured the alcohol into the second beaker, the can caught fire and then exploded. The science teacher, hearing the explosion ran in from the adjoining room and used a fire blanket to put out the fire that had engulfed Connett causing severe burns. Connett sues the teacher and the school district alleging negligence and failure to adequately instruct and supervise students in the use of chemicals in school laboratory. The trial court granted the school district's motion for summary judgment.[212] The plaintiff appealed to the Wyoming Supreme Court.

Issue:

1. Whether the court erred in granting summary judgment and thereby holding that there was no issue of material fact on the question of the instructor's alleged negligence in failing to properly instruct and supervise John Forrest Connett in his use of alcohol and burner in the school laboratory?[213]

Holding:

1. Yes. "We conclude here that there are present in this record issues of material fact which cannot be decided as questions of law"[214] as to whether the teacher was negligent in properly instructing and supervising Connett in his use of alcohol and burner in the school laboratory.

---

212. Summary judgment motions are brought when there are no issues of material fact and the court can decide based on those facts the liability of a party as a matter of law. In this case, the trial court ruled as a matter of law that the science teacher was not negligent as a matter of law. The Wyoming Supreme Court reversed and remanded for trial.

213. Connett v. Fremont Cty. Sch. Dist., 581 P.2d 1097,1099 (Wyo.1978).

214. *Id.* at 1104.

Analysis:

In finding that there were issues of material fact regarding the science teacher's negligence the Wyoming Supreme Court, after discussing the requirements and standards for determining a summary judgment motion in the context of comparative-negligence statute, proceeded to examine the record.[215]

On the central issue of supervision, (including instruction) the court pointed out several inconsistencies in the record as to whether the science teacher had properly instructed and supervised Connett while he was in the laboratory. Connett could not recall that the science teacher had ever given him instructions relative to the use of alcohol around fire and neither could the teacher. There was no evidence that the can containing alcohol had any instructions or warnings on it. One of the students in the class who was in the adjoining room with the science teacher could recall that the science teacher had given instructions regarding the flammable effects of alcohol during a safety lecture at the beginning of the year, but Connett was not yet a member of the class at that time. This same student indicated that the science teacher had not given any safety instructions on the day Connett was injured and this was consistent with both Connett's and the science teacher's testimony. This student also testified that the science teacher, while he was in the adjoining room, could not see where Degner and Connett were working and had spent almost all of the time engaged in cleanup but that he might have stepped into the doorway to see what Degner and Connett were doing. The science teacher testified that he did not see Connett and Degner together, could not hear their conversation, even though the student who was working with the science teacher could hear the conversation. The record showed that the science teacher had hearing difficulties, that he was in the room with the other students for approximately 20 to 30 minutes, and that neither he nor anyone else undertook to supervise Degner's experiment. The science teacher's testimony conflicted with the student's. The teacher indicated that he was working in a position that allowed him to see Degner and had him under constant watch. However, by his own admission he never saw Connett at Degner's worktable, the place where Connett was injured. These inconsistencies present an issue of material fact as to the teacher's negligence in supervising students and therefore require reversal of the trial court's issuance of summary judgment in favor of the district.

The Wyoming Supreme Court then proceeded to explain the duty of care owed by the school to the student. Indicating that the science teacher had testified that boys of this age in circumstances such as this require "full supervision, to the best of your ability," the court explained that this was correct because included in the duty of care which the school board owes to a child is a duty to supervise.[216] After a discussion of the cases discussing the duty of the school where lack or insufficiency of supervision is involved the court held that the duty of care owed to students is

> that care which a person of ordinary prudence, charged with the duties involved, would exercise
> under the same circumstances. That which constitutes proper supervision depends upon the facts

---

215. The issue of how to apply the requirements of a summary judgment motion, which concludes that there are no issues of material fact, to a 50 percent comparative-negligence statute was one of first impression for the Wyoming court. While accepting that summary judgment is a poor device for deciding questions of comparative negligence, the Wyoming Supreme Court indicated that what was contemplated by the comparative negligence statute was an examination of the totality of the causal negligence to determine the contribution made by each party and then by examining the "respective contributions to the result" a determination can be made as to who is the most negligent and by how much. This ability to compare assumes that the things to be compared are known and can be placed on the scales. *Id.* at 1100. In short, if there are issues of material fact, there can be no summary judgment because not all the facts causing the accident can be weighed. If all the issues are known, then the determination of who caused the most harm, and their relative contribution to the final result can be determined.

216. Connett v. Fremont Cty. Sch. Dist., 581 P.2d 1097, 1102 (Wyo.1978). "A school agency has a duty to supervise the conduct of children on school premises at all times and to enforce pertinent rules or regulations, and a failure to do so can constitute actionable negligence . . . [citations omitted]." *Id.*

and circumstances attending each event. In order that the tort be actionable, the lack of supervision must have a causal connection with the accident and resulting injury.[217]

The court concluded that the alleged negligence of the teacher charged with inadequate supervision was a question of fact that needed to be determined by a jury. However, the court made clear that this duty of supervision was not constant, rather, "[a]bsent special dangerous circumstances, a school district does not have the duty of providing constant supervision of all movements of all pupils at all times." [218] The court then proceeds to describe what it means by special circumstances requiring constant supervision: "Classroom connected injuries have led to recovery where the activity involved was inherently or potentially dangerous, such as working with guns, operating shop machines, learning to swim . . ."[219] The court indicated that it was not necessary for the plaintiff to prove that the very injury that occurred was foreseeable in order to establish that the failure to provide necessary constituted negligence as this would impose too high a burden. Rather, "it is sufficient if a reasonably prudent person would foresee that injury of the same general type would be likely to happen in the absence of such safeguards."[220] As applied to the facts of this case then, the plaintiffs must show—not that the science teacher should have foreseen that Connett *would* use the alcohol as he did, but that 14-year-old seventh grade boys *might*, if confronted with these or similar circumstances, so misuse the flammable liquid and that injuries such as did occur would likely occur in the absence of adequate safeguards or supervision. Finally, the court stated

> . . . we would observe that the school owes the student the duty to supervise his activities. This duty becomes more imperative in the classroom, and risks of danger are foreseeable, and thus the degree of care higher, where young, inexperienced students are handling substances which for them are potentially dangerous.[221]

Comment:

For all practical purposes, Connett appears to require that during a laboratory where hazardous chemicals are used the duty of supervision is constant.

---

217. *Id.* at 1102–03.
218. *Id.* at 1103.
219. *Id.*
220. *Id.* at 1104.
221. *Id.*

Bush v. Oscoda Area Schools,

405 Mich. 716, 275 N.W. 2d 268 (1979), *sub appeal,* 109 Mich. App. 373, 311 N.W. 2d 788 (Mich. Ct. App.1981)

Concepts:

- Administration Negligence
- Chemical Storage/Security
- Class Size
- Conducting Class in an Unsafe Area
- Defective Building Exception
- Duty To Instruct and Warn
- Duty To Supervise
- Lab Design
- Non-Science Classroom
- Safety Equipment
- Science Facilities

Facts:

Tracy Ann Foxworth, a 14-year-old student at Oscoda High School, was enrolled in Introductory Physical Science. The class originally meeting in the chemistry lab had been rescheduled in order to accommodate increased enrollment and was meeting in a math room in the interim. The chemistry laboratory was equipped with a safety shower, ventilation or exhaust hoods, sink's enclosed storage areas, stationary laboratory desks and water and gas outlets. The substitute room was not so equipped. The classroom teacher had previously complained to the principal about the overcrowded conditions existing in the classroom and the increased potential for accidents.[222]

The students were expected to perform lab work in the substitute classroom. The class laboratory schedule provided for the use of heat approximately eight to ten weeks into the semester. In the chemistry laboratory, the students used gas burners connected to permanent gas supplies. In the substitute room, the students used alcohol burners. The alcohol for the burners was stored in the chemistry lab and transported to the substitute classroom in a plastic jug. Before school, the classroom teacher poured enough alcohol into the jug to fill the burners for that day's classes. The jug had an open top. The jug, along with the alcohol burners, was put on top of a counter at the rear of the classroom. Students filled their burners from the jug, and then carried them to their desks. The classroom teachers then lit their burners at each student's desk. Safety goggles were worn during the experiment. After the completion of the experiment, students were to extinguish the burners and return them to the back counter. After one lab session, Tracy Ann was returning her burner to the counter at the back of the room when she noticed a lighted burner. As she picked it up and attempted to put it out, an explosion occurred setting her on fire causing second and third degree burns.[223] Tracy Ann panicked. Another teacher entered the room. The fire extinguisher, which was kept at the opposite end of the room, was given to the classroom teacher and she put out the fire.

---

222. She said "[y]ou cannot keep sending us this many students and expect us to do lab work in rooms this size where the tables move too easily. It's just too crowded." "When you throw more students in that classroom * * * [y]ou have more hands to get into things, more bodies in the small amount of space, more confusion at times. People sometimes bump into each other. You tend to have more clumsiness occurring and it's just too hard to manage too many students." Bush v. Oscoda Area Schools, 405 Mich. 716, 275 N.W.2d 268, 270 (1979).

223. This was Tracy Ann's original story. In her second version she said that she decided to see what would happen if she brought a lighted match over the top of the alcohol jug. This caused an explosion from which she received second and third degree burns. In a subsequent appeal, the court noted that Foxworth's original deception does not

In her complaint to recover for her injuries she stated cause of action under a "defective building" exception to a Governmental Tort Liability Act, alleging that the improper design of the classroom (temporarily being used as substitute for a chemistry lab) and the absence of safety devices rendered it unsafe as a science classroom, and that the classroom was therefore "dangerous and defective" and the proximate cause of Tracy Ann's injuries.

Tracy Ann sued the school district, the superintendent, the principal and the science teacher. At trial a jury awarded Tracy Ann $295,000. However, the jury also found that Tracy Ann had been 44 percent negligent under comparative negligence principles. The trial court accordingly entered judgment in the amount of $162,839.60 with interest at 6 percent per annum from the date of filing the complaint (July 19, 1974). The trial court granted dismissal of the claims against the school district on grounds that they were immune from suit. However, the trial court found the teacher and the principal negligent. Judge Peterson explained why the teacher should be held liable:

> As to the defendant teacher she . . . is charged by the complaint with personal negligence in the conduct of her class, both in acts of omission and commission, including conducting the class under inadequate and unsafe conditions, allowing storage of alcohol in a damaged container, leaving spilled alcohol exposed to ignition sources, failure to properly handle and store the alcohol when open lamps were in use proximate thereto, and failure to warn and supervise the students in handling alcohol and flame. We think there is a fact issue for the jury as to the conclusion that may be drawn regarding the conduct.[224]

As for the negligence of the principal, the court stated that

> [w]e reach the same result, not because of the allegation of in-class negligence of the teacher, but because of the risk inherent in conducting a class of this kind in a room which is not equipped for the purpose. As principal of the high school, curriculum, scheduling, and room assignments would not only be within his knowledge but his direct responsibility. The removal of the class from the laboratory to the mathematics room was his responsibility. He must be presumed to know the nature of the class, that it would involve chemicals, fumes, alcohol, and open flame alcohol lamps, and that the room to which the class was transferred had no vents or any safety features of the laboratory. We cannot say that all reasonable men would agree that no negligence could be inferred under these circumstances.[225]

A number of appeals ensued and the case eventually reached the Michigan Supreme Court.

Issues:

1. Whether the complaint was sufficient to state a cause of action against the school district under defective building provision of Governmental Tort Liability Act on the theory that improper design of the classroom and absence of safety devices rendered it unsafe as a science classroom and that classroom was dangerous and defective and a cause of injuries to students?

2. Whether complaint was sufficient to state a claim for negligence against individual defendants?

Holding:

1. Yes.

2. Yes. The complaint did state claims against the individual defendants.

---

have any bearing on the defendant's challenge to the evidence. <u>Bush v. Oscoda Area Schools</u>, 311 N.W.2d 788, 791 (Mich. App. 1981).

224. <u>Bush v. Oscoda Area Schools</u>, 405 Mich. 716, 275 N.W.2d 268 (1979).

225. <u>Bush v. Oscoda Area Schools</u>, 275 N.W.2d 268 (1979).

Analysis:

The most important issue before the Michigan Supreme Court was whether the school district could be found liable under a "defective building exception" to the Michigan Governmental Tort Liability Statute. The Court of appeals had earlier indicated that a school district was not immune from suit for negligence and had found it unnecessary to decide whether the plaintiff had also stated a claim under the defective building exception. As the court noted the two claims were not equivalents. The plaintiff's negligence theory was predicated on the school district's and building principal's failure to "exercise due care in holding the class in a non-laboratory room, scheduling too many students in the classroom and failing to adequately supervise the class." [226] The defective building theory was based on the lack of safety devices in the classroom. The majority of the court neatly steps around the governmental immunity limitation that had until this decision applied to schools. According to Justice Ryan, in a strong dissent, the operation of public schools had always comprised a "governmental function" and therefore school districts and their employees were immune to suit. [227] The majority however, rather than attempt to overrule the will of the legislature found that the defendants were not immune from suit as they fell squarely within the defective building provision of the Governmental Tort Liability Act which read in relevant part:

> Governmental agencies have the obligation to repair and maintain public buildings under their control when open for use by members of the public. Governmental agencies are liable for bodily injury and property damage resulting from a dangerous or defective condition of a public building . . .. [Citation omitted].

The school district argued, unsuccessfully, that their duty to the student was only to "repair and maintain" and Foxworth had not alleged such failure. The Michigan Supreme Court, analogizing this statute to a similar defective highways provision, held that the term "repair and maintain" extends to a "dangerous or defective condition of a building," [228] and further held that "[g]overnmental agencies are subject to liability for a dangerous or defective condition of a public building without regard to whether it

---

226. *Id.* at 271 n.7.

227. *Id.* at 274–76. For a very revealing look at what the plaintiff's complaint contained, Justice Ryan in his dissent excerpted the complaint to illustrate that all of the activities alleged by the plaintiff fell within and comprised a governmental function. From a perspective geared to safety in the classroom, these excerpts reveal that the school allegedly was negligent in holding the physical science class in the classroom rather than in the lab for a myriad of reasons including:

18 (a) . . . holding a class in a room which was not designed, equipped or constructed for the performance of chemistry experiments involving the use of extra hazardous substances such as alcohol when they knew or should have known that this would be dangerous to students and particularly would deny them access to the shower-type device available in the chemistry lab.

(b) They scheduled too many students in the class such that overcrowding resulted, equipment and supplies were congested, storage space was lacking and proper supervision by the teacher was difficult or impossible.

(c) They failed to warn, instruct and supervise or provide adequate warning, instruction and supervision for the students as to the handling of their equipment and extra hazardous and inflammable substances such as alcohol, and allowed spilled alcohol to lie on the counter contrary to good housekeeping practices, when they knew or should have known that alcohol would be exposed to sources of ignition in the form of matches and burning alcohol lamps.

(d) They failed to handle, store, or put away a large quantity of an extra hazardous and inflammable substance, alcohol, in a place not exposed to an open laboratory area when burning alcohol lamps would be in use by many student partners . . .

(e) They failed to store a large quantity of . . . alcohol in a safe container, but chose a damaged and split container which had originally contained another type of fluid and was not designed to dispense alcohol in the presence of a source of ignition.

(f) They failed to have the fire alarm equipment in proper working order or energized and did not train and instruct students and personnel how to operate the alarm and extinguisher equipment.

(g) They failed to follow laboratory requirements set out by the United States government, which advanced funds for the construction of the school and equipment, when the Defendants had agreed to observe these requirements. *Id.* at 275, n. 3.

228. *Id.* at 272.

arises out of a failure to repair and maintain."[229] This conclusion opened the door to step around the governmental immunity claimed by the school district, and the court quickly defined what a "dangerous or defective condition" might entail. According to the court ". . . *a building may be dangerous or defective because of improper design, faulty construction, or the absence of safety devices.*"[230] [Emphasis added.]

Noting that the majority of the Court of Appeals had indicated that whether or not a building was dangerous or defective was a question of the intended use or activity for which the building was intended, the Michigan Supreme Court stated that ". . . the question whether part of a building, in this case a classroom, is dangerous or defective is to be determined in light of the "uses or activities" for which it is "specifically assigned" in this case a physical science class."[231]

The court concluded that whether the room was defective when used as a physical science classroom and whether the defect was the cause of Tracy Ann's injuries was a question for the jury. The court, possibly worried about a flood of litigation, clarified that the lack of certain safety devices did not render the classroom defective per se as it ordinarily was unnecessary to install safety equipment in classrooms. However, the court felt that in determining whether a place is safe one must consider the use or purpose it serves:

> A school is not a school because it is called one, but because it is used and functions as one. If a hospital is converted into a prison, the building must be maintained as a safe prison, not as a safe hospital. The room in which Foxworth was injured had by use become a physical science room, and therefore had to meet the standards of a physical science room although once it had been a mathematics room. . . . The school district claimed that increased enrollment necessitated conducting physical science classes in non-laboratory rooms. We recognize that circumstances change and temporary accommodation must be made so that business may continue while adjustments are being made. In such situations it might be reasonable to change temporarily the use of a building or room. . . . [232]

> A governmental agency is not subject to liability for a dangerous or defective condition unless it had "actual or constructive knowledge of the defect and, for a reasonable time after acquiring knowledge, failed to remedy the condition or to take action reasonably necessary to protect the public against the condition. . . . Temporary use of an unconverted room may have been reasonable provided the school district took appropriate action to protect the students until permanent protective measures could be provided.[233]

Comment:

School administrators take note of this case because it has important implications in overcrowded facilities. This case stands for the proposition that principals can be held liable for injury if they schedule classes improperly or holds them in inappropriate facilities. In addition, the dissent perhaps indicated that in the absence of immunity the actions of the district in this case might have amounted to negligence:

> Simple logic compels the conclusion that a building or a classroom is to be used in accordance with the purpose for which it was designed and constructed and that while the failure to do that may amount to negligence, it surely does not constitute the building defective. . . . It is eminently clear from examination of the . . . complaint that the essence of plaintiff's claim relates to the allegedly improper use of the classroom as a Physical Science laboratory despite the fact that it was neither designed nor equipped for laboratory experiments. As such, the alleged tortuous

---

229. *Id.*
230. *Id.* at 272–3.
231. *Id.* at 273.
232. *Id.* at 273.
233. *Id.* at 273–4.

conduct does not relate to a dangerous or defective condition in the building but, rather, to the conduct of the school authorities in utilizing as a science room which was properly designed, constructed and equipped for teaching mathematics.[234]

The Michigan Supreme Court also opened the door for the argument that overcrowding of a facility might constitute negligence if the principal assigns students in such a manner that the use to which the laboratory is being put is unreasonable. Thus, for teachers working in poor facilities and overcrowded conditions, it is imperative that the school district be placed on "actual notice" of the existence of conditions constituting a threat to the safety of students and teachers. The appropriate remedy for teachers is to first contact their principal or other administrator in charge of classroom assignments requesting a move to a properly equipped classroom. If the request is denied, then teachers may act by filing of a grievance based on unsafe working conditions via their union representative. In the absence of a grievance, teachers should document their efforts to remedy the situation with site or district administration and put such efforts in writing. In addition, as this case demonstrates, the science teacher's unheeded complaint about the conditions was not enough to shield her from liability. Therefore, teachers must go the extra step and refuse to conduct laboratory experiments in conditions where such experiments may, by happenstance, go awry, resulting in serious injury to themselves or their students. A red flag for liability should go up any time there is the absence of safety equipment such as showers, eyewashes, chemical spill stations, goggles, ventilation, etc. This case demonstrates how the good intentions of a teacher, performing to the best of her ability in abhorrent conditions, can result in teacher liability.

Finally, to add insult to injury, Tracy Ann recanted her original version of the story about how the explosion occurred, and on yet another appeal, 311 N.W.2d 788 (Mich. App. 1981), the appellate court held that "[I]t does not appear to us that Foxworth's original deception has any bearing on Defendant's present challenge to the evidence. . . . The fact that Ms. Foxworth was more responsible for the explosion than was originally believed in no way negates the fact that there were inadequate safety devices."[235]

---

234. *Id.* at 277.
235. *Id.* at 291.

Nielsen v. Community Unit School Dist. No. 3,

90 Ill. App. 3d 243, 45 Ill. Dec. 595, 412 N.E. 2d 1177 (Ill. App. 1980)

Concepts:

- Chemical Labeling
- Chemical Packaging
- Defective Equipment Theory
- Duty To Supervise
- Immunity Statute
- Safety Equipment

Facts:

Thomas Nielsen was injured when a container partially filled with either methanol or ethyl alcohol exploded or burst into flames during physics class. The container ignited when another student lit a match and placed it near the container. Apparently, the container was incorrectly labeled as floor wax and, as alleged, the container was too large for the storage of this hazardous material, allowing the contents to expand into a dangerous gaseous state. Thomas brought suit against the district under two theories of liability, for negligence and for willful and wanton conduct.

Issue:

1. Whether, under the circumstances the plaintiff's negligence count is barred as a matter of law because the school district was immune from suit on the basis of ordinary negligence.[236]

Holding:

1. No. [A]lthough plaintiff's negligence allegations contain some elements of both improper supervision and defective equipment, we find the plaintiff's negligence count is based primarily on a defective equipment theory. Plaintiff's primary allegation is that the school district knew, or should have known, that the container was defective and dangerous instrumentality. Plaintiff's negligence count should not be barred as a matter of law."[237]

Analysis:

The appellate court, after first determining that for ordinary negligence claims the plaintiff would have to prove willful and wanton conduct by the school and its employees, distinguishes the two separate functions of the school district to provide supervision and control of the student, and to provide equipment. In providing equipment for students, the school district is not held to the higher willful and wanton standard of care, but is held to only a duty of ordinary care in providing equipment for its students. Therefore, the court concluded, "[a] school district may therefore be held liable in ordinary negligence for providing equipment which is known, or should have been known, to be defective or dangerous."[238] The court acknowledged that this rule only applies to school districts and has not been extended to individual teachers. In addition, the appellate court noted that the Supreme Court had extended the duty of care in

---

236. In Illinois at the time this case was decided the Illinois Supreme Court had ruled in <u>Kobylanski v. Chicago Board of Education</u>, 63 Ill.2d 165, 347 N.E.2d 705 (1976) a few years earlier that sections of the education code conferred upon educators the status of parent or guardian to the students in both disciplinary and nondisciplinary matters and consequently in suits involving educators for improper supervision, the plaintiff must prove not that the educator's conduct was negligent but "willful and wanton." <u>Nielsen v. Community Unit School Dist. No. 3</u>, 412 N.E. 2d 1177, 1178 (Ill. App. 1980).

237. *Id.*

238. *Id.*

Lynch v. Board of Education of Collinsville Community Unit Dist. No. 10, 82 Ill. 2d 415, 45 Ill. Dec. 96, 412 N.E. 2d 447 (1980), by holding that a school district has a duty to not only provide safe equipment, but has an affirmative duty to provide equipment to prevent serious injuries. The appellate court concluded that plaintiff's complaint contained elements of both inadequate supervision and of defective equipment and failure to provide other protective devices but that the primary thrust of the complaint was defective equipment and therefore should not be dismissed as a matter of law by the court.

Comment:

Nielsen demonstrates another way that courts have slid around the immunity statutes insulating school districts and their employees from liability. The point of the last two cases should make clear, that the fact that a particular state has an immunity statute protecting school districts and employees, does not mean when the injuries are serious enough the court will not make policy and find away around the immunity statute.

Nielson is also a case about the duty of school districts to provide the necessary safety equipment to students (and staff) to prevent serious injuries. Here the teacher's liability flowed from the fact that the container, improperly labeled as floor wax, contained a highly flammable substance. The court considered the improperly labeled container as defective equipment. Applying the principles of Nielsen to other typical lab situations, such as broken goggles, torn aprons, flammable chemicals being transferred or transported in makeshift containers, etc. all of these situations be considered as providing defective equipment to the student. As such, school districts and teachers have a duty to take affirmative steps to repair such equipment or prevent students from using defective equipment. In addition, under the holding of Lynch v. Board of Education of Collinsville Community Unit Dist. No. 10, 82 Ill. 2d 415, 45 Ill. Dec. 96, 412 N.E. 2d 447 (1980), cited by the Nielsen court, school districts have an affirmative duty to provide equipment to prevent serious injuries. This duty is twofold. First, school districts have an affirmative duty to provide personal safety equipment to the student, meaning primarily safety goggles and safety aprons. Second, school districts have a duty to provide safety equipment in the laboratory to prevent injuries from becoming more serious if the personal safety equipment fails, for example, fire extinguishers and fire blankets, fume hoods, eye washes and showers, first aid kits, chemical neutralization kits, Material Safety Data Sheets, and other equipment to reduce the threat of injury to students.[239]

---

239. The chemistry teacher should be required to take appropriate first aid and other training to meet the duty of care, and this training should be taken on a regular basis in order to meet the changing conditions and practices in the high school laboratory.

Kush ex. Rel. Marszalek v. City of Buffalo,

59 N.Y. 2d 26, 462 N.Y.S. 2d 831, 449 N.E 2d 725 (Ct. App. 1983)

Concepts:

• Chemical Storage/Security

Facts:

David Kush, an eight-year-old who liked to play along a path behind the school, one day found some plastic sandwich bags containing what appeared to look like sand. He began to play with them along with some matches that he had found earlier. The plastic bags contained some magnesium powder and some potassium nitrate that two 15-year-old students had stolen from an unlocked chemistry room and adjacent storeroom located on the fourth floor of the school. The 15-year-old students were hired to assist the janitorial staff at the high school during the summer as part of a summer youth program sponsored by the school board. The two boys had gone to the chemistry lab while the adult employees were on coffee break with the intention to take the chemicals and drop them out the window. They planned to return to pick up the chemicals after work that day. However, before that could happen, David, as was his habit, walked along a well-trodden path that wound its way along the building. The chemicals exploded and David received second-degree burns to his hands, arms, and face. David sues the school board for negligence and the jury finds the board liable for the infant's injuries. The board appeals and presents two issues:

Issues:

1. Whether the school board breached its duty of care to the minor plaintiff by failing to secure dangerous chemicals stored on school grounds?

2. Whether the school board's breach of this duty of care proximately caused David's injuries?

Holding:

1. Yes. "Where the school purposely maintained a store of chemicals, some of which were inherently dangerous, and recognized that, in the environs of the school, a serious hazard would arise if deliberate safeguards were not in place, reasonable care required the securing of the chemicals in such a way that their unsupervised access could not be readily obtained by children, and school which failed to adequately supervise its student employees and failed to adequately secure the dangerous chemicals breached that duty."[240]

2. Yes. The "school's liability for plaintiff's injuries was not affected by the intervening acts of the 15-year-old student employees, since the intervening acts of the employees in taking the chemicals was itself a danger to be reasonably foreseen.

Analysis:

The Court of Appeals first held that the school board owed a duty of care to David since it was foreseeable that children would be on school grounds[241] even though school was no longer in session for the year and that school authorities were aware that children played on the grounds in the summer. The court then turned to the issue of what constituted reasonable care under the circumstances and whether the board met that standard. The court emphasized that the school kept a store of "dangerous" chemicals on the property and knew that they could cause "grave" harm to children, and that because of this the

---

240. Kush ex. Rel. Marszalek v. City. of Buffalo, 462 N.Y.S. 2d 831, 834 (Ct. App. 1983).
241. "By their very nature, a school and its playground attract children." *Id.* at 833.

superintendent had issued regulations entitled "Safety in the Science Classroom and Laboratory."[242] The regulations clearly stated that students should not be permitted in any of the science rooms unattended or unsupervised, and that the science rooms were to be kept locked when not in use. Combustible materials should be locked in a fireproof cabinet.[243] Concluding that the school board could have averted the danger at little cost and great ease by simply locking the chemicals in a fireproof cabinet, a remedy that was already in the board's regulations, the court held that the jury acted rationally in finding that the school board had "failed to exercise reasonable care under the circumstances by failing to secure the dangerous chemicals from unsupervised access by schoolchildren."[244]

On the issue of whether the board had breached its duty of care to David Kush, the court of appeals indicated that the school board's duty comprised two elements and that the board had breached its duty in both instances. First, the board had a duty to adequately supervise its student employees. Second, the board had a duty to adequately secure the dangerous chemicals. The court felt that the board had breached this duty of supervision by permitting the students to be left alone for 30 minutes each day when the rest of the staff went for their coffee break in the school's basement, allowing them the opportunity to roam about the building. The board argued that the students were employees and were acting outside the scope of their employment. The court rejected this argument and declared that the board's duty was not predicated on its status as employer, rather, the "control and supervision of school-aged children present within the building, whether as students or employees, is an essential part of defendant's duty to secure dangerous chemicals from the children's access."[245] As for the failure to secure the dangerous chemicals, the court pointed to testimony which showed that on the day of the accident, the door to enter the chemistry lab was unlocked, the door connecting the lab to the storeroom was unlocked, and the chemicals in contravention of the board's own regulations were not stored in a locked fireproof cabinet designed for the storage of chemicals.

Turning to the second issue, whether the board's breach of the duty of care proximately caused David Kush's injury, the court concluded that the board's negligence was a substantial cause of the events which produced the injury because the board's duty was to take reasonable steps to secure the dangerous chemicals from unsupervised access by children, and in breaching that duty, not only was it foreseeable that there would be theft of the chemicals by the student workers but also that the theft of the chemicals was a natural and foreseeable consequence of the circumstances created by the board.[246] Consequently, the court indicated, the board would not be relieved of liability because such theft was foreseeable and the board failure to guard against such conduct would not relieve them of liability when the act occurred.[247]

---

242. *Id.* "Defendant maintained on the school premises a store of dangerous chemicals for use in science classes. Defendant recognized that unsupervised access to these chemicals by children created a grave risk of harm to all present on the school grounds. The dangers inherent in many of the chemicals stored at the school included flammability and toxicity." *Id.*

243. A chemistry teacher, on staff for 21 years also testified that as a general practice special security measures were necessary for chemicals that "would be likely to cause trouble . . . if gotten in poor hands. *Id.* at 834.

244. *Id.*

245. *Id.*

246. *Id.* at 835.

247. *Id.*

Brazell v. Bd. of Educ. of Niskayuna Schools

161 App. Div. 2d 1086, 557 N.Y.S. 2d 645 (3d Dept. 1990)

Concepts:

- Chemical Storage/Security
- Chemical Theft
- Consistent Enforcement of Rules
- Duty To Instruct and Warn
- Failure To Follow Instructions
- Responsibility for One's Own Actions
- Safety Rules

Facts:

Colin Brazell was in his science class one afternoon and assigned, with his lab partner, to measure approximately 5.0 grams of sodium chlorate and put it aside for use by the next class for an experiment. After making the measurement, Colin decides to place an unspecified extra amount in his pants pocket so that he could take it home to burn with matches. Another student had told him that the chemical would burn and sparkle like firecrackers when ignited. The teacher specifically had told the class to never remove chemicals from the classroom and had gone over safety procedures in the classroom with him. At about 10:00 p.m. while in his bedroom with his two younger cousins, Colin claims the chemical in his pocket spontaneously ignited burning his leg.[248] Colin sues the teacher and the school board for negligence claiming that the defendant negligently supervised Colin allowing him to have access to dangerous chemicals without adequate warnings or precautions. The defendant raised the defenses of contributory negligence and brought a motion for summary judgment claiming that Colin's act in stealing the chemicals was the sole proximate cause of his injuries. The trial court denied the school's motion for summary judgment and the school appealed.

Issue:

1. Whether Colin's intervening culpable act in intentionally stealing the chemicals constitutes a superceding force absolving the school of liability?

Holding:

1. Yes. "[I]t is our opinion that even if the science teacher was negligent in any way by reason of being unable to watch some 28 students every minute of the time they were there, Colin's intervening culpable act of intentionally stealing the chemical constituted a superseding force absolving defendant from any liability."[249]

Analysis:

The appellate court, distinguishing Kush, indicated that in this case Colin's class was supervised, the rules were clear, and there was no evidence of anyone other than the teenage boys that the chemicals were being taken. Unlike Kush, the chemicals in this case were stolen while the class was in session, and the fact that the boys were able to sneak some chemicals out of the room without the teacher's knowledge does not make the outcome (the burning of Colin's leg) a probable one because " . . . a series of new and

---

248. Colin claims that there were no matches in his room, but the police recovered two matchbook pieces from the scene.
249. Brazell v. Bd. of Educ. of Niskayuna Schools, 557 N.Y.S. 2d 645, 646 (A.D. 3d Dept. 1990).

unexpected causes intervened and had to intervene" before the injuries to Colin, some seven to eight hours after the theft, could occur."[250]

Comment about chemical storage and theft:

Theft of chemicals is a recurrent theme in these cases. All chemistry teachers should know that certain types of chemicals are attractive to students. These include strong acids and bases, and those that cause fires and explosions. Consequently, teachers need to be on guard about limiting student access to these chemicals by storing them properly in secure cabinets and storage areas. In addition, teachers must keep track of the use and the quantities of chemicals in the classroom. For this reason, storerooms must be inventoried frequently and accurately. Equipment and chemicals must be put away after their use and never left where a student would have access. While it is often convenient to have on hand quantities of chemicals used on a regular basis, such as 1.0 M HCl and 1.0 M NaOH, the duty of care requires that even these chemicals need to be securely stored. All chemicals should be stored in a properly ventilated, locked storage area.

Another important question to ask is "Do I really need this chemical?" Often chemical storerooms contain chemicals, equipment, and other substances inherited from decades ago. If you have not used the chemical in the past five years, then it is very unlikely that you will ever use it and it should be disposed of properly. The rationale in most districts is probably, that my budget is so low that I cannot afford to buy chemicals and other equipment later because the money will not be available. Therefore, I will buy large quantities when the funds are available and store them until I need them. This practice, borne out of necessity, carries with it risks for both teacher and student. Teachers should examine their current practices and then sit down with the department head and the administrator in charge of the department's budget and problem-solve to arrive at a solution where funds can be rolled over into different years to promote current ordering and shipment of laboratory materials. Unlike previous years, shipping methods have significantly improved, with most supplies being shipped in a few days.

---

250. *Id.*

Usher v. Upper Saint Clair School Dist.,

87 A.2d 1022 (Pa. Cmwlth. 1985)

Concepts:

- Immunity

Facts:

  James Usher, a student in a chemistry class, was out of his seat and watching a demonstration performed by his teacher next to a sink counter where the experiment was being conducted. The teacher accidentally dropped a flaming beaker he was holding and some of the flaming liquid splashed on James' face burning him. The student sues the school district for the injuries to his face, alleging in his complaint that the teacher was negligent in failing to take adequate measures to control the area immediately surrounding the experiment. The school district raised, as a defense to liability, governmental immunity under a provision of that state's Political Subdivision Torts Claims Act, and moved to dismiss the case by summary judgment. The trial court grants the request dismissing the case. The student appeals on the ground that the negligent conduct of the teacher was directly related to the care, custody, or control of real property and therefore falls within a specific exception to governmental immunity in this case.

Issue:

1. Whether the alleged negligent conduct was directly related to the care, custody, or control of real property, one of the specific exceptions to governmental immunity enumerated in the act precluding summary judgment and dismissal of the complaint?

Holding:

1. No. "[A]lleged negligence of school teacher in failing to properly conduct a chemistry experiment and in failing to take adequate measures to protect student from injuries sustained when teacher dropped a flaming beaker which splashed flaming liquid on student's face was not related to care, custody, or control of real property and, hence, did not preclude school district from raising immunity as a defense to student's negligence action."[251]

Analysis:

  The court in a brief opinion indicated that the exception in the statute related to the care of real estate, and nothing in the plaintiff's complaint alleged the failure of the teacher to control real estate. The court believed the allegations amounted to nothing more than a failure to properly supervise, and as such subject to the defense of governmental immunity.

Comment:

  This case and the next case are important because they reveal that there are a few states that have immunity for professional negligence. Teachers must be aware of the local laws that affect them for better or worse.

---

251. Usher v. Upper Saint Clair School Dist., 487 A.2d 1022 (Pa. Cmwlth. 1985).

Duross v. Freeman,

831 S.W.2d 354 (Tex. App.—San Antonio 1992)

Concepts:

- Immunity

Facts:

Leslie Miller, a middle school student, was participating in an experiment using potassium hydroxide (KOH)[252] "a dangerously caustic chemical compound."[253] Some of the dry KOH came in contact with Leslie's thigh. However, because the KOH was in crystalline form it did not begin to burn her until it encountered the moisture of her skin. Because KOH is an alkaline substance, "the effects of the injury were not felt until the injury had progressed."[254] Later in the day, Leslie sought out the school nurse for help who told her there was no time to help her, and sent her home. By the time Leslie got home, the injury was severe. Immediately upon reaching her home, she went to receive medical treatment. The parents later sued the school science teacher and the nurse for negligence in supervising the handling of the dangerous chemical and for delay in treating the injury as well as for injuries sustained by the delay in treatment that caused "severe, permanent, disabling, and disfiguring injury requiring reconstructive surgery."[255]

Issue:

1. Whether the student was precluded from pursuing negligence claims against the science teacher (for negligence in supervising the handling of a dangerous chemical) and the nurse (for delay in treating the injury)?

Holding:

1. Yes. Under the Texas Education Code, "a professional school employee is not personally liable for acts done within the scope of employment, and which involve the exercise of judgment or discretion, except in circumstances where disciplining a student, the employee uses excessive force or his negligence results in bodily injury to the student."[256] "While we sympathize with Leslie's plight . . . we are, as an intermediate appellate court, bound to follow the majority holdings of [the Texas Supreme Court]."[257]

Analysis:

This case is not as much about negligence as it is about the policy decisions of a legislature and the duty of a court to follow precedent. Specifically, the case turns on the question of whether school personnel are immune from ordinary negligence. The court majority is very sensitive to the fact that Leslie was severely injured by apparently a negligent teacher and nurse. What troubles the majority most is where the Texas Legislature had drawn the line in deciding when an injured student had the right to go to court for injuries sustained by a negligent school employee. As the author of the opinion notes:

> For this author at least, it is troubling from a public policy standpoint that our corporate citizens have unfettered access to the courts for redress of perceived tortuous grievances, but children, whose well being has been entrusted to fiduciaries known as parents and teachers do not have access . . . . Recognizing that school personnel are conscientious, careful adults an overwhelming

---

252. The court misidentifies the chemical formula of potassium hydroxide in the case as POH.
253. Duross v. Freeman, 831 S.W.2d 354, 355 (Tex. App.—San Antonio 1992).
254. *Id.*
255. *Id.*
256. *Id.* at 356.
257. *Id.*

majority of the time, they, like other human beings, have occasional lapses of reasonable care for which the law has developed a remedy known as the negligence cause of action.[258]

The court goes on to intimate that they do not believe that there "should be wholesale litigation between teachers and students" but there should be some attempt to address what the court calls "unusual and extreme circumstances" such as the one before the court and calls on either the Texas Supreme Court or the Texas Legislature to recognize the wisdom and justice of providing some remedy in these circumstances.

In a scathing concurrence [259], Justice Peeples identifies the effect of removing immunity for ordinary negligence:

> A statute making it easier for students to sue teachers and administrators would pit them against each other, diverting money, time, and mental effort from education to litigation. Schools would pay a high price when those involved in litigation (and perhaps their colleagues) gave depositions instead of lectures; produced documents instead of learning; attended trials instead of classes; listened to legal advice instead of student reports. While the lawsuit inched its way toward trial, the matter would occupy the minds of everyone, diverting attention and mental energy from the education task. . . . [T]he student body would gossip about the lawsuit. The authority of all educators would be undermined. We would read more articles asking why Johnny can't read, and whether our students have fallen further behind the Japanese. Teachers might wonder why they took up teaching instead of the law. . . .[260]

Comment:

The concurrence by Justice Peeples reads like a dissent and provides a strong rationale as to why science teachers should receive limited immunity from acts of ordinary negligence. However, to the parent faced with this situation, the denial of the right to have a child's serious injuries redressed, particularly if that child is maimed, seems particularly unfair. Insulating teachers and school personnel from their own acts of negligence, removes an important component from the duty of local school boards and their districts to act reasonably to ensure the safety of students and employees on their campuses and permits them to shirk their responsibilities to provide such safe environments.

---

258. *Id.*
259. In a concurrence, the author agrees with the decision of the court, but not the reasons for arriving at that decision, or just has something else to say that needs, in their opinion, to be said.
260. Duross v. Freeman, 831 S.W.2d 354, 357 (Tex. App.—San Antonio 1992).

District of Columbia v. Howell,

607 A.2d 501 (D.C. App. 1992)

Concepts:

- Administration Responsibility
- Age Level–Appropriate Experiments
- Duty To Instruct and Warn
- Duty To Supervise
- Educational Value of an Experiment
- Inappropriate Experiment Selection
- Safety Funding
- Science Funding
- Teacher Inexperience
- Teacher Training

Facts:

Nine-year-old Dedrick Howell attended a summer school enrichment program designed to provide hands–on education for gifted and talented eight and nine-year-old children. The program's teacher, A. Louis Jagoe, held a master's degree in chemistry and a Ph.D. candidate at The American University. Before the start of the program, the teacher had informed the staff that he wanted to do a "luminescence experiment, a "cold-pack" experiment, and that he wanted to make sparklers with the children."[261]

At the beginning of the class on making sparklers, the teacher "distributed his recipe for sparklers to the children and also wrote it on the black board. "Along with other chemical ingredients, the recipe called for the use of potassium perchlorate as the oxidizing agent. Potassium perchlorate was described at trial as an extremely unstable and highly volatile chemical often used to make rocket fuel. Commercially made sparklers are not made with potassium perchlorate.

> The children scooped the chemicals, including the potassium perchlorate, out of jars, ground up the mixture in mortars. While they were combining the chemicals, Jagoe ignited three different chemical mixtures at the front of the room with a butane lighter. . . . The children continued to grind the material, while a counselor distributed pieces of metal hangers to be dipped into the mixture at a later time. Dedrick Howell was specifically told not to dip the hanger in the material until instructed to do so. Moments later the chemicals exploded in front of Dedrick. The chemicals burned at 5,000 degrees Fahrenheit, and Dedrick was burned over 25 percent of his body including his hands, arms, chest, and face. He was rushed to Children's Hospital. His burn treatment in the following months included several stays in the hospital and rehabilitation centers, multiple skin grafts, surgery to reopen the scars that constricted his movement and circulation, painful physical therapy that was continued at home, both in-patient and out-patient psychotherapy.[262]

Dedrick and his parents sued the District of Columbia and the American University for injuries sustained. After a 10-day trail, a jury awarded eight million dollars to Dedrick individually for pain and suffering, one million dollars to his parents for past and future medical expenses, and one million dollars to each of Dedrick's parents individually for loss of parent–child consortium. The jury found the District of Columbia (which runs the schools) negligent under several alternative theories:

---

261. District of Columbia v. Howell, 607 A.2d 501, 503 (D.C. App. 1992).
262. *Id.* at 504.

1. The principal of the school had failed to exercise ordinary care for the safety of the children in the summer program;

2. The director of the program had failed to exercise ordinary care and because he was an apparent agent of the District, his negligence was attributable to the District;

3. The chemistry teacher, Jagoe, was also negligent and his negligence was attributable to the District because he was an independent contractor engaged in an inherently dangerous activity;

4. The director and Jagoe had violated District of Columbia regulations against manufacturing fireworks; and

5. The district, by permitting the presence and use of dangerous chemicals, failed to maintain the school premises in a reasonably safe manner.[263]

     The District appealed.

Issue:

1. Whether the District of Columbia was liable for the negligence of its independent contractor, Jagoe?

Holding:

1. Yes. "Because we conclude that there was ample evidence from which the jury could properly find Jagoe to be an independent contractor performing inherently dangerous work for the District of Columbia, thus making the District vicariously liable for his negligence, it is unnecessary for us to consider other grounds of liability."

Analysis:

     In holding the District vicariously liable for Jagoe, an independent contractor, the court concluded that while "an employer generally is not liable for injuries to third parties caused by an independent contractor over whom (or whose work) the employer has reserved no control"[264] there are exceptions for those who employ an independent contractor to do work of any kind that involves "a risk, recognizable in advance, of physical harm to others which is inherent in the work itself, or normally to be expected in the ordinary course of the usual or prescribed way of doing it, or that the employer has special reason to contemplate such a risk under the particular circumstances under which the work is to be done."[265] The court on this basis that concluded that "a jury reasonably could find the required risk of physical harm and knowledge of the risk by the District of Columbia, because the principal, the District's supervisory employee, knew that Jagoe intended to make sparklers with young children as part of the "hands-on" chemistry class [and] . . . therefore had reason to know of the specific risks likely to arise from the manner in which the contractor performed his assigned [job].[266] Charged with knowledge of the danger, the [principal] reasonably could have been expected to prohibit the experiment or at least to inquire beforehand about the manner in which Jagoe intended to conduct it.[267]

Comment:

     This case had a couple of interesting twists. The teacher in this case, Jagoe, was declared bankrupt during the trial and was dismissed as a party.[268] That is, the person responsible for the little boy's injuries was dismissed from the lawsuit.

---

263. *Id.* at 502.
264. *Id.*
265. *Id.* at 505.
266. *Id.*
267. *Id.* at 506.
268. *Id.* at 502. fn.1.

This case also demonstrates that the principal of the school needs to be aware of what is going on in the science classroom. Testimony during the trial indicated that the principal had in her possession the following facts:

1. The principal had learned during the employment interview that Jagoe intended to make sparklers and Jagoe had repeated that he intended to make sparklers during a meeting of staff where the principal was present;

2. While the students were performing the experiment, the principal had stepped into the room for a moment and observed the children wearing goggles or glasses;

3. She also observed Jagoe lighting the chemicals, with a fire extinguisher on the table next to him. The ignition created what she described as a "puff" about the size of a baseball, accompanied by a flash of colored light.

4. The principal acknowledged that she had never been in an elementary school classroom where the children had been required to wear goggles.

5. When the principal was asked if she was surprised that Jagoe was igniting materials in front of eight and nine year olds, one of them her own son, she stated that she was not really surprised but was unsure of what was going on.[269]

These facts, according to the court, made it reasonable to conclude that the principal, and therefore the District, reasonably should have known of the risk of the teacher's activity. The short lesson offered by this case is that if someone is seriously hurt, the deep pocket is going to pay. Districts need to be aware that in extreme circumstances, involving major injuries, a court will, as long as there is no established case precedent or statutes to the contrary, bend the law to achieve justice. When compared with Duross v. Freeman, 831 S.W.2d 354 (Tex. App. San Antonio 1992) *supra*, the Howell court appears much more willing to impose liability on the District, whereas in Freeman the court felt that in order to preserve justice they needed to follow case precedent established by the Texas Supreme Court.

The appellate court also reversed part of the damage award to the parents holding that the award to the parents for loss of parent–child consortium must be reversed because the District of Columbia did not recognize that type of claim. In addition, the court reversed the award for future medical damages because the evidence did not support the award.

Howell provides guidance for science teachers as well. All teachers need to be aware of the safety issues involved in every lab they perform with students. At first reading, the teacher appears to be incredibly lacking in judgment. How can a Ph.D. candidate in chemistry believe that the sparkler lesson was appropriate for eight- and nine-year-olds? In addition, why was he permitting these students to grind with a mortar potassium perchlorate that he should have known was highly unstable? The key to understanding this decision is not by questioning the teacher's knowledge of chemistry, but rather, by examining his experience as a teacher. Jagoe was young, excited about teaching, and highly motivated to share what he knew was an exciting experiment with his students. The problem was that Jagoe overestimated the level of maturity of his students and the risks involved in using apparently large amounts of an explosive chemical. He did not look at the capabilities of his students because he did not know how to assess them. An experienced teacher would not have made this mistake. This was a rookie teacher making a huge error that unfortunately maimed a small child. The questions really in need of attention in this case are those related to the training and supervision of teachers. Just because someone has a degree in a subject does not mean that individual is now qualified to teach. More importantly, chemistry teachers need continuing training on safety related to their subject matter. Very little training is available on the safe handling of chemicals, safe experimental design, and managing students in the science classroom.

---

269. *Id.* at 504.

Finally, principals should be very guarded about underfunding science labs when teachers request additional safety equipment. As this case and several of the other cases discussed in this section illustrate, when the school district does not provide proper safety equipment and a safe learning environment, a court is willing to find liability for those negligent acts.

Cazsador by Cazsador v. Greene Cent. Sch.

220 A.D. 2d 862, 632 N.Y.S.2d 267 (3d Dept. 1995) *amended on reh'g,* 1996 N.Y. App, Div. Lexis 128, *appeal denied, without op.* 87 N.Y.2d 812, 664 N.Y.S.2d 145, 666 N.E.2d 1059 (1996)

Concepts:

- Duty To Instruct and Warn

Facts:

Donna Cazsador brought a negligence action against the school for damages sustained when, during a frog dissection, some of the preservative present in the tissues of the frog came in contact with her face and arms causing " a burning sensation and stinging discomfort when the affected areas came in contact with perspiration, hot water, and sunlight, and that red blotches would appear following physical exertion such as jogging or running" more than six years after the incident. At trial a jury awarded Donna $20,000 for past and $10,000 for future pain and suffering. On the main action, liability was apportioned 10 percent against Donna and 90 percent against the defendant school. The school in turn sued the frog supplier (Ward's Natural Science Establishment, Inc.) for contribution and at trial liability was divided up with the school being held 15 percent responsible and the frog supplier 85 percent responsible. The school and Ward's both appealed the decision.

Issue:

1. Whether school and frog supplier were negligent in failing to provide a warning of the dangers associated with long-term contact of the chemical preserving the frog with human skin?

Holding:

1. Yes. Evidence supported a jury finding that the preservative constituted a dangerous product because it contained varying concentrations of acetone, formalin, and methanol and it was "undisputed that neither [Wards] or the [school] provided any warning of the dangers associated with the solution's long-term contact with human skin."[270]

Analysis:

The appellate court neatly disposes of the argument that Donna's injuries were not foreseeable. In short, the court ignores the fact that there had been no other reported cases where chemical burns had resulted from human contact with the solution. More distressingly for science teachers, once the court concluded that the preservative was a dangerous product, it did not matter that the science teacher had taken appropriate precautions of providing students with protective eyewear and rinsing the frogs in clear water before handing them out.

Comment:

This case illustrates a fundamental principle that teachers must think about when they plan experiments for the classroom: Does the experiment involve some type of chemical that a court might consider a dangerous product? The problem with the Greene decision is that at the time, there were possibly a million such preserved frogs throughout the nation, in every part of the United States. The court, in reaching its decision, incorrectly applied the law in this area by declaring the product defective and unreasonably dangerous based on a single instance of an abnormal allergic reaction. While clearly the court was sending a message that Wards should make the product safer, that is not in fact what happened after this case. What Wards and every other biological and chemical supply company do now is provide

---

270. Cazsador by Cazsador v. Greene Cent. Sch. 632 N.Y.S. 2d 267 (A.D. 3 Dept. 1995).

warnings about the dangers of the product. This case is not about negligence, for in fact the teacher was not negligent at all in the performance of the duty of care. The teacher provided safety equipment, and then rinsed excess preservative off the frogs.

The court's message to science teachers, and the jury's message in awarding damages, is that the teacher (and the supplier) must provide warnings of potential hazards. The teacher must think about potential hazards to certain chemicals in the laboratory setting. The supplier has a duty to warn the teacher of potential hazards and the teacher has a duty to read those warnings and communicate the potential for harm to the students as appropriate. Material Safety Data Sheets ("MSDS") fulfill the manufacturer's purpose of providing useful information that teachers have a duty to read. Having such safety sheets in the classroom providing relevant safety information to the teacher may relieve the supplier/manufacturer from liability and expose the teacher to liability for the negligent failure to read the information related to the chemical, and pass that information on to the students. This entire case would not have happened if the supplier had printed warnings about the preservative, the teacher had then read those warnings, and finally communicated those warnings to the student. The case should also send a message to every science teacher, that even those products that they are most familiar with can, on rare occasions, have unintended and unforeseen consequences that even reasonable efforts to prevent harm might not work. Allergic reactions are common and foreseeable. Here the lesson is, if a teacher even remotely thinks that someone could get hurt performing an experiment, the teacher should warn the student. Teachers should require students to list the chemicals used in the laboratory in the prelaboratory report, and include the safety information they have researched using the MSDS. If time is a factor, teachers could photocopy the relevant safety information and provide it with the laboratory information given to students and reviewed with them before the lab.

B. Shop Cases

The following cases are included because they add to the discussion of liability for failure of the teacher, administrator, or school board to conform their actions to the relevant duty of care. It is important to note that these cases take place in other settings, but are relevant to the duty issues found in chemistry and other science classrooms.

Goodman v. Pasadena City High School Unified Dist.,

4 Cal. App.2d 65, 40 P.2d 854 (1935)

Concepts:

- Eye Safety
- Negligence Analysis

Facts:

Le Roy was a 13-year-old student at a junior high school who was in the second semester of an auto mechanics class. Just before the accident, Le Roy, having disobeyed his teacher's direction to go sit in a corner away from the other working students and "write up his lesson,"[271] was standing approximately 12 feet away from a vise with a group of other boys, watching three boys pound aluminum in a vise. After watching for about three minutes, a piece of the aluminum broke off and the projectile struck Le Roy in the eye, destroying it. The student sued the school alleging that the school was negligent in not requiring the students to wear goggles while in the shop. At trial, Le Roy is awarded $15,000 for his injuries, and his father receives $2,000 for injuries to his son. The school district appealed.

Issue:

1. Whether the school district was liable for failing to require the shop students to wear goggles?

Holding:

1. No. The school district was not liable for failing to require goggles for shop students because, as the court pointed out, there was "no proof that any school authority of the district knew that aluminum shattered when pounded, although the pupils had been advised as to the danger in striking steel implements together."[272] In addition, the court noted that the "students had all been advised to wear goggles when working around the emery wheel, but at no other work in the shop was it deemed advantageous to wear goggles. Finally, it was not shown that any instructor knew that goggles were necessary for the safety of a spectator within the shop."[273]

Analysis:

This early case illustrates in the view of the court that there was no "substantial evidence" in the record that "there existed such danger which was known, or ought to have been known, to the authorities." A modern analysis would find this same practice negligence. This case demonstrates a central principal in negligence analysis. As more information becomes known about a particular practice, and as standards in the industry change, the failure to conform one's practice to the industry standard is evidence of negligence. In some instances, even if the industry standard is being met, a court using benefit–burden analysis described earlier may conclude that the burden on the individual to change his practices is outweighed by the harm that may occur if the practice is not changed. Applied to this case, the burden on the school district to provide safety goggles is minimal compared to the harm that might result from them not being provided, such as the loss or destruction of an eye.[274]

---

271. Goodman v. Pasadena City High School Unified Dist., 4 Cal.App.2d 65, 66, 40 P.2d 854 (1935).
272. *Id.*
273. *Id.* at 66–7.
274. *See* Scott v. Independent School Dist. #709, 256 N.W.2d 485 (Minn. 1977).

Ohman v. Board of Education of City of New York,

300 N.Y. 306, 90 N.E.2d 474 (N.Y. 1949), *reh'g denied,* 301 N.Y. 662, 93 N.E. 2d 927 (1950)

Concepts:

- Duty To Supervise

Facts:

On November 15, 1938, at about 2:15 p.m., Herbert Ohman, a thirteen-year-old pupil in drawing class 7-B, at Public School No. 238, Brooklyn, . . . sustained a severe permanent injury when struck in the left eye by a lead pencil. The pencil had been thrown by a classmate in the direction of a third classmate with the remark "Here is your pencil." The boy for whom it was intended ducked and the pencil hit the plaintiff who was standing directly behind him. The accident occurred while the teacher in charge was temporarily absent from the classroom for the purpose of sorting and storing in a corridor closet an issue of schoolroom supplies, a routine task forming part of her usual duties.[275] Ohman sues the teacher and the school district for negligence. At trial Ohman wins, and defendants appeal. The appeals court reverses the trial court and directs a verdict in favor of the defendants and dismissal of the complaint from which Ohman appeals.

Issue:

1.   Whether the teacher's absence from the room was the proximate cause of Herbert's eye injury?

Holding:

1.   No. "The most favorable inference . . . is that the teacher was not in the room when the accident occurred. Nonetheless, it does not follow that such absence was the proximate producing cause of the injury, which was due, as we see it, to the tossed pencil. Whether it was done mischievously and heedlessly or wantonly and willfully, or with the serious purpose of returning the pencil to its owner, it was the act of an intervening third party which under the circumstances could hardly have been anticipated in the reasonable exercise of the teacher's legal duty toward the plaintiff." [276] "There is no proof of similar accidents, nor can anyone seriously contend that a pencil in the hands of a school pupil is a dangerous instrumentality. This is one of those events which could occur equally as well in the presence of the teacher as during her absence."[277] Judgment affirmed.

Analysis:

In reaching its decision, New York's highest court stated that:

The testimony as to the length of time the teacher was out of the room is conflicting (which is not at all surprising as nine years elapsed between the date of the accident and the trial) but whether for "more than an hour" as contended by the plaintiff or "less than a minute" as shown by the defendant's witnesses is wholly immaterial."[278]

Ignoring the lack of supervision entirely, the court goes on to say that

it does not follow that such absence was the proximate producing cause of the injury, which was due, as we see it, to the tossed pencil. Whether it was done mischievously and heedlessly or wantonly and willfully, or with the serious purpose of returning the pencil to its owner, it was the

---

275. These are the facts offered by the majority opinion in support of its holding that the teacher's absence was not the proximate cause of Herbert's injury.
276. Ohman v. Board of Education of City of New York, 300 N.Y. 306, 308–9, 90 N.E.2d 474, 475 (N.Y. 1949).
277. *Id.* at 310.
278. *Id.* at 308.

act of an intervening third party which under the circumstances could hardly have been anticipated in the reasonable exercise of the teacher's legal duty toward the plaintiff.[279]

The two dissenting judges in this case in a strongly worded, lengthy, and sarcastic dissent noted:

When a large number of children are gathered together in a single classroom, without any effective control or supervision, it may reasonably be anticipated that certain of them may so act as to inflict an unintentional injury upon themselves or their classmates. Children have a known proclivity to act impulsively without thought of the possibilities of danger. It is precisely this lack of mature judgment which makes supervision so vital.[280]

The dissent also pointed out the apparent failure of the majority to include the relevant facts before the court in making its decision:

The facts, thus ascertained, are these: Herbert T. Ohman (hereinafter called plaintiff) was a pupil in class 7-B of a Brooklyn public school. On the day of the accident, he was 13 years of age. At 1:00 p.m. on that day, his class met in room 411 for what was scheduled to be a double period of drawing instruction. The teacher referred to above was supposed to be in charge of the drawing class in that room. We shall refer to her hereafter as teacher.

Plaintiff, together with other boys, had been picked by a lower grade teacher who was in charge of school supplies to assist in carrying such supplies from a ground-floor stockroom to different portions of the building. At about 1:15 p.m., plaintiff delivered some supplies, i.e., "a few baskets and some books that came in the baskets," to room 411. The teacher was not there at the time. Another pupil, one Lupo, was standing in front of the classroom. He said that the teacher was out and that she had left him in charge of the class. At that time, a few of the pupils "were fooling around and talking in the class." They were "throwing balls of paper and smacking somebody in the back of the head . . . and things of that sort." Plaintiff left the supplies and returned to the stockroom. There, he was given another load of supplies which he carried to the library—also located on the fourth floor. En route, at about 1:45 p.m., he saw the teacher sitting on a stool inside a supply closet or storeroom on the fourth floor. She was sorting paper on shelves. This storeroom was about 48 from the nearest door of room 411 and was around an L-shaped corner. It was about 25 feet from the nearest door of room 411 to the corner and about 22 or 23 feet from the corner to the storeroom.

Plaintiff then made two more trips to the library with supplies. Each time, he passed the storeroom and saw the teacher there on a stool or stepladder. On his next trip, he again delivered supplies to room 411. When he entered the room, the teacher was still absent. He observed that the wicker baskets he had previously deposited there "were being kicked around in the front of the room, just the same way as it was the last time. 'The pupils' were throwing things around and talking to each other and doing as they pleased." While he was sorting out the supplies at the platform in front of the room, plaintiff was hit in the leg by a basket that had been kicked. He then brought some of the supplies to the storeroom where the teacher was still working. At her direction, he put them on the floor and returned to the supply room on the ground floor. This time, he was given a stack of six long boxes containing paint. He had to rest his chin on the topmost box to keep it from tipping to the side. In this fashion, he carried them up to room 411. It was about 2:15 p.m. Plaintiff was preceded into the room by one De Mauro, another 13-year-old pupil, who was also bearing supplies. De Mauro dropped his supplies in the front of the room and started to walk to the rear by way of the center aisle. Plaintiff then entered the room by the rear door and started to walk up the

279. *Id.* at 308–9.
280. *Id.* at 314.

center aisle. The teacher was still absent from the room and the children, as before, were walking around, throwing things, "fooling around" and "having a lot of fun in her absence." At that point, Lupo, the boy who had been left in charge of the class, called to De Mauro, "Here is your pencil." With that, he threw the pencil at De Mauro. It was an overhand throw and it was fast. De Mauro ducked out of the way, and plaintiff, who was behind him, was hit in the left eye by the point of the pencil which came spinning through the air at him. The point entered the center of his eyeball, lacerating the cornea and piercing the lens capsule behind the cornea. After many operations, he is practically sightless in that eye.[281]

The dissent also took issue with the principal of the school's testimony as to the adequacy of the supervision:

The principal testified that "If the teacher was required physically to go outside the immediate confines of her classroom in connection with her teaching and was still consciously supervising the classroom, she violated no regulation." He said that the storeroom 50 feet down the hall and around the corner was within "the immediate confines" of the classroom. If the teacher were there for *five* minutes, he said it would depend upon the teacher and the class as to whether there was proper supervision. He admitted that "If the teacher neglected her class during that entire 10-minute period, I would not regard that as proper supervision." Nor would he regard it as proper supervision, he stated, if the teacher were away for *an hour and fifteen minutes.*[282]

Finally, the dissent suggests this "better reasoned" holding to the case:
There can be no doubt that the jury was justified in finding, upon this evidence, that the teacher was absent from her classroom for an hour and fifteen minutes, i.e., from one o'clock, when the class met, until two fifteen, when the accident occurred; and further, that such failure, under the standards set by the principal, constituted a failure of supervision or improper supervision on her part. Likewise, the jury was justified in finding that the principal was negligent in failing to adopt adequate regulations, ensuring proper supervision of classes, in his school and in assigning or permitting the performance of additional duties by the teacher, during scheduled teaching hours, so that she was away from her classroom for an hour and fifteen minutes.[283]

The dissent felt that it was foreseeable that a classroom full of children would be playing and become unruly if left alone, unsupervised, and unattended for 75 minutes. As such, the dissent would reverse the appellate court decision and remand for a new trial.

In what can best be described as an exclamation point on the case, the dissent summarized the very reason why chemistry and other teachers need to take their duty seriously: "Parents do not send their children to school to be returned to them maimed because of the absence of proper supervision or the abandonment of supervision."[284]

---

281. *Id.* at 310–11.
282. *Id.* at 311.
283. *Id.* at 312. The dissent stated that
    [h]ere, the jury could find that, because of the teacher's absence from the classroom for over an hour, the pupils became progressively more restless and unruly, that they were throwing and kicking things around the classroom, and that Lupo, the appointed monitor, in keeping with the prevailing spirit of horseplay and disorder, threw the pencil at De Mauro, who ducked out of the way so that it spun past him and hit plaintiff in the left eye. It is a legitimate inference upon this record that the exercise of greater supervision, or, indeed of any supervision, on the part of the teacher would have averted the accident and its tragic aftermath. *Id.*
284. *Id.* at 310.

Comment:

Ohman, decided in 1949, would not have turned out the same way today. As school has become larger and more crowded, a fact noted by the Ohman dissent, [285] the need for supervision is increased. In short, the more bodies in the room, the greater the need for increased supervision.

---

285. The dissent identified a developing trend regarding population:

In New York City, as time passes and we become more communal in practice as a result of population growth, economic pressure and other factors, we shall be more and more dependent upon kindergarten and grade school teachers, as well as baby sitters and day care nursery school directors or nurses in the basements of New York City housing and similar developments, for child care as well as education of our children. In New York City, the situation materially differs in degree from that existing throughout the rest of the State. The Legislature seems to have recognized this fact and, as a result, in 1937, added two sections to the Education Law [which] … provided for the direct liability of a board of education in a city having a population of one million or more inhabitants [and a section that] imposed a somewhat less direct liability upon a board of education, trustee or trustees in any school district having a population of less than one million. Consequently, a high standard of supervision and care in the crowded schools of New York City, requiring as they do part-time classes in order to accommodate the number of pupils, should be imposed upon principals and teachers. *Id.* at 311.

Ross v. San Francisco Unified School Dist.,

120 Cal.App.2d 185, 260 P.2d. 663 (1953)

Concepts:

- Duty To Instruct and Warn
- Duty To Supervise
- Eye Safety
- Maturity of a Child
- Safety Equipment

Facts:

Vernon Ross, a 15-year-old ninth grade junior high student, is asked by his shop teacher, Ferrari, to polish the teacher's horse reins (personal property) which were made of leather and had silver rings along the length of each rein. The teacher directed the student to use a high-speed circular buffing machine in another teacher's class. On January 4, 1951, Ross started working on the reins alone in the metal shop. Ferrari had let him into the room and turned on the machine, which required a key. Ross worked for a half hour without incident and left. Ferrari did not warn Ross about the danger of working with a flexible leather strap. The teacher had instructed Ross in the proper use of the buffing machine in the past.

The next day, Ross again was directed by Ferrari to complete the job he had started the previous day. Ross went by himself to the metal shop, where another teacher was taking roll to begin a class. Ross went to the tool locker where the safety goggles were kept. He had obtained a pair of goggles from the tool locker the day before, and on this day only found two pairs of goggles. One of the pairs of goggles was obviously broken, and so Ross selected the other pair. The teacher finished taking roll, and came over and turned on the buffing machine for Ross. Before beginning the buffing operation, Ross attempted to put on the goggles, but found that a strap was broken. Ross immediately reported to the teacher in the room that the goggles were broken. The teacher told Ross to go get another pair from the locker. Ross searched several lockers and cupboards not finding a single pair, except for the broken pair he had first spotted. Ross returned to the buffing machine and started buffing the reins without goggles. He worked on the reins for about 15 minutes before the accident occurred.[286] No one approached Ross while he was working. The teacher was in the middle of the room and remained there at all times. "Vernon polished all of the silver rings on one of the reins, and was half way through the other, when the accident happened. The rein upon which Vernon was working became entangled in the buffing wheel, causing the long leather band to revolve rapidly. A sliver of the buckle flew off and pierced Vernon's left eye,"[287] resulting in permanent destruction of the eye. Ross sues the district for negligence in failing to properly maintain the buffer and supervise its operation.

At trial, the court, after testimony from Ross that:

1. He knew that "safety goggles should be worn while operating the buffer";[288]

2. When he had taken the sheet metal course, he "had been instructed upon safety precautions, and was given a test upon safety regulations";[289]

3. He "had always been instructed always to use safety goggles when he operated the buffer";[289] and

---

286. Other testimony indicates that he may have worked on the reins for as long as 30 minutes before the accident occurred. Ross v. San Francisco Unified School Dist., 120 Cal.App.2d 185,189, 260 P.2d. 663, 666 (1953).
287. Ross v. San Francisco Unified School Dist., 120 Cal.App.2d 185,189, 260 P.2d. 663, 666 (1953).
288. *Id.* at 190.
289. *Id.*

4. "[P]rior to the accident he had used the buffer some 75 or 80 times, and on each occasion had worn goggles,"[290] directed a non-suit on the ground that such evidence demonstrated that Ross was guilty of contributory negligence as a matter of law. Ross appealed.

Issue:

1. Whether Ross's evidence that he had been told to wear goggles and knew he should have worn goggles was sufficient evidence to support a finding that Ross was contributorily negligent as a matter of law.

Holding:

1. No. "[I]t seems clear that whether Vernon's actions, under the circumstances, constituted contributory negligence or whether defendant was negligent in its maintenance of or supervision over the buffing machine or in its supervision of Vernon's actions while operating the machine and what was the proximate cause of the accident, were fact questions that should have been left to the jury."[291]

Analysis:

The appellate court, carefully stepped around the contributory negligence issue. Recognizing the harshness that would result from such application, courts had chipped away at its strict application by carving out a child exception. For the science teacher, the court's analysis of the facts provides some important lessons. The appellate court indicated that

> [t]he above evidence would *obviously* support findings that the school district was guilty of negligence in its maintenance of and supervision over the buffer. The failure of the defendant to have an adequate supply of unbroken goggles on hand, the failure of Friersen to keep a watch on Vernon to see that he had found and was using goggles, the failure of Ferrari or any one else to warn Vernon of the danger of the long flexible reins becoming enmeshed in the buffer would support findings that defendant was negligent and that such negligence was a proximate cause of the accident. It is also true that Vernon's evidence to the effect that he had been told to wear glasses and knew that they should be worn *might* support a finding of contributory negligence.[292] [Emphasis added.]

The court, citing a long string of previous court precedent, then gave the minor plaintiff a boost:

> The barring of a plaintiff, particularly a minor, on the ground that he has been guilty of contributory negligence, as a matter of law, is a rare occurrence, and will only be done in the clearest of cases." . . . In the instant case, we are dealing with a minor. In determining whether a minor has been guilty of contributory negligence as a matter of law, a much more lenient rule in favor of the minor is applied than applies to adults. . . .In <u>Foley v. California Horseshoe Co.</u>, 115 Cal. 184, 47 P. 42, the court held that a different standard applied to a boy of 14 operating machinery than would apply to an adult, and held that even where such boy proceeded with a certain process in the face of a known danger, he was not barred, as a matter of law, because his knowledge of the danger and the precautions that should have been taken were not inconsistent with that lack of judgment that creates the need for the special protection of children.[293] Thus,

---

290. *Id.*
291. *Id.* at 193.
292. *Id.* at 190.
293. The court goes on to add:
  It would be barbarous to hold them to the same accountability as is held the adult employee, who is an independent, free agent. Their conduct is to be judged in accordance with the limited knowledge, experience, and judgment which they possess when called upon to act. * * *
  So here the child might well be expected to comprehend the likelihood of accident, and to know how to provide against it, when engaged in his usual employment in front of the machine. But when he is sent to the rear of it, and in among the wheels and mechanism, to perform a novel duty, we cannot say as matter of law that he entered upon

mere knowledge of the existence of the danger will not necessarily bar a child while it might bar an adult.[294]

Finally the court, hammering home the point that no matter how large a mistake a child makes they are, after all, only children, cites <u>Mastrangelo v. West Side U. H. School Dist.</u>, 2 Cal.2d 540, 42 P.2d 634, wherein

> a 16-year-old high school student was nonsuited in an action brought for his injuries received in a class chemical explosion. The boy had picked out the wrong chemical from the shelf, failed to follow the printed instructions in the textbook, and mixed the chemicals contrary to such instructions. Nevertheless, the judgment of nonsuit was reversed, it being held that, because the teacher knew that the boy was going to perform the experiment and did not supervise him while performing it, it could not be held that the boy was guilty of contributory negligence as a matter of law.[295]

Comment:

This case is instructive for a number of reasons. First, chemistry teachers should recognize that their duty of care in some cases extends to rooms beyond where they are present (Ferrari in this case) and in some cases extends to students working in their room who are not their own students (the metal shop teacher). Supervision is a primary concern of the court in this case. The outcome would have been different in this case if Ferrari had called the metal shop teacher and said, "Please watch Ross." The metal shop teacher's error was in not ensuring that Ross had working goggles. If the goggles had not been broken, then a court would have looked at this case differently. Second, the court demonstrated a principle of law applicable today: Children are not held to the same standard as adults for the mistakes they commit that causes harm to *themselves*. There is a strong public policy supporting that children need the protection of society from the negligent actions of others, but also from their own negligent actions.

---

its performance with a full appreciation of the increased dangers and risks, and with sufficient judgment to know how to avoid them. These matters and the further question whether the minor duly exercised such judgment, as he possessed, must, therefore, as a rule, be left as considerations of fact for the jury's determination; and it would be an exceptional case which would present them as unmixed questions of law for the determination of the court. <u>Ross v. San Francisco Unified School Dist.</u>, 120 Cal.App.2d 185, 192, 260 P.2d. 663, 667 (1953).

294. *Id.* at 191–2.
295. *Id.* at 192–3.

Lilienthal v. San Leandro Unified School Dist.,

139 Cal.App.2d 453, 293 P.2d 889 1st Dist. (1956)

Concepts:

- Class Size
- Duty To Supervise

Facts:

Leonard Lilienthal, a student in a metal craft class, was struck in the eye by a sharpened piece of pencil-shaped metal that had been retrieved from a sheet metal bin by another student. On the day of the accident the class assembled in the shop room, but because of noise from partition construction work, the teacher, after about ten minutes, took them outside on the lawn. While in the shop room Tom Accatino, one of the students, saw a "homemade knife" in the sheet metal bin. The bin was for the purpose of storing short, small, odd pieces of metal, including pieces that had been used before but have a "certain salvage value." Tom picked up the knife and held it while he was in the shop room.

When the class reassembled outside on the lawn the students sat in a semicircle around the teacher. There were 28 boys in the class. The class, engaged in reviewing a written examination on safety, had been in session on the lawn about half an hour when the accident happened. In the course of this review, the teacher would read a question and the correct answer and then look up from his paper to see if the students had any questions. Before the accident happened, some of the boys had been flipping the instrument into the ground. Plaintiff testified that he had seen Tom Accatino flipping the knife four or five times. He saw no one else flipping the knife. Tom testified that he had seen three or four boys throwing the knife around. He named Chris Canazero as one of them. Student Jack Golden saw Chris Canazero throwing the knife into the grass two or three times before it hit plaintiff's drawing board and bounced into the latter's eye. The teacher testified he did not see the knife before the accident and that his first knowledge that anything had happened was when he heard plaintiff's outcry. The knife, when it was being flipped on the lawn, made practically no noise.

Issue:

1.   Whether the teacher knew or should have known in time to avoid the accident that the students had been throwing the metal piece for about 30 minutes before the accident?

Holding:

1.   Yes. "We think there was evidence for the jury on the question whether the teacher knew or should have known of the knife throwing. The evidence tending to prove that the knife throwing had been going on for some 30 minutes plus the teacher's own testimony that the students were facing him and were all plainly visible and that he looked up frequently and viewed them to give them a chance to ask questions, would, we think, warrant the jury to infer that he did observe these knife throwing activities (if the jury disbelieved his testimony that he did not see what was going on in front of him) or that he was inattentive and careless in failing to observe such an activity which was going on over such an extended period of time."[296]

Analysis:

The court, citing Mastrangelo v. West Side Union High School Dist., 2 Cal.2d 540, 42 P.2d 634, felt that even if the teacher had not seen the knife being thrown around as he had testified, that he should

---

296. Lilienthal v. San Leandro Unified School Dist., 139 Cal.App.2d 453,456, 293 P.2d 889, 891 1st Dist. (1956).

have seen the knife being thrown had he used ordinary care in observing his students. Had he done so, he would have been able to avert the injury to the student.[297]

Comment:

This case demonstrates that the failure to provide adequate supervision can sometimes be tantamount to a finding of negligence for the teacher and the school district. As often happens in the laboratory classroom, the teacher's attention is drawn away from the students for a large variety of reasons: Teachers are expected to provide individual attention to students to ensure learning and to correct technique in the laboratory to prevent accidents. This means that other students are not receiving due care and attention at that time. This problem is magnified when the environment is not set up for a large number of students. In many classrooms students are packed into laboratories designed for 20 students, but are now required to seat 40 students at a time.

---

297. "Even if the jury believed the teacher's statement that he was unaware of any knife throwing until the occurrence of the accident and plaintiff's outcry, they could have inferred that if he had used ordinary care in the use of his power of observation and his opportunity to observe he would have become aware of the knife throwing in ample time to put an end to it and thus could have avoided the accident." *Id.*

Calandri v. Ione United School Dist.,

219 Cal.App.2d 542, 33 Cal. Rptr. 333 (3d Dist. 1963)

Concepts:

- Duty To Instruct and Warn
- Duty To Supervise
- Foreseeability of Harm
- Take Home Experiments
- Unauthorized Experiments

Facts:

In an action by Calandri, a 15-year-old boy who was injured by the explosion of a toy cannon made by him in his school's shop class, a jury verdict in favor of the school district and the shop-training teacher was reversed. A new trial ordered on the ground that the trial court failed to instruct the jury on the standard of conduct required of an adult dealing with a child was prejudicial error. Calandri lost two fingers and a portion of the palm and wrist of his hand as the result of an explosion.

The students in the shop class were assigned regular projects. Upon completion of the assigned projects, they were permitted to undertake projects of their own design, which, in the case of Calandri, a freshman, consisted of the construction of a model bronze Revolutionary War–type cannon. Students had chosen this same project in earlier years. The design required the use of a metal lathe and drill press (used in drilling out the bore, the touch holes, and the "pan") and was approved by the teacher, who considered it good practice on the lathe. The cannon was mounted on blocks of wood, rather than on wheels or carriages, and there was other evidence justifying an inference that the cannons were being made to be fired. Further evidence showed that the other boys had fired them, using ball bearings as projectiles, and there was evidence that the teacher knew about this, although he denied such knowledge. The teacher at no time warned the plaintiff or any of the other boys who had completed similar projects, of the dangers involved in firing this type of cannon. In addition, he had not given any instruction regarding the type of fuse that could be used safely, nor as to how a fuse should be applied. The plaintiff testified that he had spoken with the teacher and obtained some information from the teacher as to where gunpowder might be purchased to use in firing the cannon.

After the cannon, which was over 5 inches long and 1_ inch in diameter at the breach, and with a bore of slightly more than one-fourth of an inch in diameter, was completed, it was graded by the teacher and was taken home by Calandri.

At home, Calandri fastened the cannon with baling wire to a block of wood, and, in a shed behind his home, proceeded to load it for transport outside of the city limits for firing. In the shed, Calandri took a shotgun shell apart, setting aside the shot and powder, and then loaded the cannon by its muzzle, stuffing successively, powder, rag wadding, shot, and further wadding. Finally, Calandri then mixed other powder with match-heads and worked that combination into the touchhole with some "thin instrument." Either simultaneously or within a few seconds thereafter, the cannon fired, resulting in the severe injury to Calandri's hand.

Issue:

1. Whether the school owed the student a duty of care for a model "cannon" project constructed at the student's home resulting in injuries to the student?

2. Whether the teacher, Gebhardt, was negligent in failing to warn Calandri regarding the dangers involved in loading and firing the cannon?

Holding:

1. Yes. A school owed a duty of care to its pupils when, as a part of its curriculum, it included instruction involving the use of dangerous instrumentality, and notwithstanding the injury occurred off the school premises.

2. Yes.

> We think it absurd to say, as respondents contend, that these cannons, although denominated as 'toys' are not dangerous instrumentalities. Proof lies in the fact that one was capable, of, and did, blow off part of a boy's hand. Respondents stress the fact that the cannon did not blow up; that it functioned as it was supposed to function. The statement is only half true. It was not supposed to prematurely and unexpectedly discharge its projectiles as happened here. A jury could conclude reasonably that instruction and supervision of the making of the cannon should have included a warning as to its potentialities to main and even kill, and particularly of the eccentricities inherent in the operation of the touch hole and 'pan' and of safety practices to be observed in the fusing and firing of the cannon.[298]

Analysis:

The court held that the school owed a duty of care to the plaintiff, since it, as a part of its curriculum, included instruction involving the use of an instrumentality which the court found was dangerous, and that the question of whether the school had exercised due care had been properly submitted to the jury as a fact question. However, the court ordered a new trial because of refusal of the trial court to give an instruction on the care required to be exercised for the safety of a child, which in effect states that "one dealing with children must anticipate the ordinary behavior of children" and that the fact that children usually cannot and do not exercise the same degree of prudence for their own safety as do adults, imposes a duty to exercise a proportional vigilance and caution on those dealing with children, and from whose conduct injury to a child might result.[299] The court said that such instruction was required in this case, since the injured pupil was constructing a dangerous instrumentality as a part of a course supervised by the teacher.

The court noted that a jury could have reasonably concluded that instruction and supervision of the making of a cannon should have included a warning as to its potentialities to maim and even to kill, and particularly as to the eccentricities inherent in the operation of the device and of safety practices to be observed in the fusing and firing thereof. The court did not find any significance to the fact that it was

---

298. <u>Calandri v. Ione United School Dist.</u>, 219 Cal. App 2d. 542, 54933 Cal. Rptr. 333, 337 (3d Dist. 1963).
299. The <u>Calandri</u> court in a lengthy discussion analyzes the role that foreseeability of the harm plays in a negligence analysis:
    A finding of negligence turns upon two elements, first, the existence of a duty to use care, and second, a breach of such duty by the creation of an unreasonable risk of harm. [citations] A third element necessary to establish actionable negligence, is proximate cause. [citations] Inquiry into proximate causation, however, presupposes an affirmative finding of negligence, based upon the dual occurrence of a duty and its breach. [citation] A duty of care, owed by the alleged wrongdoer to the injured plaintiff or to a class of which he is a member, is indispensable to negligence liability. [citation] One factor in the delineation of duty is the foreseeability of harm. [citation] Foreseeability is equally pertinent in the exploration of proximate cause, especially where an intervening act plays a contributory role in the accident. [citations] Divergent results are possible and judicial disagreements arise by approaching negligence determination through the gateway of duty, on the one hand, or proximate causation on the other. [citations] . . . To the extent that existence of a duty of care turns on conflicting evidence as to the reasonable foreseeability of injury, the question may be one for the jury. Initially, however, presence of a duty rests upon factors other than foreseeability, and its existence is primarily for judicial determination. *Id.* at 548–49.

understood that the firing of the cannon would be conducted off the school premises.[300] The court also rejected the contention that the plaintiff was contributory negligent as a matter of law, taking the position that both contributory negligence and proximate cause were normally fact questions in the absence of compelled inferences to the contrary; that this was particularly to be emphasized where a minor's alleged negligence was involved, when much more lenient rules in favor of the minor were to be applied in view of the "heedlessness, impulsiveness, and forgetfulness of youth."

Comment:

Much like the Ross case, Calandri shows that courts are going to hold children to a much more lenient standard than adults. Teachers make thousands of decisions each day, not all of them related to the functioning of the class. In some cases, a teacher's failure to predict what a reasonable child will do with an object will expose them to potential liability for failure to supervise. As Ross and Calandri both show, teacher's have duties of supervision that extend beyond the boundaries of their classrooms. In Ross, the injury occurred in another teacher's classroom with the teacher present, and yet the teacher, Ferrari was found negligent. In Calandri, a project of the student's own selection and construction, which was never intended by the teacher to be fired at school but was approved by the teacher, turns that project into the teacher's negligence. How was Calandri's teacher negligent? The teacher should have known that the cannon was a potentially dangerous object, and that to a freshman student, it was highly likely that "a working model" would likely be fired. The second mistake was approving the project. Without the teacher's approval, the court would have concluded that Calandri was operating on his own and that the school had no responsibility for the unauthorized project. When assigning laboratory experiments, projects, or any activity, the science teacher needs to ask himself or herself if there are any possible dangers to the student that may occur by the student's use, or foreseeable misuse of the equipment and chemicals used in the activity. Ross and Calandri teach that chemistry teachers have a duty to take reasonable precautions to supervise and warn their students concerning the danger of equipment. Calandri shows us that teachers need not only guard against foreseeable uses of equipment or chemicals, but also against foreseeable misuses as well.

---

300. Moreover, if the teacher knew that these playthings were being made to explode gunpowder, we can find no significance, comforting to respondents, in the fact (earnestly argued by them) that it was understood such explosions would be conducted off the school premises. Would Mastrangelo . . . have been decided differently had the making of gunpowder been assigned as homework? We think not. *Id.* at 549–50.

Matteucci v. High School District No. 208, Co. of Cook,

4 Ill.App.3d 710, 281 N.E.2d 383 (Ill. App. 1972)

Concepts:

- Duty To Instruct and Warn
- Duty To Supervise
- Experiment Selection
- Foreseeable Uses And Misuses
- Safety Training for Students
- Self-Designed Experiments

Facts:

Lawrence Matteucci, almost 15 years old, was a high school student enrolled in basic wood shop. The course curriculum included the use of saws, lathes, and jointers. There were about 24 students in the class. The injury occurred while Lawrence was using a circular bench saw that had been fitted with an aluminum guard above the saw blade. There is some dispute about whether the guard was always used. The teacher testified at trial that he almost always used the guard except on those rare occasions that it was necessary to cut at an unusual angle because the guard blocked the ability to follow the cut. Lawrence and several other students testified that the teacher and some of the students had in the past used the saw without the guard. On the day of the accident, Lawrence had been using the saw, and had just finished turning off the power and was walking around the machine when he slipped on some "sawdust, or it could have been anything."[301] "As his feet came out from under him and he started to fall, he attempted to catch himself and his hand came in contact with the blade of the saw which was still revolving." The teacher testified at trial that

> the jointer and the bench saw were the most dangerous machines in the shop. They were close together so that "they could be easily observed" by the instructor. His testimony was that it was rather important to give close supervision to students using this equipment. He testified that he demonstrated the proper use of the bench saw to the entire class and that he "checked out" most of the students on the bench saw, including plaintiff. The witness also wanted to stand by each individual student when they were using the machine. In addition, the teacher testified that he used, in this class, a textbook explaining safety procedures for the machines. Also a list of safety rules for the bench saw was mimeographed and given to the students at the inception of the course. These rules advised use of a metal guard on the bench saw.[302]

The jury returned a verdict for Matteucci and the school district appealed the trial court's denial of the school district's motion to direct a verdict in their favor.

Issues:

The court addressed several issues in the case but three are relevant to this discussion:

1. Whether the school district was negligent in supervision and instruction of Matteucci in the safe operation of the saw;

2. Whether the school district's negligence was the proximate cause of Matteucci's injuries because Matteucci had slipped on the sawdust that he had created while using the saw and this was an intervening cause that broke the chain of causation relieving the school district of liability; and

---

301. Matteucci v. High School District No. 208, Co. of Cook, 4 Ill.App.3d 710, 715, 281 N.E.2d 383, 387 (Ill. App. 1972).

302. *Id.* at 385–6.

3.   Whether Matteucci was contributorily negligent as a matter of law.

Holding:

1.   Yes.

> Safe use of this dangerous instrumentality certainly required due care from the instructor with reference to instruction of the students as to proper use of the machine and proper supervision to enforce necessary rules of safety. . . . We hold specifically that, in circumstances as shown by this record, where a high school class is obliged to use admittedly dangerous machines, there is a duty upon the instructor, as agent of the school, to exercise due care in instructing the students in safe and proper use of the machines and also a duty to exercise due care in proper supervision of the students in use of the machines as a part of regular school activities. . . . This record presents conflicting evidence as to very important facts regarding both instruction and supervision by the teacher. Under these circumstances, the issue of negligence was one of credibility for determination by the jury. In such case, we cannot substitute our judgment for the verdict.[303]

2.   Yes.

> The evidence here left room for difference of opinion on this issue between reasonable men. Under circumstances of this type, the question of proximate cause is definitely for the jury. The jury was amply justified in finding that accumulation of sawdust beneath a machine of this type was reasonably foreseeable so that it did not constitute an independent, intervening cause of plaintiff's injury and did not break the causal connection. The trial court acted properly in refusing to direct a verdict on this ground." [304]

3.   No. " [T]he difficulty with defendant's argument is the standard to which plaintiff, as a minor 14 years old, must be held. The issue of contributory negligence was one for the jury. The trial court acted properly in denying the motion to direct the verdict on this ground.

Comment:

The Matteucci court, like Ross and Calandri, shows an unwillingness to disturb the verdict of the jury. There is little analysis presented in the case as the court in deciding the issues before it on appeal made clear: questions of fact are for the jury to decide. This case again shows how a high duty of supervision will be imposed when there are serious accidents. The teacher and school district are placed in the position of proving a negative every time there is an accident. That is, rather than the burden being on the plaintiff to prove by a preponderance of the evidence that the teacher and school were negligent, they are placed in the very difficult position of proving that they were not negligent. Since, as this case clearly demonstrates, almost everything that results in harm is foreseeable, teachers have a difficult task in proving they were not negligent. Chemistry teachers are then faced with difficult decisions when choosing activities for their students. If the task presented to the students possibly might result in harm to the student, then the teacher must, as much as practical, design the lesson to ensure the safe performance of the task by the students, while minimizing the risk of harm.

---

303. *Id.* at 386–7.
304. *Id.* at 387.

Scott v. Independent School Dist. #709,

256 N.W.2d 485 (Minn. 1977)

Concepts:

- Eye Safety
- Failure To Follow a Regulation

Facts:

Richard Scott was a seventh grade pupil in a junior high school industrial arts class. He was in the process of drilling a hole in a plastic domino when the drill bit became stuck in the plastic. After another student had gotten a pipe wrench to hold the domino in place, he turned the electric drill press on again. The drill bit snapped off and a tiny piece of it became imbedded in his left eye. At the time of the accident, Scott was not wearing his safety glasses. At the beginning of the year an individual pair of safety goggles was assigned to each industrial arts student who did not already have shatterproof prescription glasses. The students were instructed to wear safety goggles, but the rule was not consistently enforced. The Minnesota legislature had enacted a safety statute that required the wearing of protective eye gear by students engaged in industrial arts classes. The trial court found the school district "negligent per se" and liable as a matter of law and allowed the jury to rule on the issues of contributory negligence and damages. The jury awarded a total of $63,000 in damages. However, it found Scott 10 percent contributory negligent and the school division 90 percent negligent, thereby reducing the award of damages to Scott from the school division to $57,100. The school district appealed to the Minnesota Supreme Court.

Issues:

1. Whether the school district was negligent per se in failing to properly supervise and enforce the wearing of protective safety goggles in an industrial arts class as required by a state statute;

2. Whether in enacting the statute, the Minnesota Legislature intended to preclude consideration of contributory negligence on the part of the student;

3. Whether Scott was contributory negligent in failing to wear the goggles; and

4. Whether the award of $60,000 for permanent injury to the eye was excessive.

Holdings:

1. Yes. [T]he conduct of the school district clearly constituted negligence per se.

2. No. The legislative intent here does not appear to make liability absolute on the part of the school district. Such a construction would place a nearly impossible burden on a school supervisor.

3. Yes. The evidence did indicate that there were signs warning the students to wear safety glasses and that safety glasses were provided at the beginning of the school year. Thus, the record adequately supports the trial court's decision to direct a verdict against the school district but to allow the issue of contributory negligence to go to the jury.

4. No. "We have already indicated there was adequate evidence to support the jury's verdict. As to the amount, $60,000 for a permanent injury to an eye is not excessive.

Analysis:

The Minnesota Supreme Court in a rather straightforward analysis, indicated that on the facts before it the school board was negligent per se:

With certain exception, violation of a statute may constitute negligence per se. . . . Negligence is the breach of a legal duty. It is immaterial whether the duty is one imposed by the rule of common law requiring the exercise of ordinary care not to injure another, or is imposed by a statute designed for the protection of others. . . . All that a statute does is to establish a fixed standard by which the negligence may be determined. To constitute negligence per se, four elements must be satisfied:

The court may adopt as a standard of conduct of a reasonable man the requirements of a legislative enactment or administrative regulation whose purpose is found to be exclusively or in part

(a) to protect a class of persons which includes the one whose interest is invaded, and

(b) to protect the particular interest which is invaded, and

(c) to protect that interest against the kind of harm which has resulted, and

(d) to protect that interest against the particular hazard from which the harm results.

Under this standard, the conduct of the school district clearly constituted negligence.[305]

The court then tackled the issue of whether contributory negligence of the student would be a bar to recovery under the statute. The court in holding that the legislature did not intend to preclude contributory negligence of the student in determining liability, indicated that to construe the statute in such a manner would make "liability absolute on the school district."[306] The court noted that such a construction would also place a "nearly impossible burden on the school supervisor. For example, even if the supervisor instructed a student every day in the use of safety glasses, but while the instructor left the room or was working with another student a student lifted off the glasses temporarily and was injured, liability would follow."[307]

The court, after concluding that it was not error to submit the issue of contributory negligence to the jury, stated:

The evidence of negligence on the part of the defendant was adequate for the court to hold as a matter of law it had violated the statute. At best, supervision in this class was sporadic. At times it was non-existent. Students were allowed to come and go almost at will.[308]

The court then held that there was adequate evidence to support the jury's verdict and that "$60,000 for a permanent injury to an eye is not excessive."[309]

The final issue before the court was an interpretation of Minnesota's maximum tort liability statute. The court held that a school district that did not have insurance coverage to meet its maximum statutory liability, but which in good faith did attempt to procure such coverage, and such insurance was obtainable, was liable for the difference between the insurance coverage and the statutory limits.

Comment:

Scott leaves little doubt that the failure to consistently enforce a regulation enacted by a state legislature or other governing body is tantamount to an admission of negligence. In finding the teacher negligent per se, the court significantly reduced the plaintiff's burden of proving a negligence cause of action, requiring the plaintiff only to prove his damages proximately caused by the defendant's negligence. Scott is a critical case, applicable to all teachers. There is an enormous amount of regulation that affects the

---

305. Scott v. Ind. School Dist., No.709, Duluth, 256 N.W.2d 485, 488 (Minn. 1977).
306. *Id.* at 489.
307. *Id.*
308. *Id.*
309. *Id.*

chemistry classroom. Chemistry teachers need to ensure that their classroom practices and procedures comply with the existing regulations. Laws and regulations change frequently and often it is very difficult to keep up with the changes, some of which may significantly impact the chemistry classroom. Appropriate teacher training directed to reviewing legislation affecting the chemistry classroom on a regular basis is required in order to meet the duty of care. Scott also demonstrates an important principle: Chemistry is taught nationwide, but each state legislature and court system has placed different requirements and responsibilities on the classroom teacher. It is critical that chemistry teachers are familiar with the local rules that affect their potential liability.

Lawrence v. Grant Parish School Bd.,

409 So.2d 1316, 2 Educ. L.R. 1234 (La. Ct. App.), *cert. denied,* 412 So.2d 1110 (La. 1982)

Concepts:

- Administrative Negligence
- Consistent Enforcement of Rules
- Defective Equipment
- Duty To Supervise
- Failure To Fix Safety Problems
- Informing the School District of Problems
- Role Modeling
- Safety Equipment

Facts:

Bruce Lawrence was a 14-year-old student in Bernard Harrison's agriculture class where he was learning welding. "The classroom was situated in a building containing numerous welding booths." [310] The building also contained power equipment that had been stored in the building for some time prior to the accident under the authority of the Grant Parish School Board. A power saw that was easily accessible to the students was stored in the back of the building."[311] Mr. Harrison and the students used the saw periodically. "Immediately prior to the accident the saw had been in use by another student in Bruce's class. At the time of the accident, the saw had an extension cord attached to it, which was plugged into the wall socket. The blade of the saw had been cranked up, but the safety guard had not been reinstalled. . . . The safety guard was not on the saw when it had been stored by the School Board."[312] Mr. Harrison had instructed the students at the beginning of the two six-week class sections, to not use the power equipment. In addition, "at the beginning of the class session the students were given a list of rules, over 200 in number, regarding the use of equipment in the class."[313]

Bruce Lawrence was using the power saw during the class period, when the accident occurred. "He was attempting to cut a piece of wood when either the wood jumped up, or he cut through the wood, causing his hand to come in contact with the saw blade. The blade severed the index finger of his right hand at the proximal phalange and further caused damage to his fingers, hand and thumb resulting in several surgical operations."[314] At the time, Mr. Harrison was out of the classroom, as was his habit, as he frequently left the classroom. Lawrence sued the School Board, the principal, and Mr. Harrison for negligence. At trial, the jury determined the principal was not negligent, and could not reach a determination on the teacher, Harrison. However, the School Board, which was tried by a judge, was found liable for its own negligence and vicariously liable for the negligence of its employees. The judge also held that Lawrence was free from fault concluding that Lawrence was neither guilty of contributory negligence nor had Lawrence assumed the risk. Lawrence was awarded $70,000 for his injuries. The School Board appealed.

Issues:

1. Whether the trial court erred in holding the School Board liable for both its own acts of negligence and for the negligent acts of its employees;

---

310. Lawrence v. Grant Parish School Bd. 409 So.2 1316, 1318 (La. App. 1982).
311. *Id.*
312. *Id.*
313. *Id.*
314. *Id.*

2. Whether the trial court erred in holding that Bruce Lawrence was not contributory negligent;

3. Whether the trial court erred in holding that Bruce Lawrence had not assumed the risk; and

4. Whether the trial court erred in awarding excessive damages.

Holding:

1. Yes.

   (a) School Board Negligence:

   The law is well settled that in order for a school board to be liable it must have had actual knowledge or constructive knowledge of a condition unreasonably dangerous to the children under its supervision. The school board had actual knowledge of the existence of the saw—it ordered its storage. The record shows that it knew of the dangerous condition in which the saw was stored. It knew young children were present in this class daily, and, therefore, owed a duty to exercise a greater degree of care to these students. . . . Despite the duty, the saw was stored with a blade, without a safety guard, in an operative condition in a classroom in which these students were attending. . . . We agree that the School Board might have prevented this accident by either properly storing the saw outside of the contact of the students, removing the saw blade, or installing a locking mechanism to keep the machine from being turned on without a key, or placing a barricade around the power saw. A rope with a keep out sign would have been the least it should have provided. It failed to exercise any of these duties, thus becoming liable for the injuries sustained by Bruce Lawrence through its own negligence.[315]

   (b) Employee Negligence:
   "The acts of Bernard Harrison were clearly a legal cause of the accident. Had he been present in the classroom the accident probably would not have happened.[316]

   Harrison as a teacher owed a duty to the minor to supervise him at all times during the class period due to the presence of inherently dangerous equipment. Harrison breached this duty when he left the shop area leaving the students unsupervised. He knew a power saw was present in the classroom. He further knew that it had been in use from time to time. He also knew that the safety guard was not on the saw. He testified that he did not know the blade on the power saw had been positioned ready for use or that an extension cord was already attached and plugged in. He should have observed this. These acts and his failure to act to protect the minor constitute fault on behalf of Harrison causing injury to Bruce.[317]

   [The principal] was also aware that the saw had been stored in the welding shop. He knew that it was in working condition. He further knew or should have known that 13- or 14-year-old children were apt to use the saw. As principal of the school, he owed a duty to the students to see that the saw was stored either in a safe manner, or stored in a place or barricaded whereby students could not get hurt. He failed to discharge this duty. There are many things the defendants could have done to protect Bruce and other students . . . . The cost of these protective measures is negligible and there is no excuse for the inactions of the defendants.[318]

2. No. "Bruce Lawrence's only wrong was to use a saw he was told not to use. This simple disobedience does not constitute contributory negligence. The duty of the school board encompassed acts such as those of Bruce Lawrence and his classmate. It is foreseeable that kids will do things they are told not to

---

315. *Id.* at 1318–9.
316. *Id.* at 1319.
317. *Id.*
318. *Id.* at 1320.

do. The School Board owed a duty to all students to not store a dangerous power saw in an area that was easily accessible to students. The School Board knew or should have known that someone would attempt to use the saw as plaintiff did."[319]

3.   No. "Bruce Lawrence had never before used a power saw nor was he instructed in its use, it cannot be said that he assumed any known risk by his actions."[320]

4.   No. "[I]n the assessment of damages, discretion must be left to the trier of fact. . . .The evidence shows that after the accident, it was between one and two hours before Bruce was taken to the hospital. He testified that he experienced severe pain during this period. Bruce's index finger was completely severed and had to be picked up from the floor and taken to the hospital. The saw blade made deep cuts into Bruce's thumb, fingers, and hand. . . . For the rest of his life, Bruce will have a permanent disfigurement and impairment in his right hand. His thumb is pinned and thus restricts his motion. . . . Bruce has a 50 percent disability of his right hand. . . . Bruce is right handed. . . . We find no clear abuse of the trial court's "much discretion" in awarding $70,000.00 in general damages."[321]

Analysis:

The Lawrence court makes quick work of the school district and the teacher in this case. The court indicated that the district had "actual knowledge or constructive knowledge" of a piece of equipment it considered "dangerous," with or without the guard and that the school district had carelessly stored in a room where it could be accessed, and was accessed, by the teacher and the 13- to 15-year-old students he taught. The court implied knowledge because the school district ordered the equipment stored, and stored it in a room where children were present on a daily basis. The fact that the school district had this information and failed to take action to prevent student access, either by disabling the saw, or by locking it up, putting up a "rope with a keep out sign," at a minimum, was unreasonable for the court.

The teacher's liability turns on his own admission that he was frequently out of the room when the welding machines were in use, had used the saw himself, knew that students were using the saw, and in the court's view "the students were left alone, unsupervised, with welding equipment in use, and power equipment present. When the accident happened, the teacher was out of the room. If he had "been present in the classroom the accident probably would not have happened."

Once the court decided the guilty should pay, it made them. Of significance is the court implying that the only thing Lawrence did wrong was in using the "saw he was told not to use."[322] The court's decision paints the teacher and the district of being negligent in failing to protect students from themselves.

Comment:

Lawrence appears to reward students for failing to follow the rules in handling an instrument that at ages 13 to 15 they should realize is quite dangerous. For the chemistry teacher, students often do not realize the potential for harm in the materials that teachers casually handle, often without safety equipment. When mixing chemicals for the lab, or dispensing them for students, it is important that the teacher follows the same safety rules set out for students. While this point is not made immediately obvious from the facts of Lawrence, the court in reaching its decision seems to focus on the fact that the teacher had used the saw before the accident. If the teacher can use the saw, then the students believe that they can use the equipment in precisely the same manner.

Lawrence's teacher was his model for the handling of the equipment, in this case, a saw. In the chemistry classroom, teachers are expected to model safe techniques for handling of chemicals and other equipment. If the teacher does not wear an apron, safety glasses, and other protective equipment, a court, much like the Lawrence court, could find that despite teaching students the rules, the failure of the teacher

---

319. *Id.*
320. *Id.*
321. *Id.* at 1321.
322. *Id.* at 1320.

to enforce and reinforce those rules may be unreasonable particularly when students are handling dangerous or hazardous equipment and materials. The court is not chastising Harrison for failing to instruct the students and Lawrence. They obviously had received sufficient safety instruction. The court in this case is pointing to whether the teacher reinforced that instruction and the importance of maintaining a safe working environment. The court, is intimating that it is pointless to teach rules when the teachers actions are inconsistent with those instructions. There is no indication that the teacher followed his own safety rules, enforced the more than 200 such rules he gave the students, and did not seem to concerned that students might be injured using the equipment because of his frequent absences from the room while students were working. The fact that Lawrence disobeyed the instruction not to use the saw in the eyes of the court is inconsequential because the teacher was not around to enforce the rules anyway. This case is about consistency in enforcing the rules, and the failure to enforce, model, and teach the rules will be viewed harshly by the court.

Not to be ignored in this case is the fact that the teacher left the room while students were working with welders. The court disproved of the teacher leaving the students unsupervised so they could get into trouble. While leaving the room is an obvious mistake for the <u>Lawrence</u> court, the practical reality is that sometimes teachers need to leave their rooms unattended for brief periods. The question of when a chemistry teacher can leave their room unattended is a question of fact. Certainly, there should be no "hazardous or dangerous" chemicals or equipment in use by the students, or which the students have access. It is foreseeable that students will find ways to get into trouble when the teacher leaves the room. However, as <u>Ohman</u> instructs, not every time a teacher leaves the room is it foreseeable that students will injury themselves. However, <u>Ohman</u> is distinguishable from <u>Lawrence</u>, in that the instrumentality causing the injury was a pencil, whereas the instrumentality here is a power saw without a guard. <u>Lawrence</u> and <u>Ohman</u> read together seem to indicate that if the instrumentality causing harm to the student is one provided by the school or the property of the school and is by its very nature hazardous or inherently dangerous, then the failure to properly supervise the students is negligence. If the instrumentality is not provided by the school or the school's property or not by its nature hazardous or inherently dangerous, the teacher's presence in the room will not be taken by the court as a significant factor in determining fault for the accident.

Roberts v. Robertson County Board of Educ.,

692 S.W.2d 863 (Tenn. App. 1985)

Concepts:

- Documentation of Teacher Training
- Duty Of Care
- Duty To Instruct and Warn
- Duty To Supervise
- Record Keeping
- Standard of Care

Facts:

Wallace Glen Roberts, Jr. suffered a serious head injury when a fellow student, William Edward Yount asked him for help in using a drill press during a vocational agriculture class taught by Mr. Billy Ross Ballard. Wallace was a freshman at Greenbrier High School and enrolled in Vocational Agriculture I class with 22 other students. According to the State Board of Education, the class was one of two required before students could take classes that are more specialized. Ballard had taught the class for the past 16 years. He did not rely on a written lesson plan but "generally relied upon his memory and his philosophy on teaching the students."[323]

Mr. Ballard testified that he taught "safety" in each one of his classes, although [it] is not clear . . . the exact nature of the instruction Roberts' class received. This instruction took several forms including handouts, films, signs posted in the shop, and shop demonstrations on each piece of equipment. It also appears to have involved general safety rules as well as specific operational rules with regard to each piece of equipment.[324]

Mr. Ballard's three main general safety rules were: (1) that the machinery could not be operated when he was not in the shop; (2) that "horseplay and horsepower don't mix"; and (3) that students should not talk to or distract persons who were working with the machinery.[325] There was some doubt as to what rule (1) meant, with various shop students testifying to different versions and Mr. Ballard testifying to two different versions. One version had the machines not being used when he was not in the building, the other version when he was not in the shop area itself. Mr. Ballard also testified that he had given specific operational rules for each piece of equipment. The drill press had a sign located near it that had a list of eight safety precautions. Roberts' class had received a demonstration of the drill press by Mr. Ballard earlier in early November. Yount had not participated in the demonstration because he was using welding equipment in another area of the shop at that time. There was no evidence that the students' instruction had "included warnings to the students of the dangers attendant to more complicated uses of the drill press or instructions concerning how students should help each other use the drill press."[326]

On the day before Christmas vacation, Yount spoke with Mr. Ballard about using the drill press to drill a hole through a fourteen-inch piece of wood he was using to make a lamp base. This was not one of the basic uses for the drill press and Yount had never attempted to drill through such a large piece of wood before. Mr. Ballard gave Yount a special long drill bit that he kept in his desk in order to accomplish the task. This bit was much longer than the bit the students were familiar with and Ballard testified that he had "instructed Yount to wait before he started to use the drill bit because he wanted to be present to observe

---

323. Roberts v. Robertson County Board of Educ., 692 S.W.2d 863,866 (Tenn. App. 1985).
324. *Id.* at 867.
325. *Id.*
326. *Id.* at 868.

the student's work. Yount went into the shop and set up the drill press as best as he new how. He then waited for Mr. Ballard."[327]

Mr. Ballard left the shop to go and retrieve a soft drink machine. He had promised the students free soft drinks that day. At the time Yount was ready to use the machine, Ballard was near the outside entrance to the shop building. The drill press could not be seen from where Ballard was located.

Yount waited for approximately 10 minutes for Mr. Ballard to return to the shop. . . . When Mr. Ballard did not come in, Yount asked . . . Roberts, to assist him in drilling a hole in the lamp base. Roberts had been helping another classmate use a hand saw, and this was the first time he was aware that Yount desired to use the drill press. . . . Roberts had never been instructed or warned concerning the danger of what Yount was doing or the manner in which people could be injured when using a longer drill bit.[328]

At Yount's request to hold the piece of wood while the hole was drilled, Roberts knelt down next to the drill press and held the piece of wood firmly in both hands. His face was approximately 10 to 12 inches away from the drill itself. Yount turned on the drill, and in an instant, the long drill bit deflected at an angle of approximately forty-five degrees striking Roberts on the right temple. The drill bit caused a long cut and skull fracture from Roberts' right temple to behind his right ear. He fell back immediately from the machine, and other students came to his aid and carried him into Mr. Ballard's office. Mr. Ballard did not know what had happened until one of the students came to get him.[329]

Roberts filed suit against the Robertson County Board of Education, the school superintendent, the high school principal, and his vocational agriculture teacher, Mr. Ballard alleging negligence. The defendants filed a third party complaint seeking contribution and indemnity from Yount on the theory that it was his negligence that caused Roberts' injuries.[330] The case was tried before a judge in accordance with Tennessee law. The trial court dismissed Roberts' action after "determining that Mr. Ballard had not breached the duty of care he owed to his students and that Yount's intervening acts were the proximate cause of Roberts' injuries."[331] Roberts appeals.

Issues:

1. Whether Ballard owed a duty of care to Roberts;

2. If Ballard owed a duty of care to Roberts, whether Ballard was negligent for failure to furnish adequate instruction and supervision and whether Ballard's negligence was the proximate cause of Roberts' injuries;

3. Whether the school board was liable for Roberts' injuries.

Holdings:

1. Yes. "The standard of care for school teachers and administrators is that of a reasonable person in such a position acting under similar circumstances."[332]

    [W]e find that a high school vocational teacher has the duty to take those precautions that any ordinarily reasonable and prudent person would take to protect his shop students from unreasonable risk of injury. The extent of these precautions must be determined with reference to

---

327. *Id.*
328. *Id.* at 869.
329. *Id.*
330. *Id.* at 865.
331. *Id.*
332. *Id.* at 870.

the age and inexperience of the students involved, their less than mature judgment with regard to their conduct, and the inherently dangerous nature of the power driven equipment available for their use in the shop.[333]

2. Yes. "Based on our *de novo*[334] review . . . we conclude that the evidence supports a finding that Mr. Ballard was negligent and that his failure to furnish adequate instruction and supervision to his vocational agriculture students was the proximate cause of Roberts' injuries."[335]

3. Yes. "Mr. Ballard candidly conceded that Roberts would not have been injured had he been present in the shop supervising Yount's use of the drill press. We agree. This provides a basis, independent of any consideration of Yount's actions, to hold Mr. Ballard, and thus, the local school board, liable for Roberts' injuries.[336] Mr. Ballard acting in his capacity as a teacher, was an agent of the Robertson County Board of Education. Thus, . . . the County is liable for his negligent acts . . . . We do not find that this record contains adequate proof to find that the school's principal, Steve Moss, was negligent.[337]

Analysis:

The appellate court, after a lengthy discussion of the applicable facts, turned to the question of the negligence of the school officials in this case. Indicating that the trial court had determined that Mr. Ballard "had a duty to properly supervise and instruct his students,"[338] the appellate justices felt that it was necessary to define this duty more precisely and to describe more carefully the scope of the teacher's standard of care. Discussing prior court precedents, the justices determined that that the standard of care for "school teachers and administrators was that of a reasonable person in such a position acting under similar circumstances."[339] The court noted that courts have also recognized that this "standard of care can be related directly to the underline{nature of the persons} to whom the duty is owed and the circumstances giving rise to the duty. [Emphasis added]." In arriving at its holding, *supra,* the court concluded that a "high school vocational teacher has the duty to take those precautions that any ordinarily reasonable and prudent person would take to protect his shop students from the unreasonable risk of injury."[340] The court added that the extent of those precautions must be analyzed in light of the "age and inexperience of the students involved, their less than mature judgment . . . and the inherently dangerous nature of the . . . equipment available for their use. . . ."[341] Applying this revised definition of Mr. Ballard's duty to the students, the court stated that "[I]n order to discharge this duty, it is incumbent on a teacher, at a minimum, to instruct his students in the safe and proper use of the equipment, to warn the students of known dangers, and to supervise students to the extent necessary for the enforcement of adequate rules of shop safety."[342]

Turning to the issue of causation, the justices intimated that

[w]ith specific reference to the conduct of teachers, we do not impose upon them the duty to anticipate or foresee the hundreds of unexpected student acts that occur daily in our public schools. Verhel v. Independent School District No. 709, 359 N.W.2d 579, 586 (Minn. 1984). However, like other courts, we have no hesitation in holding a teacher or local school system to

---

333. *Id.* at 870–71.

334. *De novo* review means that the court will examine the trial record without any inferences or presumptions as to the correctness of the verdict. However, the trial court's findings of fact are presumed correct. Accordingly, the appellate court will affirm the trial court's decision unless an error of law affecting the result has been committed or unless the evidence preponderates against the trial court's findings of fact.

335. Roberts v. Robertson County Board of Educ., 692 S.W.2d 863,872(Tenn. App. 1985).

336. *Id.* at 873.

337. *Id.* at 873 n. 13.

338. *Id.* at 869–70.

339. *Id.* at 871.

340. *Id.* at 870.

341. *Id.* at 871.

342. *Id.*

the duty of safeguarding students while at school from reasonably foreseeable dangerous conditions including the dangerous acts of fellow students.[343]

The court then proceeded to conclude that Mr. Ballard was negligent and that his failure to furnish adequate instruction and supervision was the proximate cause of Roberts' injuries.[344] The court stated that there were four separate aspects of Mr. Ballard's conduct justifying this conclusion:

> First, Mr. Ballard had a practice of permitting inexperienced freshman students to remain in the shop area unsupervised in the presence of fully operational power-driven equipment which, if used improperly, could cause serious injury. Second, there was no proof that Mr. Ballard ever instructed his students in the proper technique for assisting others in operating shop machinery. Third, there is no proof that Mr. Ballard ever gave his students any instruction concerning the ways a drill press could cause injury if it was not used properly. . . . Fourth, Mr. Ballard gave Yount a drill bit knowing that he had never used the drill bit before and that he was eager to use it during that class period.

Finally, the court stated that the evidence supports a conclusion that Mr. Ballard was aware that Yount did not know how to properly use the longer drill bit and that Mr. Ballard knew that this drill bit could be dangerous if used improperly. Mr. Ballard also knew Yount intended to use the drill bit on that day because it was his last opportunity to do so before the Christmas vacation. Rather than keeping the drill bit and having Yount wait for him in the shop area until he could come and supervise his work, Mr. Ballard instead gave Yount the instrument that caused Roberts' injury. "Providing the drill bit to Yount, knowing at the time that the shop equipment was fully operable, that other students were working in the shop area without supervision, and that Yount was eager to use the drill bit constitutes a breach of Mr. Ballard's duty to supervise his students properly and provides a sufficient basis for judgment in Roberts' favor. [345]

After finding Mr. Ballard liable, the court swiftly passed judgment on the school board, indicating that Mr. Ballard was acting in his capacity as teacher and therefore was an agent of the school board. The school district argued that Yount's actions were an intervening cause and the proximate cause of Roberts' injuries. The court, without making any determination as to Yount's negligence, which was still to be decided, held that Yount's actions were not "independent, intervening causes sufficient in and of themselves to excuse the negligence of Mr. Ballard or the local school system."[346]

After a discussion of the inapplicability of a motion for a directed verdict to the present case, the appellate court, reversing the trial court entered a judgment for Roberts in the amount of $25,000 predicated upon the following facts:

> . . . Roberts' family sustained approximately $4,225 in medical bills as a result of this injury. Further, Roberts . . . was hospitalized for ten days and experienced moderate pain for sometime thereafter. His surgical treatment required that his head be shaved, and thus for some time after the accident he was subjected to the ridicule and teasing of his peers. This embarrassment to a 14-year-old boy can be as painful as the injury itself. His treating physician determined that this injury has caused a permanent weakening of his skull . . . and that this injury has resulted in a five percent disability to the body as a whole.

Comment:

Robertson is *the* duty case. The court takes the time to define the scope of the duty precisely as a modification of the reasonable person test (ordinarily reasonable person in the position of the person under the circumstances) taking into account the characteristics of the person to whom the duty is owed. In this

---

343. *Id.* at 872.
344. *Id.*
345. *Id.*
346. *Id.* at 873.

case, Mr. Ballard failed to modify his instruction to accommodate the characteristics of Roberts' class of freshmen. The result in this case may have changed if Roberts possessed different characteristics. For example, if this was an advanced class of seniors with numerous hours of instruction, and specific training related to the use of the large drill bit.

Robertson is also a record-keeping case The court intimates that part of the rationale for holding Ballard negligent, other than the fact that Ballard admitted he was negligent for failing to properly supervise the students, was that Ballard could not provide evidence that he had in fact provided safety instruction. Ballard was an experienced teacher, who was no longer guided by a written lesson plan. This case may have turned out differently had Ballard followed a written lesson plan that provided information as to what instruction he was providing his students. Teachers must have evidence that they are meeting the standard of care. Lesson plans, laboratory logs, safety contracts, safety notes and tests all provide documentary evidence that the appropriate safety instruction was provided to the student. The court discusses the fact that Ballard apparently provided safety instruction to his students using a variety of methods but could not provide any specific evidence of the instructions provided to the students concerning the drill press and the long drill bit. Robertson teaches that teachers must do the "necessary" paperwork.

Brown v. Tesack,

556 So.2d 84, 58 Ed. Law Rep.846, *review granted* 556 So.2d 1288, 58 Ed. Law Rep. 1378, *aff'd in part, revised in part*, 566 So.2d. 955, 62 Ed. Law Rep. 1287, *rehearing denied* (La. App. 4 Cir. 1990)

Concepts:

• Chemical Disposal

Facts:

Leonard and Gerald were playing around a trash dumpster located on the grounds of an elementary school just before the school opened for a new school year. The school is fenced, but gates are left open when school is not in session. Further, the fences have holes in them through which children and other individuals can, and do, access the schoolyard. People regularly cut across the schoolyard to get to a housing project located across the street and a major parkway that runs by the school. Because of its location the school experiences a significant amount of vandalism. A custodian is on duty at the school during the summer months. During that summer, the school had received 97 one-gallon metal containers of duplicating "Ditto" fluid for use in making copies of materials. Because of the flammable nature of the fluid and the high rate of vandalism, the school keeps the fluid under lock and key. Although the custodian denies throwing away any empty, full or partially used cans of duplicating fluid, on the date of the accident, there were a large number of cans deposited by some school employee in the trash dumpster at the school.

Leonard and Gerald took four of the partially filled cans of duplicating fluid back to the area of the project where they lived and began playing with the fluid by burning it. Other kids were also playing with the fluid, and one child had sustained a burn on top of his head. Even though another child was burned, Leonard and Gerald continued to play with the fluid. At about 7:45 p.m., Ernest Brown, saw Gerald and Leonard still playing with the fluid from the second floor window of his bedroom, and decided to join them.

Gerald was pouring the duplicating fluid from the one-gallon can into a torn plastic milk carton on the ground. . . . The fluid in the milk carton was burning. Gerald, while standing over the milk carton continued to pour the fluid into the flames. As he did so, the flames climbed the stream of fluid and entered the can. The gases produced by the burning fluid in the can forced the remaining fluid in the can to explode from the top of the can in a flaming ball of liquid striking Ernest as he came around the corner of the building to the kids who were playing with the fluid. At the moment of the explosion his head was turned quickly away from the kids; as he looked back the fluid struck him. The flaming liquid made Ernest into what could best be described as a human torch burning him and his clothing.[347]

Ernest sustained substantial and disfiguring burns to a major portion of his body. Ernest sues the school and the trial court entered a judgment finding the school free from liability. Ernest appeals.

Issue:

1. Whether, under the facts presented, the trial court erred in dismissing plaintiff's suit against the Orleans Parish School Board?

Holding:

1. No. "In this case the trial court found that the Orleans Parish School Board had a duty to properly dispose of, or "denature" the duplicating fluid. It further found that plaintiff had failed to prove that a

---

347. Brown v. Tesack, 556 So.2d 84, 86 (La. App. 4 Cir. 1989).

breach of this duty occurred, in that they failed to prove that the method of disposal was unreasonable under the facts presented. In addition, the court found that the risk that caused the harm was not within the scope of duty breached by defendant. As such it refused to impose liability upon this defendant. We are in accord with the lower court in their analysis."[348]

Analysis:

In finding the district not liable for negligence the court addressed a number of factors that it felt were decisive:

> The record reflects that the . . . school because of its unique location was subject to vandalism. It was also in an area where a large number of children would play, especially during the time of summer break. The school personnel were aware that duplicating fluid could be flammable. Precautions were taken to guard against the product being misused in that it was inventoried, collected, and stored in a double locked storeroom during breaks in the regular school year. Considering the properties of the product involved, the location of the school involved and the conditions present especially during summer break, it is clear that the . . . school board had a duty to properly dispose of the unused cans of duplicating fluid.

> In this case the subject cans were placed inside a metal dumpster located on the school grounds, on the day designated for the collection of trash from the dumpster. There is no evidence to suggest that this practice is unreasonable under the circumstance. The record is simply devoid of evidence . . . which would indicate further precautions were warranted or that defendant should have foreseen that someone would remove these items from the dumpster and allow them to fall into the hands of minors. . . . [W]e agree with the trial court's conclusion that the risk which caused the accident was not within the scope of the duty owed by the . . . School Board. The real culprit was the actions of Leonard . . . and Gerald . . . in misusing the duplicating fluid and setting it afire.[349]

The court was strongly divided. The dissenting justices strongly disagreed with the majority on whether the school board breached any duty in its method of disposing the duplicating fluid. Judge Plotkin argued that the majority misinterpreted the concepts of duty/risk and the concept of foreseeability and omitted key facts that were contained in the record:

> In determining whether the risk of harm is within the scope of the duty owed by the defendant, courts traditionally analyze the foreseeability of the risk.[350] In this case . . . the record establishes . . . that employees of the school were aware both that children from the adjacent housing project often played on the school grounds and that those children often rummaged through the trash dumpster looking for things to either take to their homes or to play with. The principal of the school and other school . . . employees also testified that the [school] experienced a lot of vandalism and break-ins."[351]

Comment:

Tesack focuses on an issue that is relevant to the chemistry and other laboratory classrooms: the safe removal of hazardous chemicals and other materials. All schools should have and follow a hazardous waste disposal program. Chemistry laboratories need to keep track of the quantities of chemicals used in the classroom and how they are disposed. Tesack focused on the disposal of duplicating fluid, but it may have easily been any of a number of hazardous chemicals or other flammable liquids found in chemistry and other laboratories.

---

348. *Id.* at 87.
349. *Id.* at 87.
350. *Id.* at 88.
351. *Id.* at 88–9.

Tesack is a reminder that teachers have a duty to properly dispose of chemicals that have a foreseeable risk of harm to those individuals who may encounter the substance. Much like Kush ex rel. Marszalek v. City of Buffalo, 59 N.Y.2d 26, 462 N.Y.S.2d 831, 449 N.E.2d 725, 11 Educ.L.R. 582 (1983) where an eight-year-old boy 'discovered' some magnesium powder and potassium nitrate and was seriously injured, Tesack extends the duty of the teacher to not only maintain and properly supervise the handling of such chemicals but also properly dispose of them. The teacher who leaves the gift of chemicals may have some responsibility if the new teacher or a student is injured when the 'gift' is discovered. For example, imagine the consequences and the liability of the new teacher who does not inspect his/her classroom for the chemicals left behind by the retired teacher when a student discovers an old, half empty, can of ether left behind on the top shelf of an unlocked cabinet that explodes in his hand. The retired teacher was negligent for failing to properly maintain and store the chemical and the new teacher for failing to inspect, and remove the can. While the Tesack court found that the school board had acted reasonably in disposing of the chemicals in the manner they did in this case by placing them in the school's trash dumpster, the strong majority in this case suggests that other courts might not find this practice reasonable, particularly when many states have enacted statutes requiring certain methods for disposing of hazardous materials such as motor oils, pesticides, and other consumer waste materials.

<u>Drake by Drake v. Mitchell Community Schools,</u>

628 N.E.2d 1231, 89 Ed. Law Rep. 239, *affirmed in part, vacated in part,* 649 N.E.2d 1027, 100 Ed. Law Rep. 280 (Ind. App. 1 Dist. 1994)

Concepts:

- Class Size
- Duty To Instruct and Warn
- Duty To Prevent Harm to Students

Facts:

For nine years the local Kiwanis group had sponsored, a "haunted house" or more accurately a "haunted grain elevator" fund-raising event on Halloween. The event took place in a grain elevator owned by a local bank.[352] The bank, for its part, never charged the Kiwanis for the use of the grain elevator for the activity.[353] In the fall of 1990, the Kiwanis again borrowed the grain elevator. The Kiwanis assumed sole responsibility to complete any necessary "cleanup" of the grain elevator before using it as the haunted house.[354] The Kiwanis approached the school and requested the assistance of the student council in putting on the event. The student council agreed to participate, and the Kiwanis and student council agreed to split the profits on a 50/50 basis.[355] The student council advisor and teacher, Ms. Wheatly,[356] at the school was

> aware that the grain elevator was potentially unsafe and could pose a danger to the students' health. Specifically, Wheatly anticipated that the students could be exposed to histoplasmosis in the grain elevator. Wheatly was knowledgeable about the disease and its causes having contracted it herself while in college. Wheatly requested that the grain elevator be inspected to make sure it was safe for students. Wheatly herself participated in the inspection and noted its dirty condition and the presence of pigeon droppings. Wheatly insisted that the Kiwanis clean the building before the students entered it.[357]

A member of the Kiwanis also inspected the grain elevator and was also concerned about the possibility of contracting histoplasmosis. Finally, one member of the Kiwanis volunteered to clean the elevator with a shop vacuum cleaner.[358]

Holli Drake, a member of that school's student council, volunteered to decorate the haunted house. Holli entered the grain elevator to make decorations before the Kiwanis had gotten around to cleaning the elevator. "The grain elevator was extremely dusty and dirty. Pigeon droppings were visible on the floor."[359] While Holli and several of the students were decorating, the Kiwanis arrived to clean the building. While they cleaned Holli and her friends remained in the building, cutting "out 10 Styrofoam tombstones, painting them, and placing them as decorations inside the elevator. Holli also helped clean the grain elevator by sweeping the ramp with a broom."[360]

On the day of the event, the grain elevator was still dusty. "Holli participated in the actual event by hiding in a plastic coffin and jumping out periodically in order to scare people."[361]

---

352. <u>Drake by Drake v. Mitchell Community Schools,</u> 628 N.E.2d 1231, 1232 (Ind. App. 1 Dist. 1994).
353. *Id.*
354. *Id.*
355. *Id.*
356. Other possible teachers in this case could have been Ms. Oatley, Mr. Barley, etc.
357. <u>Drake by Drake v. Mitchell Community Schools,</u> 628 N.E.2d 1231, 1233 (Ind. App. 1 Dist. 1994).
358. *Id.*
359. *Id*
360. *Id.*
361. *Id.*

"Several days after the haunted house event was held, Holli contracted a severe case of histoplasmosis because of being exposed to the pigeon droppings in the grain elevator."[362] She was hospitalized and her family incurred substantial medical bills and other expenses in connection with her treatment. On motion for summary judgment,[363] the court granted defendant's bank and school district's motion and dismissed them, while denying Kiwanis' motion. Holli Drake appeals the granting of the motion for summary judgment.

Issues:

1.   Whether summary judgment was appropriately entered in favor of the school?

2.   Whether summary judgment was appropriately entered in favor of the bank?

Holding:

1.   No. "Under the particular facts of this case, the School's knowledge of the specific danger in question, and accordingly, its duty to exercise reasonable care to protect its students from this danger, was independent of any duty it had to inspect the grain elevator. A reasonable jury could find the school breached its duty to exercise reasonable care to warn the students and/or protect them from a known danger, exposure to histoplasmosis. Therefore, we reverse the summary judgment in favor of the school and remand for trial."[364]

2.   Yes. "The bank is entitled to protection under [a statute granting immunity to activities that were for recreational purposes] because we hold "that Holli's participation in the "haunted house" activities were at least partly recreational in nature despite the fact that the activities were also partly for the purpose of fund-raising."[365]

Analysis:

This case is complicated by the fact that the school district claimed immunity under a provision of the Indiana Tort Claims Act which gave immunity to school districts and their employees acting within the scope of their employment, for the "failure to make an inspection, or making an inadequate or negligent inspection, of any property, other than the property of a governmental entity, to determine whether the property . . . contains a hazard to health or safety." [366] The court steps around the statute by finding a separate and distinct duty of the school district to Holli Drake:

> The Drakes concede the school is immune from liability for damages stemming from any duty it may have had to inspect the grain elevator under the . . . statute. However, the Drakes assert that the school, having specific knowledge that the grain elevator posed a risk of histoplasmosis independent of any inspection, had the duty to warn or otherwise protect the students against exposure to histoplasmosis. We agree.[367]

After an analysis of the duty of schools to the children in their care, the court discussed the relevant facts pertaining to what the school knew in order to reach its holding:

---

362. *Id.*
363. A motion for summary judgment asks the court to decide the case on the pleadings that the court has in front of it. In order for a summary judgment motion to be granted, the court must determine that there is "no genuine issue as to any material fact" and that the party moving for summary judgment is entitled to a decision as a matter of law. That is, the party bringing the motion is asking the court to decide the case without a trial because even if all the facts contained in the plaintiff's complaint were true they still would not win.
364. *Id.* at 1235.
365. *Id.* at 1236.
366. *Id.* at 1234.
367. *Id.*

In the present case, [Holli's] injuries were not caused by any failure to make an inspection or by an inadequate inspection. The inspection revealed that the grain elevator posed a risk to the students' health. Moreover, Wheatly, the school's student council advisor, was aware, independent of any inspection, that the grain elevator posed a danger to the health of the students through exposure to histoplasmosis. Wheatly had the time and opportunity to communicate this danger to her students and advise or require them to take precautions against exposure to the disease. For example, the students could have been forbidden to enter the building before it had been cleaned or could have been required to wear dust masks until the elevator was cleaned.[368]

Comment:

The court squarely places the duty on the teacher, Wheatly, to warn the students of danger that she knew about regarding histoplasmosis. The fact that Wheatly was not an expert on the disease is not a factor. Teachers have a duty to warn students of hazards to their safety and the Mitchell court blames Wheatley for not acting as a reasonable person would after she recognized the danger of students contracting such a harmful disease. This duty to warn is important. Chemistry teachers have a duty not only to warn, but as the Mitchell court points out, they also have a duty to take action to prevent harm to the student. It is not enough to simply say that pigeon droppings cause histoplasmosis, so watch out. Wheatly had an affirmative duty to take the necessary steps to protect the children. The court does not find supportive that Wheatly was concerned enough about the students to get the Kiwanis to clean up the elevator. Wheatly's failure was permitting the students to enter the elevator when she knew that the Kiwanis had not yet cleaned it up. If Wheatly had taken any type of action to prevent the students from entering before cleanup this case might have been decided differently. If the cleanup had been performed, and Wheatly thereafter testified that she thought it was safe, and that there were no pigeon droppings on the floor, and Holli still contacted histoplasmosis, a court might have decided that Wheatly's actions were reasonable under the circumstances. The Mitchell court found fault with Wheatly because she "talked the talk but didn't walk the walk." If a teacher proclaims something is dangerous, and then permits students to engage in the behavior, which the teacher knows is dangerous, then a court will find fault. If a teacher reports to the principal that they have too many students in their class to safely conduct experiments and the administrator orders them back in the room saying your contract limit is 36 students per class, and you have 36, and the teacher conducts experiments in that room—the teacher in all probability will be found liable for negligence related to that accident.

Mitchell is a lesson in "doing the right thing." If the teacher knows or should reasonably know what to do in order to prevent harm to students, then the teacher has a duty to warn the students of the hazards, and take steps to prevent the harm from occurring.

Now that we have some idea of the negligence cause of action and have examined the relevant cases we need to take a brief look at the most important defenses that influence the outcome of the negligence case, and which we saw in the presented cases, involving teachers and school districts.

---

368. *Id.*

SECTION V   Teacher Defenses

1. Immunity[369]

At common law, there was sovereign immunity that prevented just about everyone from suing the government. Our founders borrowed this concept from the English common law concept that "The king can do no wrong," and extended it to the colonies as a good idea. As time passed, the idea that wronged citizens could not sue the government became indefensible and in many cases unfair, so the federal government enacted the Federal Tort Claims Act to remedy the apparent unfairness. While many functions of the government are immune from lawsuits, there are several areas where the federal government can be sued. State governments were also immune at common law. Why is immunity important? An immunity is a defense to tort liability that is given to an entire class of persons based upon their relationship with the prospective plaintiff, the nature of their occupation, their status as a governmental or charitable entity, etc. The common law created a number of virtually complete immunities, but all of these are beginning to break down at least to some extent, by either statutory reform or judicial overruling.[370] Tort immunity is a complete bar to liability and "creates freedom from tort liability in the form of an exemption based on the nature or status of the defendant and denies the courts' jurisdiction to consider the plaintiff's claim."[371] Governmental immunity for school districts involved in tort actions still exists at common law even though in the majority of states this defense has significantly been eroded as more courts attempt to limit the boundaries of the doctrine. Many state legislatures have enacted statutes to provide immunity in certain well-defined circumstances. For example, in many states a specific exception provides immunity for claims related to the maintenance of school buildings and property. However, courts often override this immunity and hold school districts liable for injuries caused by dangerous conditions or defects existing on the school property if the school authorities had actual notice of the defect and failed to take corrective action.[372] As was discussed in Section III, this makes the reporting of hazardous conditions to the proper school administrator imperative. Proper reporting of hazardous conditions relieves the teacher of being found liable for a defective condition existing in their classroom, of which they had knowledge, and which they had negligently failed to report or correct. Depending on the jurisdiction, there are four primary exceptions to governmental (institutional) immunity:

- Governmental v. Proprietary Function Exception. Those functions of a school district that are governmental in nature and clearly serve the governmental functions of the school district will be immune from liability, whereas those functions that are proprietary in nature, serving business or

---

369. Immunity is a complex area of the law. As immunity continues to play a large role in any litigation involving school districts, the brief coverage given here is solely to highlight the effect of immunity on the litigation process and to remind the reader that one must always carefully analyze the law of a particular state to determine if a particular actor is covered by a governmental immunity.

370. Emanuel, Steven, "Torts," Fourth Edition (1991) p. 210.

371. 57 Am. Jur. 2d Municipal, County, School, and State Tort Liability § 1 (1988). A comprehensive discussion of immunity is complex and would detract from the objective of this book. Suffice to say that there are a number of situations where governmental immunity will still apply, but the results will vary significantly from state to state. In many states, the school district will be immune from suit, but the teacher will remain liable, in others, the converse is true.

372. See e.g., Velmer v. Baraga Area Sch., 424 N.W.2d 770 (Mich. 1988); Stahl v. Cocalico Sch. Dist., 534 A.2d 1141 (Pa. Commw. Ct. 1987).

commercial interests of the school district, are not immune. The problem with this test is that it is often difficult to apply.[373]

- Ministerial v. Discretionary Function Exception. Under this exception, those acts of a school district that are ministerial in nature are not immune, whereas those acts that are discretionary are immune. Under this test, the rationale is that certain governmental functions are of such a nature that they should not be subject to second-guessing by the courts in a tort action.[374] Discretionary acts are those which involve "the exercise of personal deliberation and judgment, which . . . entails examining the facts, reaching reasoned conclusions, and acting on them in a way not specifically direct, or establishing plans, specifications, and schedules where there is room for policy judgment and decision." [375] Ministerial acts do not involve discretion. Again, the problem is application. Courts have found it difficult to apply the distinction in practice. Two approaches have developed, one based on a planning-operational distinction in which the government is immune for those decisions which involve the basic formulation of policy and is liable for those decisions which involve the execution or implementation of that policy;[376] and a duty approach where school districts are immune from liability for failing to perform those duties which are discretionary, quasijudicial or imperfect, and liable for neglect or omission for failing to perform those duties which are imperative, absolute, or perfect.[377]

- Nuisance. Nuisance refers to a type of injury sustained by a plaintiff. In the education context, the type of nuisance most often referred to by the court is that of a private nuisance which is an unreasonable interference with the plaintiff's use and enjoyment of his land.[378] It is important to recognize that the plaintiff must have an interest in the land affected by the nuisance. Initially courts construed this "interest in land" requirement strictly and plaintiffs were unable to use this exception to the immunity statute of a particular state. However, judicial distaste for the immunity doctrine in some states is so great, that nuisance now is defined so broadly as to include almost any hazardous condition created or continued by the defendant with the knowledge that harm to the plaintiff was substantially certain to follow.[379] The effect of having a particular condition of the property, such as a poorly maintained science classroom, or a science laboratory without proper safety showers, fume hoods, chemical storage cabinets etc., declared a nuisance is to avoid the application of governmental immunity. Several states have recognized the exception as applicable to schools but several other jurisdictions have not made the exception applicable.[380]

- Purchase of Tort Liability Insurance. The action of school districts to purchase tort liability insurance is treated much as the nuisance exception discussed above. In some jurisdictions, the purchase of liability insurance does not act as a waiver of governmental immunity. However, in more and more jurisdictions courts are frequently determining that the purchase of liability insurance does act as a waiver of governmental immunity at least to the extent of the amount of insurance purchased. This is logical, because if school districts are already immune, then why do they have a need for such insurance? Most often, statutes determine the need for liability insurance. Consequently, the question of whether governmental immunity covers the insurance purchase, is often included in the same statute. In general, statutes either:

  (a) Provide for mandatory purchase of liability insurance and therefore waive tort immunity to the extent of the insurance coverage.

---

373. *See supra* note 381. Decisions on whether a particular activity of a school district is governmental or proprietary are all over the map.

374. Restatement (Second) of Torts § 895C(2) (b) (local government entities) (1979).

375. 57 Am. Jur. 2d Municipal, County, School, and State Tort Liability § 119 (1988).

376. *Id.* at § 121 (1988).

377. *Id.* at § 124 (1988).

378. Restatement (Second) of Torts § 822 (1979).

379. Cobb v. Fox, 113 Mich. App. 249, 317 N.W.2d 583, 3 Educ. L.R. 393 (1982), *appeal denied,* 422 Mich. 892, 368 N.W.2d 235, 25 Educ. L.R. 542 (1985).

380. *See* Rose v. Board of Educ., 184 Kan. 486, 337 P.2d 652 (1959), Cobb v. Fox, 113 Mich. App. 249, 317 N.W.2d 583, 3 Educ. L.R. 393 (1982), *appeal denied,* 422 Mich. 892, 368 N.W.2d 235, 25 Educ. L.R. 542 (1985) (both holding nuisance exception applicable. *But see* Bingham v. Board of Educ., 118 Utah 582, 223 P.2d. 432 (1950), Robinson v. Indianola Mun. Separate Sch. Dist., 467 So. 2d 911, 24 Educ. L. R. 1077 (Miss. 1985) (Both holding nuisance exception non-applicable).

(b) Provide for mandatory purchase of insurance but the purchase does not constitute a waiver of governmental immunity.

(c) Leaves the decision of the purchase of insurance to the district where such purchase constitutes a waiver of immunity.[381]

Governmental tort immunity is not the main player in the litigation process that it once was. As more judicial opinions came down squarely against the idea of giving the government free reign in committing torts against the public, all legislatures in the nation have been forced to evaluate whether the policy behind the immunity, to protect public funds, is still valid. Approximately 85 percent of the states have abrogated governmental immunity either judicially or legislatively in some part. That is, many states have carved out certain areas where immunity no longer exists, while still preserving the concept in at least a limited manner.

While the institution may not be immune to suit, in some instances, individuals in their capacity as employees of the school district may enjoy immunity in some situations, depending on the state. Again, this immunity may or may not be derived from the governmental immunity protecting the teacher. However, the immunity of teachers generally follows three patterns:

- Public school teachers are immune from liability for negligence only in connection with their discretionary functions but not in connection with ministerial ones;
- Public school teachers enjoy immunity for ordinary negligence within the scope of their duties;
- Public school teachers are not entitled to immunity from liability for their individual negligence.

Again, it is critical to note that whether a particular teacher's action(s) action in the laboratory is immune from suit depends on the state and the applicable decisional law from that state. While it would be prudent for all science teachers to find out precisely what their potential exposure to lawsuits is in their particular state, it is not always practical. The best possible approach for the science teacher, disregarding the legal effect, is to approach the laboratory setting with additional preparation and care, because the consequences of even a small mistake may have dramatic and potentially deadly consequences.

2. Contributory Negligence

The two intertwined concepts of contributory negligence and assumption of risk predate most states' legislative enactments of the 1980s and 1990s adopting comparative negligence statutes to replace these ancient doctrines and mitigate their harsh effects. This legislative trend is significant because in most of the early cases contributory negligence and assumption of risk were complete bars to recovery by the plaintiff against the teacher, school district, and school board. In a contributory negligence state, a plaintiff's own negligence barred recovery against a clearly negligent teacher or school district.

Much of the early decisional law discussed in Section IV involved either or both contributory negligence and assumption of risk. A brief review will be helpful in explaining those early results and, more significantly, show how a particular decision would change under modern comparative negligence analysis.

At common law,[382] the doctrine of contributory negligence applies.[383] The doctrine provides that a plaintiff who is negligent, and whose negligence contributes proximately to his own injuries, is totally

---

381. *See generally* 57 Am. Jur. 2d Municipal, County, School, and State Tort Liability §§ 58, 59, 60, 85 (1988). What is clear is that in all cases one must carefully consult the statute in your particular state to determine what effect the purchase of tort liability insurance may have on a school district's ability to sue. One should also remember, that this area of immunity is particularly complex, and while the school district and school board may be immune from suit, it is possible that the teacher and the building principal may not be immune.

382. The "common law" is that body of law created by courts deciding cases.

383. The information for the following discussion on the various types of defenses to negligence, contributory negligence, assumption of risk and contributory negligence appears generally, in Emanuel Torts Outline, found at http://lawschool.lexis.com/emanuel/torts/epc-tort-chapter11.htm (2.23.2000)

barred from recovering for his injuries. The plaintiff is held to the same standard of care as the defendant.[384] In addition, the same test for causation that would be applicable to the defendant is also applicable to the plaintiff. That is, the contributory negligence defense only applies where plaintiff's negligence contributes proximately to his injuries. At common law, because of the harshness of the rule contributory negligence was only a bar to a claim that was itself based in negligence. Thus, there are certain other claims where contributory negligence is not available and thus acts as a limit to the harshness of the contributory negligence rule:

- Intentional torts: Thus, the defense may not be used where plaintiff's claim is for an intentional tort, such as assault, battery, false imprisonment, etc.

- Willful and wanton: [385] Similarly, if the defendant's conduct is found to have been "willful and wanton" or "reckless," the contributory negligence defense will not be allowed. However, if defendant's negligence is merely "gross," contributory negligence usually will be allowed. The idea is that the contributory negligence defense does not apply where the defendant disregards a conscious risk of harming an individual.

Example 16: Chemistry teacher, knowing that a student with long hair is at risk of setting herself on fire while working with a Bunsen burner, fails to warn the student of the danger after seeing the student narrowly missing the flame with her hair. The student has not tied her hair back and is constantly turning her back on the open flame to talk to her friend across the aisle. The chemistry teacher reasonably knows that the student will likely suffer harm if the behavior continues. Subsequently, student is badly burned when her hair is set on fire several minutes later.

The chemistry teacher's conscious disregard of a known risk would be "willful and wanton" in this instance. Even though the student's injuries are caused, in part, to her own negligence by failing to tie back her hair and turning her back on an open flame, a court would not permit the teacher to argue contributory negligence of the student and the student would be able to recover for her injuries.

- Negligence per se: Contributory negligence can generally be asserted as a defense to a claim of the defendant being "negligent per se," i.e., negligent based on a statutory violation. However, if the statute was enacted solely for protecting a class of which the Plaintiff is a member, contributory negligence usually may not be asserted as a defense.

Example 17: There is a statute in the state that requires "all students enrolled in chemistry and biology laboratory classes must wear goggles while performing experiments." Mr. Smith, a chemistry teacher with twenty years of teaching experience, has the students performing a molar Heat of Fusion lab which only uses a scale, thermometer, ice cubes, water and a Styrofoam cup for equipment. There is little risk for injury as the students are only measuring the change in temperature of the water. Smith warns the students to not leave the thermometer alone in the cups because the thermometer will cause the cup to fall. Smith also decides that there is not enough time in the period to complete the lab if the students put on their lab aprons and their safety goggles. During the laboratory, a thermometer placed carelessly in the Styrofoam cup falls over and breaks. A piece of glass breaks loose and lodges in the eye of the student working at that station, resulting in the loss of sight in that eye. The students admit that they were careless and had forgotten that they were not supposed to place the thermometer in the cup without holding onto the thermometer.

---

384. That is, the care of a "reasonable person under like circumstances." As we shall see, this reasonable person standard is somewhat nebulous, but still, relative objective in nature.

385. "Willful and wanton misconduct is that act intentionally done or that act taken, under the circumstances known, in reckless or conscious disregard of probable injurious consequences." Albers v. Community Consol. No. 204 School, 155 Ill. App.3d 1083, 108 Ill. Dec. 675, 508 N.E.2d 1252, 1254 (1987).

In the lawsuit that follows when a student is seriously injured, the teacher argues that the student was contributory negligent for failing to follow a safety instruction. That is, but for the student's own negligence he would not have lost his eyesight. The court would not allow the defense. The teacher was negligent per se for failing to have the students wear their goggles in violation of the state statute. The statute was enacted solely for the purpose of protecting the class of chemistry and biology students of which plaintiff was a member, that is, to protect chemistry students from eye injuries while working in the lab. Note, that if the student had injured his foot because a book carried by another student had dropped on it while the students were passing each other in the lab, even though teacher was negligent per se for failing to have the students wear goggles, no liability would attach to the teacher's activities. The statute was not intended to protect students from foot injuries caused by falling books.

- Last Clear Chance: Finally, the doctrine of "last clear chance" acts as a limit on the contributory negligence defense. If, just before the accident, the defendant had an opportunity to prevent the harm and plaintiff did not have such an opportunity, the existence of this opportunity (this last clear chance) wipes out the effect of plaintiff's contributory negligence.

Example 18: In the above example, assume that there was no statute requiring the wearing of safety goggles. In addition, the student failed to hold on to the thermometer in the styrofoam cup. Teacher, who observes the student failing to follow his instruction, discovers the student's plight shortly before the thermometer falls. The teacher tries to catch the thermometer, but negligently tips the cup over breaking the thermometer and causing it to lodge in the student's eye. The student never spotted the thermometer standing alone in the cup at all. If the teacher had required the student to wear safety goggles, there would be no injury to the student's eye.

The teacher's discovery of the danger before the accident gave him a last clear chance to avoid the accident, of which the teacher failed to take advantage. This last clear chance wipes out the effect of the student's contributory negligence, and the student may recover against the teacher. In the above example, if the teacher actually discovered the student's plight, and failed to deal with it carefully, all courts would apply the last clear chance doctrine in this situation. If, on the other hand, because of the teacher's failure to require the wearing of safety goggles the teacher failed to discover the plight and thus never had a chance to deal with it, most courts would also apply the last clear chance doctrine. In some situations, the teacher's antecedent negligence may prevent application of the "last clear chance" doctrine. That is, where the teacher discovers the student's plight and tries to avoid it but is unable to do so because of their earlier negligence, most courts do not apply the last clear chance doctrine. In other words, for last clear chance to apply according to most courts, the teacher must have had an actual opportunity to avoid the harm at the last moment, not merely an opportunity that "would have existed" had the teacher not previously been negligent.

3. Assumption of Risk

A plaintiff is said to have "assumed the risk" of certain harm if she has voluntarily consented to take her chances that harm will occur. At common law, the plaintiff's "voluntary assumption" of the risk of harm is a complete bar to recovery. In the education context, most cases involving assumption of risk do not involve express assumption of risk, but rather involve implied assumption of risk. If the plaintiff explicitly agrees with the defendant, in advance of any harm, that the plaintiff will not hold the defendant liable for certain harm, the plaintiff is said to have "expressly" assumed the risk of that harm.

Example 19: Patty wants to go watch a hockey game at Dan Danger's hockey arena. Patty purchases a ticket at the box office which has on the back of the ticket given to her by Dan a "release" in which Patty agrees to "assume all risk of injury" that may result from attending the hockey game. If Patty is injured, she will not be able to sue Dan, because she has expressly assumed the risk. Nevertheless, even Patty's express assumption of the risk will not bar Patty from recovery if there is a public policy against the assumption of the risk involved. For example, if Dan's position as a unique provider of a certain service gives him greater bargaining power than Patty, and Dan uses this power to force Patty into a waiver of liability, the court is likely to find that public policy prohibits use of the assumption of risk doctrine. Public policy usually prohibits a waiver of liability for Dan's willful and wanton or "gross" negligence, and for Dan's intentionally tortuous conduct.

More relevant for chemistry teachers, is the implied assumption of risk doctrine. Even if Patty never makes an actual agreement with Dan whereby Patty assumes the risk, a court may hold that Patty's conduct was such that she assumed the risk of harm. Here, the assumption of risk is "implied." For Dan to establish implied assumption, he must show that Patty's actions demonstrated that she:

1) knew of the risk in question; and

2) voluntarily consented to bear that risk herself.

The requirement that Patty be shown to have known about the risk is strictly construed. For instance, the risk must be one which was actually known to Patty, not merely one which "ought to have been" known to her. The requirement that Patty consented voluntarily is also strictly construed. For instance, there is no assumption of the risk if Dan's conduct left Patty with no reasonable choice but to encounter a known danger or where it is not Dan's fault that Patty has no reasonable choice except to expose herself to the risk, the defense will apply. Often, Patty's assumption of risk will also constitute contributory negligence.

Example 20: Petra voluntarily, but unreasonably, decides to take a chance waiving her hand through a Bunsen burner knowing that she may possibly be burned and actively conceals what she is doing from the teacher. Petra has assumed the risk of being burned and is contributorily negligent. However, it is not always the case that the student has assumed the risk and is contributorily negligent. Sometimes conduct which constitutes assumption of risk is not contributory negligence. For example, Petra, injured, asks Dat for a ride to the hospital. Petra knows that Dat's car has bad brakes. On the way to the hospital Dat's brakes fail and the car crashes. Petra breaks her arm. This is assumption of risk, even though Petra has behaved perfectly reasonably in view of the lack of alternatives.

If assumption of risk and contributory negligence both operate as a bar to recovery, the question arises as to why the distinction is important. Distinguishing between assumption of risk and contributory negligence may be important where defendant's conduct was reckless because contributory negligence is not a defense to reckless conduct, but assumption of the risk generally is. In addition, where there is a comparative negligence statute, most, but not all states will distinguish between two types of assumption of risk: "primary" implied assumption of risk and "secondary" implied assumption. In the "primary" case, the defendant is never under any duty to plaintiff at all. In the "secondary" case, the defendant would ordinarily have a duty to the plaintiff, but the plaintiff's assumption of risk causes the duty to dissipate. In the classroom, in almost all cases, the "secondary" case applies because the teacher, present or not present as the case may be, almost always has a duty to the student. Where there is a comparative negligence statute, most states eliminate the "secondary" assumption doctrine, but not the "primary" assumption doctrine. That is, where the teacher is not already under a duty to the student, most courts will permit the primary form of implied assumption of risk to act as a complete bar to liability. However, where the teacher is already under a duty to the student, most, but not all courts will not permit the doctrine as a defense to liability.

4. Comparative Negligence

The enactment of comparative negligence statutes in almost all states today has mitigated the harshness of the contributory negligence rule. Under these statutes, a plaintiff's own negligence is not a bar to recovery but rather, reduces the plaintiff's amount of recovery in proportion to his/her own fault. A "comparative negligence" system rejects the all-or-nothing approach of contributory negligence. It instead attempts to divide liability between the plaintiff and defendant in proportion to their relative degrees of fault. The plaintiff's contributory negligence does not bar recovery but reduces her recovery by a proportion equal to the ratio between her own negligence and the total negligence contributing to the accident. Forty-six states have adopted some form of comparative negligence. Of these, only 13 states have adopted "pure" comparative negligence. The rest of the states have adopted a 50% comparative negligence statute that will completely bar the plaintiff if his negligence is (depending on the state) "as great" as the defendant's, or "greater" than defendant's. Where there are multiple defendants, and in most actions involving teachers there are multiple defendants, comparative negligence is harder to apply: If all defendants are joined in the same lawsuit, the solution is simple: only the negligence due directly to plaintiff's conduct is deducted from his recovery.

Example 21: Taking all negligence by all parties, the plaintiff is 20 percent negligent, defendant #1 is 50 percent negligent, and defendant #2 is 30 percent negligent. The plaintiff will recover 80 percent of her damages. However, if not all defendants are before the court, hard questions arise concerning joint-and-several liability. The issue is whether the defendant(s) before the court, who is/are found to be only partly responsible for the plaintiff's loss, must pay for the whole loss aside from that caused by plaintiff's own fault.

Example 22: John's (plaintiff) accident is caused by the negligence of Mr. Smith (teacher) and Bob, another student. Plaintiff sues the teacher, but cannot find or sue Bob because the student has left the country with his family. The jury finds that the plaintiff was 20 percent responsible; the teacher, 30 percent responsible; and Bob, 50 percent responsible. The plaintiff's damages total $1,000,000. It is not clear whether the plaintiff can collect the full $800,000 from the teacher. Under traditional "joint and several liability" rules, the plaintiff would be able to collect this full $800,000 from the teacher. The teacher could then later sue Bob, if he can be found, for contribution.

States have adopted four or five different approaches to these problems. Some states have completely abolished the doctrine of joint-and-several liability in comparative negligence cases. Therefore, in Example 21, the plaintiff could recover only $300,000. An important emerging approach is the "allocative" approach, by which the plaintiff and the defendant share the burden of an absent or insolvent defendant, in proportion to their own fault. As applied to the facts of Example 21, under this allocative approach, the plaintiff would bear 2/5 and the teacher 3/5 of the burden of Bob's absence. Therefore, the plaintiff would recover $600,000 total.

Courts are split as to whether the doctrine of last clear chance should survive in a comparative negligence jurisdiction. Finally, there are some circumstances where the comparative negligence statute will not apply to defendant's conduct. If defendant's conduct is not merely negligent, but "willful and wanton" or "reckless," most states nonetheless will reduce the plaintiff's damages. However, if defendant's tort is intentional, most comparative negligence statutes will not apply.

SECTION VI   Conclusion

This book has attempted to personalize the way chemistry and other teachers of science approach safety in their classrooms.[386] While teachers are not the insurers of student safety, they have specific, personal duties to students in their care. The primacy of those duties captures chemistry teachers in a cause and effect relationship to every student injury unless the practices and procedures in place in their classroom are demonstrably sufficient to meet the standard of care imposed upon them consistent with the duty of care. Robertson teaches that the standard of care is that of an ordinarily reasonable person under the circumstances taking into account the specific characteristics of the person (s) to whom the duty is owed. Once teachers understand the duty of care, they must act consistent with that duty, guarding against foreseeable risks of harm to their students. Rather than attempt to produce a manual full of specific instructions for the handling of specific hazards and situations, this book advocates a practical, conceptual approach to making the chemistry classroom safer.

Chemistry and other science teachers teach students the wonders of our world in an environment that has the potential for danger. This book identifies several areas where teachers, administrators, and school districts have exposure to significant liability for negligent practices related to breaches of the duty of care resulting in injury to students. Science teachers must examine their individual practices and procedures before tackling larger issues related to the facility and administration. To paraphrase a well-known expression: Science teachers should change the things they can change; accept the things they cannot change; and have the wisdom to know the difference.

---

386. The principles explored, as noted in the beginning of this book, are applicable generically to all teachers as they relate to student safety. While not intended as such, this book is also a guide for parents, administrators, and plaintiff's attorneys, as it is a primer of the law on safety in the science classroom.

Index

Case Index

146

Concept Index

147